Springfield Girl

a Memoir

By Martha Frances Bell White

Copyright © 2004, by Martha Dillon (maiden name: Martha Frances Bell; subsequently Martha Bell White as wife of Ray White) 410 Lynwood Blvd., Nashville, Tennessee 37205.

First paperback edition by
Howard Ray White, Jr.

Second edition limited hardback 1000 copies
Edited and published by her son John Walter White

This is the first printing of the second edition, 2004, which contains some minor edits of the first edition.

Manufactured and printed in Hong Kong by Permanent Printing Ltd. (stanso@permanent.com.hk)

For copies of this book write to John Walter White, P. O. Box 58068, Nashville, Tennessee 37205 U.S.A.

ISBN 0-9761921-0-1

Dedication

This book is dedicated to

My mother, Myrtle Simpkins Bell

My father, Walter Leith Bell

And my two sons,

Howard Ray White, Jr.

John Walter White

CONTENT

Springfield Girl a Memoir	pp 1-1
Chapter 1 – The Years Before	pp 2-10
Chapter 2 – The Little Girl	pp 11-22
Chapter 3 – The Tragedy	pp 23-29
Chapter 4 – Daddy's Sister, My Aunt Mamie, was a Dear	pp 30-38
Chapter 5 – With "Aunt Johnnie's" Help Mother and I Managed	pp 39-47
Chapter 6 – Summers with Auntie, Uncle Arthur, Aunt Effie and Uncle Clem	pp 48-55
Chapter 7 – The Remaining Grade School Years in Springfield	pp 56-65
Chapter 8 – The Junior High School Years in Springfield	pp 66-70
Chapter 9 – The High School Years in Springfield	pp 71-94
Chapter 10 – Ray White and Middle Tennessee State Teachers College	pp 95-110
Chapter 11 – A Young Married Couple	pp 111-123
Chapter 12 – Our Two Little Boys Howard and John	pp 124-142
Chapter 13 – The War Years	pp 143-166
Chapter 14 – On the Farm in Murfreesboro	pp 167-189
Chapter 15 – Early Years at 410 Lynwood Blvd.	pp 190-213
Chapter 16 – My Boys, Howard and John, and Boys' Club Camp	pp 214-233
Chapter 17 – More About Howard and John on Lynwood Blvd.	pp 234-245
Chapter 18 – Teaching Prior to Desegregation	pp 246-255
Chapter 19 – A Six-weeks tour of Europe	pp 256-263
Chapter 20 – My Two Grown Sons	pp 264-267
Chapter 21 – Dealing with Desegregation	pp 268-276
Chapter 22 – The Close	pp 277-278
Acknowledgements	pp 279-280

Springfield Girl a Memoir

It was springtime in 1918. The small four-year-old girl was standing on a heavy wire near the light pole in front of her home. Although born in Springfield, Tennessee, she had returned a year before with her parents from Detroit, Michigan, where her father had been working at the Packard plant. She was too young to be thankful that the war had ended just before her father's draft call became effective. That springtime day she was lonely and hoping for a playmate. To pass the time she was swinging back and forth with her feet on the wire. Suddenly there was a drumbeat. She heard martial music and shuffling of feet coming from the direction of Greenbrier Pike. A military band and men in World War I uniforms came into sight, marching and singing as they entered their hometown of Springfield, the county seat of Robertson County. Returning from the war, the soldiers of Robertson County had ridden the train from Nashville to Oakland Station, which was two and a half miles south of Springfield. From there they were marching into town. Now they were rejoicing over returning home. The church bells started ringing. People began to run to the roadside, straining to recognize loved ones. The little girl's mother came and stood by her. Her father and her Uncle Forrest came out of their grocery store to watch from the porch. This event is my first memory of life in Springfield, for I was that little girl.

Before I proceed to tell about my childhood years in Springfield, perhaps I should go back in time and tell about my father Walter, 34, and my mother Myrtle, 31. I will also tell about their marriage and my baby days.

Chapter 1 – The Years Before

My father was Walter Leith Bell. His parents were James (Mr. Jim) Bell (1846-1932) and Sara Frances (Fannie) Sanford Bell (1861-1909). They married in 1880. Walter grew up with his parents and four sisters – Maud, Mary Catherine, Grace (Gracie) Franklin, and Susan (Susie) Davis – on his father's farm along Greenbrier Pike, not far from Springfield. He attended school at Oakland School and Bell's School. He was a member of Wartrace Methodist Church and the local Springfield Masonic Lodge. At age 16 he moved to a Springfield boarding house operated by Mrs. Chilton and clerked at a clothing store owned by his uncle, John Davis. At this time he was a popular young man about town. He owned a handsome horse and buggy and enjoyed dancing, playing the guitar, singing, telling jokes, and fellowship with friends. He often attended the services and revivals of the churches in the area. He was considered handsome, blue-gray eyes, black wavy hair, and sleight of statute. He enjoyed the sports of fishing, hunting, and horseback riding.

The Bells were fun loving, joke telling, and musical. They loved dancing, card playing and Bible reading, and were leaders in the Methodist Church. They loved the land, nature, enjoyed hunting, fishing, farming, and horseback riding. Politics was a favorite and hotly debated subject among the Bells, who read many books and subscribed to several newspapers that offered grist to political discussions held around the fireplace. James' parents were William Leeper Bell and Elizabeth Grymes Bell. Sarah's parents were Robert Franklin Sanford and

Suzan Elizabeth Davis Sanford. These people were all Tennesseans, mostly from Davidson County and Robertson County.

My mother was Myrtle Simpkins. Her parents were Joseph Gideon (Gid) Simpkins (1850-1938) and Martha Jane Carney (1855-1908). She grew up with her parents and four brothers and two sisters. A brother and a sister had died while my mother was a child. So there remained three brothers, Perlie, Melvin and Buford, and one sister, Effie.

The Simpkins were quiet, reflective, Bible reading and serious-minded. They were middle income, hardworking farmers, teachers and ministers. Unlike the Bells, they were not given to merriment. Grandpa Simpkins owned and operated a small restaurant, featuring fish, oysters, and crabs, which were shipped in ice-packed wooden barrels by train each day. When Myrtle married he sold his home in Springfield and a home in Ashland City that had been given to his wife, Martha Carney, when they had married. He closed his restaurant, gave furniture and other household items to his children, and moved into the City Hotel where he worked as a clerk. He sold popcorn from his electric popcorn popper, which he kept outside at the street corner. He was a cripple, for one leg was shorter than the other. This deformity was the result of typhoid fever, which he had suffered as a child. He was a gentleman – quiet and mannerly, a good storyteller, and always clean, neat, and well dressed. He had a mustache.

Before marriage Daddy and Mother went together for seven years – a steady twosome. They were part of a happy group of young people in Springfield who enjoyed buggy riding, walking, play parties, revivals, songfests, and just getting together at someone's house for a meal. They enjoyed each other's company even though their backgrounds were rather different. Reverend Heron Alexander married them in Walter's buggy on December 28, 1913, in front of the Methodist parsonage at Wartrace Methodist Church near Springfield, Tennessee. Walter's sister Grace and her husband Arthur Worsham were witnesses.

Neither Myrtle's father nor Walter's father had wanted the marriage, perhaps because it meant a different lifestyle for both Grandpa Simpkins and Granddaddy Bell. Myrtle's mother had died nine years earlier, in 1908. Her sister Effie had married Clem Lane and moved to Portland. Her brother Buford had married Bertha Hancock. So, just before her marriage Myrtle, 27, was at home keeping house for her father, my Grandpa Simpkins. Walter's father, my Granddaddy Bell, owned a 500-acre farm, which he needed help in managing. His wife Fannie had also died nine years earlier, in 1908. Three daughters, Maude, Mamie and Grace, had married, and his son Walter preferred store keeping in Springfield to farming. So Granddaddy Bell was left on the farm with his young daughter Susie, age 15 years, who was going to school in Springfield and boarding with her sister Mamie during the school year.

So Myrtle and Walter had married without either parent's consent. Following the ceremony they went to Granddaddy Bell's home, where Grace and Susie had gotten together a small reception. Following their marriage they lived with Granddaddy Bell and Aunt

Susie at the Bell farm on Greenbrier Pike. Myrtle and Walter were given as their own the spare room, the upper front room of the house, which Walter's mother had previously decorated with new furniture (I still have the bed on which Myrtle and Walter slept). Myrtle and Susie shared the housekeeping duties along with "Aunt" Mandy, an African-Native American woman whose family were tenants on the farm. Walter kept his job in Springfield and either rode horseback or drove the buggy to town (1-1/2 miles) each day. With Walter's help, Granddaddy Bell, age 72, continued to manage the farm, the tenants and the hired hands.

Myrtle was considered a city girl by the country folk around Wartrace Methodist Church. She did not know how to sew, tat, knit, crochet, embroidery, or operate a sewing machine. Myrtle's clothes and her mother's clothes had been made by a dressmaker or purchased at the store. For some reason the Carney women folk did not do handwork, but had a dressmaker live with them who did all the work involving clothes. Therefore, Walter's sisters, Susie, Grace, and Mamie took as their project to teach Myrtle basic handwork technique. Many times I have heard the Bell sisters and Myrtle laugh about the long hours of hard work required to teach Myrtle how to tat, which was the handwork technique she seemed best able to master. So before I was born she had tatted trim for a sheet, pillowcases, several dresser scarves and my baby cap, which is now on my Bye-Low baby doll. During Myrtle's pregnancy she adjusted to farm life, to the Bell's boisterous and happy lifestyle, and to the Methodist Church.

Aunt Susie and Auntie have told me that my birth on November 5, 1914, was a most difficult one. Mother never said anything to me about the trauma of my birth – she spoke only of her love and joy of having me as her daughter. Mother was 28 years old and had been married for a little over ten months. And I was and would be her first and only child. She was in labor 24 hours. I was born breech. Dr. Porter stayed throughout the night until he finally had to use forceps to turn me in the birthing position and had to lacerate my mother more than normal for me to move through the birth canal. There was a great deal of fear for both our lives. Auntie came home from Nashville; Aunt Bertha with her 9-month-old son Douglas came out from Springfield to represent Mother's family. These people had to be fed and Dr. Porter's commands had to be carried out. There was no sleep in Granddaddy Bell's home that night.

When I was finally born, Dr. Porter handed me to Aunt Susie, 16 years old, and said, "Will you clean up the baby?" Many years later Aunt Susie told me, "she wrapped me in a receiving blanket, bathed me, and I smiled at her." Then she took me to Mother to be fed. Again there was trouble – mother had developed an infection in a milk gland and could not nurse me. So I was given a "sugar tit," made by placing some sugar in a piece of cloth, which is then tied and shaped in the form of a nipple, and is then dipped in warm milk. The baby sucks on this "tit" for nourishment. I do not know whether I had a wet nurse or not; but I have heard it was some days before Mother's breast cleared following lancing. Daddy and Aunt Susie's boyfriend were the first to view me following my bath. Both said I was "pretty!"

Granddaddy loved to hold me and rub my feet with mutton tallow in front of the fireplace. He always said the tallow would make my skin soft. He also liked to take me to the table at mealtime and dip my "sugar tit" in coffee, which made mother very angry, but she kept quiet about it at the time. At birth Grandpa Simpkins gave me my lovely gold locket and chain. The locket, with my baby teeth dents, is now on my charm bracelet.

Aunt Susie and Mother enjoyed each other's companionship. They would laugh and tell about their one big fuss:

I was a 1-1/2 month old baby and Mother and Aunt Susie were busy getting food ready for their big family Christmas dinner. On this particular day they were making coconut cake. The four layers of white cake turned out well; the white icing was made; the fresh coconut was grated; all was in readiness to put the cake together. Aunt Susie placed some fresh grated coconut on top of the bottom cake layer. Mother was getting ready to put icing on top of the coconut. Aunt Susie said, "No," and explained that her mother (Fannie) had always dribbled coconut milk on top of the grated coconut, then placed another cake layer on top of that following the same pattern with each layer and covering the entire cake with white icing. Mother said, "OK, they would make this cake Susie's way." But the next day Mother made a second coconut cake her way. This put Walter and the rest of the Bell's in a difficult spot. No one would say which was the better cake. Mother would continue to make her wonderful coconut cake and fluff icing, which would always be enjoyed by family and friends.

Aunt Mamie and Uncle Forrest Bell had moved to Springfield by this time to give their son, Cornelius an education at the town school, which was better than the education that was available at the little Bell School. The Bell School had been built and supported by the Bell family for both their children and other children in the community. Uncle Forrest had purchased a tobacco warehouse, where tobacco was graded, stored and auctioned. He had also purchased a general merchandising store. In 1915 Granddaddy Bell and his brother, Joe, both decided to sell their adjoining farms. They and Aunt Susie moved to town an lived with Uncle Forrest, Aunt Mamie, and Cornelius. Granddaddy Bell, Joe and Forrest each paid his share of expenses. However, from what I was told later, Granddaddy Bell provided most of the financial support. Myrtle and Walter then rented a house with a small acreage just beyond the Wartrace Methodist Church. For the first and only time mother had a home, her husband, and her baby all to herself. She said it was the happiest year of her marriage, 1915-16. Walter continued to clerk in town at the Davis clothing store.

Then World War I broke out. During this year and the next year Detroit car manufacturers were booming in expansion. They placed ads in the county papers for workers. Several of the neighborhood boys went to Detroit and worked for Packard. They wrote back glowing reports of work and salaries. Uncle Arthur, Auntie and Daddy went to Detroit so the men could apply for jobs. They found work at Packard and chose to live where the other neighborhood boys were staying. Then Mother and I went to Detroit to be with Daddy. I believe this was a happy and interesting time for Mother. With me as a toddler, our clothes and some food she made the trip by train, changing trains in Cincinnati. She said the "redcaps" were polite, helpful, and made sure she made all connections.

I wish I knew more about their stay in Detroit. But I only know a few little incidents that Mother and Auntie later reported. They boarded with Mrs. Popper. Mother, Daddy, and I shared a bedroom, and Auntie and Uncle Arthur were in another bedroom. Daddy and Uncle Arthur worked for Packard. Mother and Auntie took care of me and enjoyed big city life. There was a play park for children near Mrs. Poppers where Mother and Auntie would take me to get sunshine, swing, go down the chute, ride on the merry-go-round and play with other neighborhood children. I was very fair, almost pale, with pale blond hair and brown eyes – always dressed in feminine dresses and shoes. Mrs. Popper kept feeding me, trying to get more color in my face and to fatten me; but I came home from Detroit still pale and undernourished looking. The look would continue until my first pregnancy, which would improve my metabolism of food. While we were in Detroit we took a boat trip that Mother loved to talk about. We boarded a large boat, *Belle Island*, and traveled across Lake Michigan to a park also named "Belle Island." We spent the night on the boat and spent a few hours in Canada.

The Springfield Draft Board called Uncle Arthur home and Auntie returned to Springfield with him. Just before they left, I locked myself in Auntie's bedroom. Mother and Auntie pounded and pounded on the door and I would not open it. Mrs. Popper got someone to climb through the second story window from a ledge. They found me with Auntie's can of talcum powder sprinkling it on the border of the rug. I was walking on the border sprinkling powder, and singing a lullaby song. Because they were so happy to find me unharmed, I did not get a spanking. There is another incident in Detroit over which I should have been punished. I locked myself in the bathroom and "would not" or "could not" unlock the door. Mother was frantic and kept saying over and over, "Martha Frances, if you don't open that door I will spank you." Auntie would laugh and ask Mother how she could spank me when she could not get to me. Mrs. Popper called the fire department. Firemen had to break the window glass to get into the bathroom to unlock the door. Again, I did not get a spanking.

Eventually the Draft Board called Daddy home. Mother and I returned with him. I know nothing about the trip home except it was also by train. By the time Daddy got to Springfield, the Board was not drafting anyone because the war was drawing toward the end. I was just learning to talk when we returned to Springfield. I was a Yankee-talking 3-year old.

Chapter 2 – The Little Girl

Our Springfield home fronted on Greenbrier Pike at the corner of Greenbrier Pike and Woodland Street, which ran along the orchard side of the yard. Upon returning from Detroit, Daddy, Mother and I had moved into the house owned by Aunt Matt Davis and her son. Granddaddy Bell still lived in Springfield with his daughter, Mamie, and son-in-law, Forrest Bell. Granddaddy, Uncle Forrest, and Daddy bought a store, located in "the triangle" across the street, from Aunt Matt Davis' house and called it "Bell Brothers Grocery." Aunt Matt had recently lost her husband and needed additional income. Her husband, Richard (Dick) Davis was a brother to my great grandmother, Susan Elizabeth Davis. Therefore, Aunt Matt was my great, great aunt.

I remember Aunt Matt's house as being cold and often uncomfortable during the winter months, but comfortable other times of the year. We had to go from our heated bedroom, through Aunt Matt's unheated closed porch, through her outside porch, through our unheated dining room, and then into our heated kitchen. The bedroom was heated with a fireplace and the kitchen was heated with a wood stove. During the winter the bedroom and kitchen were warm and cozy with much love, laughter and singing. Both the Bells and the Davis' were singers. Daddy loved to sing and was determined that his small daughter would also sing. In front of the fire Daddy would sit in the rocker, hold me on his lap, and with the

Methodist hymnal in his hand, start my singing lesson. *The Old Rugged Cross* and *Love Lifted Me* were two of his favorites. He played the guitar, and on some occasions he would play singing games with me. Bless his heart, he persisted in instructing me; but perhaps I took too much after my mother, for I never became exceptionally accomplished at music. When I sang *Jesus Loves Me* on the stage at a Christmas program at Woodland Methodist Church at age five, Daddy beamed from one of the back seats. He was proud of his girl! Then when I would sing *Silent Night,* at age nine at the Christmas program at Mary F. Pepper Memorial Presbyterian Church, my mother would be so proud! As a teenager I would join my friends singing in the Mary F. Pepper Presbyterian Church choir.

Church revivals were popular during this period of my life. They were generally held under outdoor brush arbors in the summertime and inside the Springfield Tabernacle in the wintertime. It is told that, during my first time in church after arriving back from Detroit, that I, age three, stood on the seat and said in a loud voice, "When does the picture start?" In Detroit, Mother and Daddy had been accustomed to taking me to the picture show rather than to church. Were they embarrassed! But Daddy reveled in the services at Springfield. I can still visualize his happy face singing in his Irish tenor voice holding the hymnal book.

Daddy and I had a ritual for getting ready to go to church or to any special place. He would whiten my shoes, fold the leg cuffs carefully into my long white socks, and rub my gold locket and chain until they glistened. That's all I remember about dressing. But Auntie says my clothes were mostly white, hand-made by Aunt Mamie, with lace, insertion, ribbons and embroidery. They were pretty and attractive by that day's standards. Another Sunday morning stands out in my memory. Daddy and I sat under the huge pin oak tree in the bright morning sunlight while he read "Little Orphan Annie" to me on the first Sunday that it appeared in our newspaper. Sunday afternoons were sometimes spent walking to Elmwood Cemetery, which was eight blocks from our home. My first remembrance of a burial was in that cemetery. The casket was brought in a hearse drawn by horses. During the funeral, I started begging for a drink of water. Seeing a spring or cistern hydrant nearby that was dripping delicious-looking water, I threw a fit. But following the funeral, people warned me I should never drink water that drained from a cemetery.

There were six large oak trees in Aunt Matt's yard. Daddy climbed one of the tall ones in the back yard and hung a rope swing from a high limb; made a wooden seat; and called mother out of the kitchen to see me swing. I was four years old. He pushed me high and then ran under me for a higher swing. I must have panicked, for I remember vividly I could not catch my breath. I remember trying so hard to breathe, and then my frantic cries to get me out of that swing. Daddy was disappointed, but Mother pacified him by saying that I was too young for a high swing like that.

The first summer we lived with Aunt Matt, Daddy had a garden – a full and complete one. He took great pride in his vegetables and showed the garden to everyone who came to see us. The potatoes were plentiful and firm; the carrots slender and well formed; the turnips beautiful; the butterbeans were excellent; those were the vegetables I remember his talking about. That fall "we" peeled, cored and sliced peaches and apples at Aunt Mamie's – Daddy, Mother, Granddaddy, Uncle Forrest, Uncle Joe, and Aunt Mamie. The grown-ups worked the fruit as they sat in a circle, talking, laughing, and telling jokes, while Cornelius and I played. Occasionally someone would find a ripe, sweet peach or apple and hand us a slice. The men peeled the peaches and apples with their pocketknives, each one bragging about the sharpness of his blade and good qualities of his own knife (at that time the possession of a good knife was a matter of pride). The women cored and sliced the peeled fruit. This fruit was from the trees at Aunt Mamie's and Aunt Matt's. The peaches were sun-dried, and the apples were dried and sulfured. Daddy built a fruit drying rack over an outside shower stall, because it was a sunny location (he had built the shower stall earlier and provided water by extending the waterline from the garden hydrant). After spreading the fruit over the rack, Daddy built a fire below, which he kept slowly smoldering for days to keep off dew and to keep insects away. The sun would dry the apple and peach slices, which had to be turned each day. At Aunt Mamie's the peaches were placed on top of the shed to dry in the sun in the open air. During winter months, Mother would make delicious fried apple and peach pies in a skillet on top of the wood-burning stove.

Daddy was a hunter and fisherman. Mother would fry the little birds, barbecue rabbits and squirrels, and batter and fry the frog legs. I don't specifically remember

Mother cooking fish, but I do know Daddy loved the sport of fishing. While the frog legs were frying in the skillet, Daddy lifted me in his arms to see the reflex of the cooking frog-leg muscles. Mother was always afraid of Daddy's guns, especially when he regularly cleaned, oiled, and waxed them. Mother was concerned that he would shoot himself or someone else. Later, when his health began to fail, she gave Daddy's guns to Auntie and Uncle Arthur for safekeeping. Many years later, in 1976, Auntie would give them to me.

When Aunt Effie and Uncle Clem would visit, Mother would expand her round table in the dining room and have a family dinner. I remember sweet, home-canned blackberries being ladled from a pressed glass punch bowl into individual pressed glass berry bowls, mother pouring over them rich cream, which had been saved from the top of un-homogenized whole milk, and served with slices of fresh coconut cake. This was enjoyed by mother's father, Grandpa Simpkins, her brother, Uncle Buford Simpkins, his wife, Bertha, and their three children, Douglas, Martha Lou, and Mary Ruth, and sometimes also by mother's sister Aunt Effie, her husband Uncle Clem Lane and their baby, Clem, Jr. In the summer time they would sit on the front porch, talking and laughing. In the winter, they would stay longer around the dining room table, which had been extended by three extra leaves. Then they would go to the "front room" to sit around the fireplace. We children would play, and sometimes Douglas, the older one, would push the little girls just to hear us fuss.

My first Christmas remembrance is walking downtown

in Springfield at dusk, between Mother and Daddy, holding their hands. The glitter of the store windows fascinated me. We walked the length of the Main Street shopping area, and in the last store, "Hurt and Tanner," I remember seeing a huge display of dolls and toys for little girls. As Daddy held me in his arm's I looked and looked at that display. I feel sure the display was very small compared to those I had seen in the Christmas of 1916 and 1917, when we were living in Detroit and they took me to see the big department stores and Santa Claus. But, I was too young to remember those visits. Springfield, I do remember. I remember Christmas morning with the big tree in the north corner of the bedroom with popcorn strings, little round blobs of cotton thrown at random to look like snow, the little balls covered with tinfoil from China, and tinsel strips hanging from each cedar branch. There were no lights on the tree because there was no electricity in the house. Unrolled cotton batting covered the wooden tree stand, and the "sparkling snow" sprinkled upon the cotton made it glisten. Gifts were placed around the tree. Some of the toys I remember getting before Daddy died were dolls, all sizes and shapes; hand made doll clothes, a wooden doll bed with covers, a black doll buggy, black iron stove, toy cooking utensils, a wooden toy kitchen cabinet with pasteboard boxes simulating staple food stuffs (each currently in use by homemakers of the period), a small toy ironing board with a small black iron, a folding blackboard, and my own Quaker-made, red, pressed-back rocker. At age four, Grandpa Simpkins gave me a silver knife, fork, and spoon. I always had books. As I outgrew them, they were sent to Uncle Pearl's children in Cheatam county. A nursing kit was my pride and joy. It prompted me to say: "I wanna be a nurse when I grow up." At that point the adults would tease me and talk about bedpans and blood, which I resented because I thought of nursing as "doctoring."

My girl friends and I spent many afternoons under the shade of a huge oak tree with my toy nurses kit, taking temperatures, bandaging, and vaccinating each other on the upper arm with a smooth twig, bent in half. The vaccinations hurt a bit. One of us would swab an area on the other's arm with a small dab of cotton, press up a small bit of flesh, and pinch it smartly with a partially broken stick so as to leave an imprint upon the skin, which we pretended to be a vaccination. Then the vaccination would be carefully bandaged. The "vaccination" hurt, but everyone took turns at playing doctor, nurse, and patient.

I remember being at Aunt Mamie and Uncle Forrest Bell's on Batts Boulevard for a Christmas dinner with Daddy's people. Gathered there were Granddaddy Bell, Great Uncle Joe Bell, Aunt Susie Bell, Auntie and Uncle Arthur Worsham, Cornelius Bell, Aunt Maud and some of her children, Cousin Phillip Bell and his stepmother, and my Mother and Daddy. Cornelius, seven years older than I, was Mamie and Forrest's only child. Granddaddy Bell gave me a little red scooter that Christmas day. It was the type you pushed with one foot to build up speed and then coasted on as long as there was momentum. There were sidewalks in front of the house, so after Christmas dinner Granddaddy Bell decided he would show me how to ride the little red scooter on the sidewalk. He was talking to me and looking at me as he stood on the scooter when the scooter went out from under him. He fell down hard upon the sidewalk. Granddaddy Bell's hip was broken. He was 79 years old. He never fully recovered. I remember the horror of seeing him fall, the reaction of the family and the doctor arriving and blessing out my Granddaddy for trying to act so young (they were good friends). I had a guilt complex over being the cause of it all! I never remember taking the scooter home or even seeing it again. Skipping rope took the place of that little red scooter whenever I played on the sidewalk near Aunt Mamie's.

Daddy and Uncle Forrest Bell owned Bell Brothers Store. Granddaddy Bell helped finance the store, but to my knowledge he never worked there. Even though the store was at the foot of the hill below Aunt Matt's house, where we were living at the time, I rarely got to go into the store. Uncle Forrest was a stern disciplinarian and did not think children should be allowed to roam free. A little bit of everything was sold – sacks of feed, fertilizer, seeds, and farm implements were stacked on the front porch and stored in the lean-to room. The main room contained fresh produce, canned and dried foods, clothing, oil lamps and lamp oil, pots and pans, utensils for the house, and garden and farming supplies. It was a typical rural general merchandise store. For me, the most important glass counter was the one displaying penny candy. I was also drawn to the icebox that contained Cherri Colas! One morning, just across from the store, four friends and I were playing under an apple tree when my friends persuaded me that, since Daddy owned the store, he should give us all free candy and cold drinks. I knew better, but I also wanted to be the "big shot" with my girl friends, so across the road and through the back door traipsed five little girls with no money. I still can recall the stern and unbending _expression of Uncle Forrest, but Daddy was polite; too much so! We selected our candy, but no cold drinks, and we went back to our apple tree to enjoy our sack of sweets. But that night I got a lecture on the proper behavior for a little girl whose father runs a candy store. Never again did I let my friends talk me into getting free candy for them. Bell Brothers Store was inside a triangle formed by Woodland Street, Greenbrier Pike and 16th Street. It was an old, unpainted wooden structure, which had been there for many, many years.

I remember when Cornelius and Granddaddy Bell were teaching me my ABC's. Cornelius said, for me to repeat after him: "I went around the house to A; I went around the house to B – and so on until I repeated the alphabet to P. I still can remember how everyone laughed when I said, "I went around the house to P."

Grandpa Simpkins had been keeping his pony and buggy at Aunt Matt's house since selling his house and restaurant in town. He was still living at the City Hotel, where he worked as a clerk and sold popcorn from his electric popcorn popper, which he kept outside at the street corner. I have already explained that he was a cripple, for one leg was shorter than the other, a deformity caused by typhoid fever, which he had suffered as a child. Yet he remained a gentleman – quiet and mannerly, a good storyteller, and always clean, neat, and well dressed. In 1921, give or take a year, when his health began to fail, it was decided he should move to Portland, 25 miles to the east, and live with my mother's sister, Effie Lane. Daddy, Mother and I drove Grandpa's pony and buggy to Portland. I remember that day as one of the happiest days of my life. Daddy sang, laughed, told jokes and made us so happy as we rode slowly along in the buggy. We stopped at a roadside spring, where water came out of a pipe and ate the midday lunch that mother had prepared. The ride back on the train was not nearly as much fun. I was either five or six at that time.

Just a few weeks before we had taken the pony and buggy to Portland there are two incidents I remember well. We were taking a buggy ride and stopped on a hill where there were many large oak trees. This spot overlooked Springfield. We got out of the buggy and walked around. Daddy said, "This is where I want us to build our house." However, that was not to be. His health was beginning to fail. So, with his inheritance from Granddaddy Bell's estate that had come primarily from selling the farm, Daddy bought a small house on adjacent property, not far from that grove of oak trees. But we never moved in. We rented it because Daddy's health would have made moving too difficult. Granddaddy Bell's inheritance was divided among his five children. Aunt Susie bought Nashville Light and Power Company stock. Auntie made a down payment on a new house in

Nashville at 710 Porter Road. Aunt Maud bought a small house in south Springfield. Aunt Mamie made a down payment on a large house in Springfield on Batts Blvd.

I attended Woodland Street School for the first and second grade. Woodland Street School was a 2-room school building for the neighborhood children of south Springfield. It was built in the late 1800s and my half-uncle, William Bell, was the first teacher following his graduation from Peabody College (University of Nashville). My first and second grade teacher was Miss Mary Lou Williams, my Aunt Susie's closest friend. They taught me to read before I started to school. This turned against me in school because I was a smart-alec first grader. I talked back to Miss Mary Lou, laughed at the boys and girls who could not read, and turned around in my seat to see what others were doing. By the end of my first week in the first grade, Miss Mary Lou had had enough of my antics. Taking me by the hand, she led me to the blackboard, drew a circle on the board with chalk, sat me on a stool, and told me to hold my nose in the circle and stay on the stool until she told me to step down. This was the most devastating punishment I have ever received.

In spite of my punishment I loved Miss Mary Lou and continued to be taught by her at school and at my granddaddy Bell's. I enjoyed my 2-1/2 years at Woodland Street School. I led my class; received a reading award in the second grade, and played a small pump organ during lunch and recess. Aunt Mamie had taught me the piano notes and a few simple pieces of music – and I loved to try them out on the old pump organ.

Chapter 3 – The Tragedy

We went to an all day singing at Wartrace Methodist Church where Daddy and his grandparents and parents had worshiped, and where I was on the cradle roll. It was a beautiful morning. The sun was shining throughout the morning service. However, when dinner was being spread on the tables in the side yard, clouds began to gather and there were several sharp claps of thunder. Daddy said, "I have to go home." We got the buggy and home we went – a distance of one mile. It was lightning and thundering sharply by the time we got in the house. Daddy had a frantic _expression on his face. He went to the bed and crawled under the bed and drew himself up into a ball. This was my first remembrance of the beginning of the nervous breakdown that was to destroy my loving, caring, happy father. I was 6 or 7 years old.

I remember playing in the front yard under the pin oak tree one day when I heard a noise overhead. I looked up and saw a living long thing hanging from the branch above my head making a rattling noise. I had never seen anything like this before. I ran into the house to tell Mother and Daddy. Both ran out to the tree, and Daddy killed the rattlesnake with his shotgun. It was said to be one of the largest rattlesnakes ever killed in Robertson County. Mother and Daddy hugged me, cried, and thanked God for my safety. The dead snake was placed on the ground, measured, and wondered over by the neighbors and relatives. For many nights I had nightmares that the snake had fallen on me.
 At this time I was sleeping in the white iron "baby" bed because I had "graduated" from the cradle. This is the

same iron bed I now have. It had first belonged to Cornelius Bell, then to me. Next it would be used by Gracie and Arthur Worsham's son Billy, then by my sons, Howard and John. I would much later clean and paint it to be used during visits by my grandsons, Howie, Keith and David. Now I am looking forward to future great grandchildren using it.

One of my happy memories is of evenings in the warm kitchen in the winter with mother preparing the night meal. When Daddy locked the store door in the evening he would start singing. This was a signal to Mother that he would be coming home for supper, for we could hear him within our house as he left the store. I would run to the window to watch his lantern and his coming up the hill. He would stop at the window to make a face at me, run around to the door, and scoop me up into his arms & give Mother a big kiss and hug.

These happy times were short lived because Daddy was more frequently getting disorientated. He would sometimes go into the wrong house and not realize where he was – mental difficulties that greatly frightened him. Granddaddy Bell and Dr. Porter arranged for a group of doctors from Nashville to come to Springfield and exam Daddy to see what could be done. The family was at Granddaddy Bell's on Batts Blvd. when Dr. Porter gave the report of the group's medical findings. Nothing could be done. A complete deterioration of the central nervous system was worsening. Mother went into hysterics (the only time in my life I saw her out of control). I was six and one half years old at the time.

A year later Dr. Porter walked up to the back door of the house on Woodland Street and told Daddy he was going for a ride. Mother and I hugged and kissed him as he got into Dr. Porter's car. He was taken to Central State Hospital in Nashville where he was put in one of the private rooms, where doors were locked to protect patients from harm. It was mid-September 1922. I was 7 years and 10 months old.

True happiness went out of our lives. Now Mother and I were alone. What had caused Daddy's mental breakdown? I will explain the cause as it was later told to me by Daddy's sister, Grace Worsham:

Not yet married, Daddy was working in Springfield at the Davis Clothing Store and boarding at Mrs. Chilton's. One day his father, Granddaddy Bell, who folks in the region called Mr. Jim, was having trouble hiring enough field hands to get in his tobacco crop. So he persuaded Daddy to leave his work at the store and help by driving the wagon and mule team while the hands loaded tobacco as it was gathered in the fields. Since Granddaddy's big barn had burned, Daddy and the hands were unloading the tobacco into one of the barns on the adjoining farm that belonged to Daddy's sister Mamie and her husband Forest Bell. That day Daddy's sisters, Grace and Susie, and an African American servant they called Aunt Mandy prepared noon-time dinner at the Bell home for all the field hands. Work in the fields stopped when a thunderstorm arose, spitting out severe lightning. Daddy drove the mules and wagon to Mamie and Forest's barn for cover. However, a bolt of lightning came through the barn roof and passed through the coupling pole of the wagon and through Daddy, who was sitting up front on the wagon. Knocked unconscious by the lightning, Daddy fell forward onto the coupling pole and wagon tongue just behind the mules. The mules (I remember one was named Kit), after being knocked down to their knees by the lightning, got up and lunged forward pulling the wagon and Daddy with them. They burst through the barn doors and headed off toward a gully with Daddy bouncing along the ground, tangled in the reins and harness rigging. The mules jumped over the gully before being stopped by one or more field hands who happened to be within reach. Apparently the frightened mules were racing toward their stable quarters. A rescuer grabbed Daddy's foot and pulled him from the wagon. Since the accident occurred on the adjoining farm belonging to Aunt Mamie and Uncle Forest, someone ran to Mamie's house to tell her that somebody had been hurt. Mamie telephoned Grace and Susie to come over (they were at the adjacent farm in their father's house) and help whoever was hurt. When Mamie discovered that it was her brother who was hurt, she fainted and was of no help. My grandfather, who was already with Walter, must have been extremely worried. Grace and Susie ran all the way from their house, a distance of one-half mile. When they got there Daddy was on the ground, his nose was bleeding, and he was beginning to come to his senses. When Daddy saw his father, he began to curse him for insisting that he drive the mules that day. This was the one and only time anyone ever heard Daddy curse. Daddy was carried to his sister Mamie's bedroom. Dr. Porter came. Grace stayed up all night with Daddy. Daddy was exceedingly hot with a burning sensation all over his body. He would scream and relive his experience in his sleep. The next day he was moved to his father's house. For many weeks he remained in his father's bedroom where a fire was always kept and where two beds were available. Grace waited on him.

This happened in 1910 or 1911, following Daddy's mother's death and before Grace's marriage. Daddy had to be tended like a baby. He was in extreme pain. Doctors from Nashville came by train to assist Dr. Porter in treating Daddy. They agreed it was a miracle that he lived through this experience, which would become the eventual cause of his death. Many friends, neighbors, and relatives came to see Daddy and the wagon. Some of them took as souvenirs pieces of the coupling pole, which was splintered into small pieces.

Daddy had been courting Mother since 1906. And he had asked her to marry him, but Mother had not yet given her answer. Visiting him often during his convalescence, and seeing him so badly wounded, Mother made up her mind that, if Daddy lived, she would marry him. Daddy's sister, Grace thought Mother must have loved Daddy deeply to marry him with so much uncertainty about his future health. Daddy did recover sufficient to marry, and the wedding was held in December 1913. I was born eleven months later, in November 1914.

So that was the story of the tragic accident that befell Daddy.

After Daddy had become too sick to work at Bell Brothers Grocery across the street, it was sold to two

Davis brothers, John and Dick, and the store was afterward known as Davis Brothers Grocery. John and Dick Davis were my great uncles.

A new life style began for Mother and me. After Daddy was taken to the hospital in Nashville, Mother and I continued living at Aunt Matt's. As often as possible we would ride the train to Nashville to visit Uncle Arthur and Auntie. They would drive us out Murfreesboro Road to visit Daddy in the red brick hospital. Mother and I would sit in the lounge with Daddy and talk about our everyday life. Sometimes Daddy knew us; sometimes he didn't. Several months later our visit had to take place in the hospital room because Daddy was unable to leave his bed. The last visit with him was on July 3, 1923. I was eight and a half years old. Daddy was very calm, very weak, and was running a high fever. He wanted me lifted up by Mother to give him a hug and kiss just before we left. Mother wanted to go back to see him on July 4, but the hospital would not allow visitors on a holiday. Mother cried most of the day. The next morning around seven o'clock came the telephone call that Daddy had died just before midnight. That was July 4, 1923.

Henry & Bell Undertakers came to the hospital for the body. Mother kept asking for Daddy's personal items; that is, his Masonic ruby ring and his Masonic gold pocket watch with chain and fob. She never got them, or any other personal items. It was raining and darkness had fallen when the hearse, followed by Uncle Arthur's car with Auntie, Aunt Susie, Mother, and me, left Nashville by way of Old Nashville Pike, White's Creek Road and Joelton. This was a slow procession in the rain, in the dark, and over gravel roads. At the foot of the hill at Hinkle's chair factory and store, the hearse had a flat tire. The kind people in the Hinkle store invited us in to wait until the tire was repaired. Daddy's body was placed in the front guest bedroom at the Springfield house where Uncle Forrest, Aunt Mamie and Granddaddy Bell lived. Just before the casket was closed for the funeral, I was lifted up to see Daddy, and mother leaned over to kiss him goodbye.

The funeral procession went to Elmwood Cemetery in Springfield. Daddy was buried at the foot of his mother's grave. We were seated on folding chairs. Many people were there. I remember the Masonic ceremony that was held over the open grave after the casket had been lowered into the grave. A number of items were placed on the casket, each representing a Masonic ritual. Mr. Luther Davis and two other Masons conducted the ritual. I remember very little about the funeral because, as a grieving 8-1/2-year old girl, I didn't understand a lot of what was going on. Mother kept her composure throughout the funeral. Years later, when I was a teenager, I was with mother at a relative's funeral when a family member screamed and fainted as the casket was being lowered into the grave. Mother said, "Never behave like that. Always behave like a lady and keep your emotions under control." My mother was a Christian lady all of her life.

Mother sold the house on the hill near the grove of oak trees. Over future years she used the money to buy a piano and pay for my music lessons and my college education.

Chapter 4 – Daddy's Sister, My Aunt Mamie, was a Dear

When Daddy went to the hospital our lives completely changed. The income from the grocery store stopped, and Mother had to find ways and means of supporting me. Before her marriage to Daddy she had worked at the telephone company where her brother Melvin was a pioneer in surveying, planning and installing telephone wires, circuits and stations through-out Middle Tennessee – and later in the State of Mississippi. Myrtle's best friend, Sara Carter, was secretary and treasurer of the Springfield unit. Myrtle's family friend, Mr. Tomlinson, was station manager – so Mother had no trouble in getting her old job back. I continued attending Woodland Street School and we continued to live at Aunt Matt's. While Mother worked, Aunt Matt looked after me, or I stayed with Aunt Mamie and Granddaddy Bell. We continued living with Aunt Matt until the year following Daddy's death. Miss Dovie Lynn McCrary was my third grade teacher at Woodland Street during the fall session. She lived next door to Aunt Matt's, and I had known her for several years. Again, I received the reading award.

During this period in my life Mother and I attended Woodland Street Methodist Church. Uncle Buford (Mother's brother) and his family attended the church and lived on Woodland Street between Aunt Matt's and the church. I spent many happy hours playing with my cousin, Martha Lou Simpkins, daughter of Uncle Buford. However, they never really took care of me. I never remember eating a meal at their house (except later in life at family gatherings) or any special attention from Aunt Bertha.

Following the school day at Woodland Street School I would go home to Aunt Matt's. She would feed me my supper and listen to my lessons and tuck me in my bed. On cold days there would be a big fire in the kitchen fireplace and I would enjoy putting a broom straw in the fire to watch the end glow with fire. Aunt Matt soon put a stop to that – she told me it would "make me wet my bed!" Mother, at this time, was at home in the morning to see me off to school, and she would walk with me to the street. Then she worked until after dark at the telephone office. She would walk alone from downtown to Aunt Matt's (about 1 mile) in all kinds of weather. Only one time was she afraid she said. Two men in a car stopped and tried to talk her into getting in the car with them. She would not talk to them but reported them to the policeman the next day. After that she never had any trouble when returning home after dark.

During the summer between my second and third grades I spent the day hours at Aunt Mamie's and Granddaddy Bell's. This was an enjoyable time for me even though Daddy had died that summer. There were several children in the neighborhood and much activity at Aunt Mamie's house. In the house there were Granddaddy Bell, his brother (uncle Joe), Aunt Susie, Aunt Mamie and Uncle Forrest and their son Cornelius. There was also "Aunt Mandy," an older woman who was half African American and half Native American, in the basement doing washing and ironing, and her adult daughter worked in the kitchen. ("Aunt Mandy's parents had been slaves owned by William Leeper Bell.) All Bell family gatherings were held here. On her way home in the evenings Mother would stop at Granddaddy Bell's for me and we would walk together the three-quarter-mile trip home to Aunt Matt's. I remember many little stories about that summer of 1923, spent at Aunt Mamie's while Mother was at work.

Aunt Mamie liked to teach me things – notes on the piano, cooking, and sewing. No one ever told me to stop "banging" on the piano – so, little by little, I picked up a few selections to play.

I remember one day that summer when the Bells were having a family barbecue, and the hustle of three servants, "Aunt Mandy" and her daughters, in the kitchen. They had sent me to the living room to be with the men and visiting aunts (to be out of their way). Then Aunt Mamie asked me to come back to the kitchen so she could show me how to make cold slaw. I stood in a chair so I could see what she was doing to the cabbage, cut into a large mixing bowl. Here are her instructions: chop the fresh, green cabbage with a sharp knife with clean, direct cuts so as not to crush and bruise the edges of the cabbage. Begin to pour pure apple cider vinegar slowly over the cabbage – just enough to delicately coat the cabbage pieces – then with hands turn cabbage over and over to cover cabbage with vinegar. Add sugar and salt to taste. Again, mix slowly and carefully the entire bowl full of cabbage. By coating cabbage first with vinegar there will be less water drawn from the cabbage by the salt and sugar. This is old-fashioned slaw to be served with barbecue, potato salad, baked beans, salt-risen cornbread. Following this meal we had cold watermelon from Granddaddy Bell's garden.

Another way to entertain me was with magazines and fashion books. In the front guest bedroom Aunt Mamie kept her sewing machine, fashion books and notions. I would sit on the rug in the middle of the floor surrounded by pattern books, my dolls, odds and ends of fabric, lace, ribbons, buttons, and there plan my new wardrobe for the dolls. After my selection, she would draw the outline of the pattern on cloth, I would cut on the line and with a large needle and thread attempt to sew 2 pieces together – then decorate the dress with lace or ribbons or buttons. As an 8-year old I made some funny looking doll clothes – but I always got a compliment from Aunt Mamie, "Aunt Mandy," and Granddaddy Bell.

One day Aunt Mamie was cleaning and oiling her sewing machine with a turkey feather. So I learned to oil, clean, and operate a sewing machine when I was 8 years old. But I did not have the love of sewing that Aunt Mamie had. She made all my clothes (dresses, coats, blouses), allowed me to help select the pattern and go with her to Randolph House clothing store to select the material. I never made any articles to wear (except as a ninth grader in home economics Class when I made an apron, dress and pajamas) until my home economics college courses in college. Later I began sewing for my boys. I always bought my clothes. I would depend on Aunt Mamie and her exquisite fashion sense and skill for my clothes until I was 18 years old.

When Aunt Mamie was busy, I was the responsibility of "Aunt Mandy," the elderly woman of Indian and African descent who had worked for the Bells all her life. It was fun to be in the cool basement and on the concrete porch and "help" Aunt Mandy with the washing and ironing. She was patient with me when I played in the wash water washing my doll clothes. She strung up a low clothes line for me to hang my doll clothes on to dry; helped me sprinkle them for ironing; stood me in a chair so I would be high enough to the ironing board to iron my doll clothes. In the kitchen she was patient with me in showing me how to dry dishes. The pantry was a room with shelves from ceiling to floor. I remember stacks and stacks of dishes. The everyday dishes were the brown ivy leaf earthenware in sets of 24. I have one plate from this set, which belonged to my grandparents Bell. Occasionally Aunt Susie would do the ironing and entertain me with stories of the farm.

There were several children in the neighborhood. All of them were older than I, except Bess Alice Clinard (she would marry Tom Estes, who was my age and my special playmate from Woodland Street School). Cornelius was 7 years older than I and had a bunch of neighborhood boy friends that enjoyed baseball in his backyard. I begged and begged to play; but the boys didn't want me interfering with their game. I cried; Aunt Mamie said they should let me pretend to play; they put me in the backfield; naturally, I tried to catch a hit ball. It went through my 8-year-old hands and hit my mouth directly on my new permanent front teeth. No more playing ball with the boys – a loose front tooth kept me from wanting to play. The dentist said to leave the tooth alone – it would firm. As a result I have had a yellow front tooth to show for my ball game – a firm but slightly yellow tooth.

The boys dug a tunnel of about 4 feet length to a little underground room, which they had dug out under the carriage house. They said this was their clubhouse. I watched them haul out dirt and begged to go see the clubhouse. I was about 8 years old and I did not understand it was merely a black hole in the earth. Finally, Aunt Mamie said she would watch me as I crawled through the tunnel. Upon entering I found Cornelius and a friend sitting next to a burning candle in the middle of the dirt floor. This candlelight threw funny shadows on them and the surroundings. I began to cry. I was afraid to crawl back through the dark tunnel and had difficulty getting my breath. So with Aunt Mamie outside the tunnel urging me forward, and Cornelius in the back of me urging me forward, I got out into the sunlight and threw myself into Aunt Mamie's arms – never again did I ask to "see" the boy's club house!

At Christmas time and the Fourth of July, Cornelius had great delight in begging me to hold sparklers and throw firecrackers and bombs. I was afraid of them. Again I would go crying to Aunt Mamie, who was kind and considerate of me – never berating me for being afraid, or being a crybaby. She was a dearly beloved aunt. She knew I liked yellow cake with chocolate icing or sauce and would make it especially for me. She also would save the "pulley-bone" of the chicken for me. But Cornelius would take the "pulley-bone" from the platter of fried chicken first, if he had a chance – just to hear me fuss and demand it was "my" piece of chicken. Aunt Mamie would make him give it to me. Granddaddy, Uncle Forrest and Uncle Joe would never interfere with any argument between Cornelius and me, and Aunt Mamie would usually decide in my favor. Cornelius was constantly getting me into trouble. However, he was a great brother type for me whom I loved and looked up to. He would hold me in his arms, and as I grew older, hold me by my hands and dance all over the house humming or singing. Later, when they had a radio he would turn the dance music up loud and dance me around the house.

Granddaddy Bell would buy large pieces of beef or pork from the back of a farm wagon when someone killed beef or slaughtered hogs. I remember these huge pieces of meat piled on the kitchen table and "Aunt Mandy" and her daughter getting it ready for cooking. Live chickens, gallons of sweet milk, dozens of eggs and pounds of butter would be bought from farmer's wagons. Behind the house were stables for the horses and a large vegetable garden. "Aunt Mandy's" family, including her other daughters and grandchildren, had to be fed as well as Granddaddy Bell's family. "Aunt Mandy's" family lived behind the main house and its lot in a small cabin facing an alley, which served the other African Americans servants who likewise lived behind the houses where they worked. When the Bell's had big family dinners, I would go with Aunt Mamie to the back fence with food for "Aunt Mandy's" children and grandchildren, but I never remember one of the children being around Granddaddy's house – they stayed in their cabins beyond the fence. There was a servant's room in the basement, but it was used for storage and grape wine that Aunt Mamie made for the sacrament for Wartrace Methodist Church. Granddaddy Bell always took responsibility in paying for any healthcare required for anyone in "Aunt Mandy's" family.

One day Cornelius asked me if I would like something good to drink. He showed me how to open the spigot and run some of the wonderful sweet grape wine into my mouth. He also drank some wine. The adults caught onto this and the winemaking apparatus and wine disappeared. Where? I don't know. No one ever said anything to me about it.

I remember Granddaddy Bell bought a wooden barrel full of raw oysters packed in ice. The oysters were placed on the kitchen table, and everyone participated in shucking and eating the raw oysters, except me. Cornelius chased me all over the house, dangling a raw oyster between his fingers, saying he would make me eat it. I never did. Today, I won't, either.

The neighborhood children decided to have an entertainment night for the adults. The basement was chosen as the place; a curtain was hung; a play was written and parts given out. Much time was given over to practicing before the given night. I don't remember the outcome of the night except there were several chairs occupied by adults in front of the curtain. We obtained a penny from each person who came.

My best friend, Bess Alice Clinard lived three doors north of Aunt Mamie's house. It was fun to visit her and climb the narrow steps out of the kitchen to the servant's upstairs room, which had been turned into a playroom for Bess with her dolls, games, etc. She moved when she was 10 to the country where her family built a house, and kept a garden, horses, chickens and pigs. Her brother, Orman, would drive a car to school each day so Bess and he could attend Springfield schools.

Aunt Mamie and Uncle Forrest had a large touring car, with window coverings to be put up in cold or rainy weather. Aunt Mamie had a long wide scarf to cover her head and shoulders when riding to keep the dust from settling in her hair and on her clothes. Some of the creeks did not have bridges, so through the water the car must go. Also, the roads were of gravel. I loved riding in this car, staring out the window and asking questions about the countryside. To keep the dust down on the street someone had to water them each day. Aunt Mamie's water for the house came from a cistern and had a water pipe going to the front yard from which the street was watered. It was special for me to hold the hose with my Granddaddy Bell's help. The house had a tin roof, which resounded with noise during a rainstorm. These times I would sit on the floor in the large upstairs bedroom at Aunt Mamie's house in front of a bookcase and read school books – any books I could find – and play with an old clock that played chimes was kept above the bookshelves. Mother would clean Aunt Mamie's house on her days off from work – dust, polish, mop, etc. to help repay her for taking care of me and sewing for me. So Mother always told me not to feel obliged in anyway to Aunt Mamie because she had repaid Mamie by working around the house.

Chapter 5 – With "Aunt Johnnie's" Help Mother and I Managed

At the time Daddy died, financial troubles increased for my mother. She had only a part time job with the telephone company – not enough to support the two of us. She fought relatives and community leaders to keep me as her daughter. Auntie and Uncle Arthur offered to adopt me. Aunt Effie and Uncle Clem offered to adopt me. Aunt Mamie and Uncle Forrest wanted to adopt me as well. The Masonic Lodge wanted to send me to the orphanage on Franklin Road. My mother said no to each one.

One fall day Mr. Davis and another Mason came to see Mother in regard to sending me to the orphanage and the Springfield Masonic lodge chapter paying my way. They presented Mother with a beautiful basket of fruit. She was so angry with them that she threw the basket and fruit back in their faces and said, "If the Masons would pay their credit bills at the store, she wouldn't have any trouble with money." Again, I repeat, my Mother was a Christian lady with a great depth of determination. She was determined to keep her daughter and this she did! Although Bells Brothers Grocery had been sold, Mother still owned the past due accounts receivables. I remember those stacks of credit bills (unpaid), which Mother saved until just before her death. She would say that she knew she could not collect them, but it kept her perception of people from getting dull – many times she would say if that person would have paid his bills she would respect him and give him her support. So all of my Mother's business dealings were colored with who had paid my Daddy's grocery store bills or who had not. It would have cost too much to take so many people to court. Daddy had also invested in an independent tobacco warehouse with Uncle Forrest and Granddaddy Bell – all of this was lost just before the depression. So my side of the Bell family went from wealth to middle income to poor a few years before the Great Depression.

Mother went to talk to her brother, Buford, about so many people wanting to adopt me and to seek his advice. Buford was not at home, but his wife Bertha, was. Mother told her why she wanted to see Buford. Aunt Bertha, thinking that mother wanted money, became angry and told Mother, "Don't expect any help from them that she would not allow Buford to help her, he had to support his own family." I was there; I heard her angry voice. I saw my Mother turn away, take my hand, and sobbing and crying, walk slowly back to Aunt Matt's and to her few hours of telephone work. True to her word, Aunt Bertha and Uncle Buford never, in any shape, form, or fashion, helped my Mother and me!

So to my father's family I am deeply indebted for education, love, affection, and material advantages, which they so generously gave to me. Poor as Mother and I were, we maintained our social standing and the respect and friendship of the better-quality people of Springfield. I was invited to join the best teenage clubs; enjoyed being invited into the wealthy homes; and was a member of a small select group of friends. Uncle Forrest was my legal guardian until he died when I was 14 years old.

In the fall I returned to Woodland Street School. But a diphtheria outbreak prompted a Board of Education ruling that every student had to have an immunization shot. As I was pale and underweight, Dr. Porter would not consent or give me a shot. I stayed out of school three or four weeks, each day begging to go back to school. Mother took pity on me and took me to Dr. Freeman (another doctor in Springfield) for my vaccination. I developed a bad reaction – high fever, out of my head, and aching joints. Dr. Porter stayed by my bedside for hours and overnight. I remember being cooled in tepid water and Mother and Dr. Porter trying to bring me out of my delirium. Mother berated herself that she had gone against Dr. Porter's instructions. In about a month I was well enough to go back to school. I kept my schoolwork up because Miss Dovie Lynn, my teacher, would bring it home to me. In the meantime Mother had gained a full-time job at the telephone company, so she was working full time. She wanted to be nearer town for work and her church, the Presbyterian Church, and wanted me to go to the town school. This Christmas was a big one – large Christmas tree, many gifts, a folding table (for my dolls), tea china set for 4, my very own fountain pen, and a blackboard on a stand. Soon after Christmas my life entered a new phase, because we moved from Aunt Matt's to "Aunt Johnnie" and "Uncle Will" Orndorf's home on Fifth Avenue East, Springfield.

"Aunt Johnnie" was not my real aunt, but Mother and I considered her family. As a girl, Johnnie was in great difficulty because her mother had died and her father was an alcoholic and unable to properly care for her. So my great, great grandparents, Sarah Catherine Elizabeth

Featherstone and Jesse W. Davis, had taken Johnnie into their home to be a body servant and companion for their granddaughter Sarah Frances Sanford, who was four years younger. This arrangement had allowed Johnnie to attend school with Sarah at the same time that she earned her room and board as a body servant. My grandmother loved Johnnie like a sister. And Johnnie was grateful for the Davis family's generosity in giving her a home (In the 1870 census Johnnie is listed as a domestic servant). She had married Will Orndolf and lived on some land, just two blocks from the courthouse, which had been in the Orndolf family since pioneer days. They were good middle class people, and we were lucky that they had some space in their home that we could rent for an affordable price. I do not know how the arrangement was made with "Aunt Johnnie" and "Uncle Will" for Mother and me to live with them.

This move meant a changing environment, a different school and a different church – a complete change for me. I was nine years old. We had a back bedroom behind the living room. "Aunt Johnnie's" house was smaller than any I had lived in before. We were cramped for space. My playthings had to be put in the doorway of a servant's house, which was also used as a storage house. It was no fun to play by myself in this dusty crowded spot. There was room for only one full bed in the bedroom, so for the first time I had to share a bed with my mother – which I did until I was 15 years old. Our kitchen was Aunt Johnnie's summer kitchen. It had a concrete floor, which was cold as kraut during the winter. We reached it by going across a closed-in narrow walkway, unheated, with screen doors at each end.

Mother stored her trunks against the wall in this walkway. Extra furniture was stored in the servant's house, some were given to Aunt Effie, and some things were stored at Aunt Matt's. (Later, when Mother went to get some lamps and a wash and pitcher set she had left at Aunt Matt's, she found that Aunt Matt had sold them – Mother cried privately over this because they were her mother's.)

Even in this crowded condition I adjusted and grew to love "Aunt Johnnie" and "Uncle Will" – they were good, kind, thoughtful people and gave me the run of the house; treated me like a granddaughter, and were staunch Presbyterians. "Uncle Will" operated a saddle shop. I would watch him by the hours as he would cut, sew, make, and repair anything leather. At home he had a cow, chickens, and a large garden. I would follow him to milk the cow. One day he let me try to milk, but I could not get any milk. Sometimes he would allow me to go to the attic above the shop and look at the old magazines stored there (I know now that they were *Godey* magazines. I wish I had saved them; they would now bring a lot at an antique market). On Wednesday and Sunday nights I would stay at home with "Uncle Will" while Mother and "Aunt Johnnie" would walk up "pull-tight" (Fifth Avenue) to church. I would crank up the old Victoria, changing the records and finding records "Uncle Will" wanted to hear. "Going Out To Aunt Mary's" was his favorite. We would then sit in rocking chairs in front of the living room fire and play cards. For the first time I was taught to play cards (no gambling or spot cards were allowed) Flinch, with numbers on them, was our game. "Uncle Will" died when I was in the 5th grade – I missed him so.

Mother would see me off to school, for she worked the afternoon-to-evening shift. I had a good hot breakfast with a tablespoon of cod liver oil and a packed lunch. "Aunt Johnnie" would be at home in the afternoon to greet me; give me a snack, supper, hear my homework, and tuck me in bed for the night. Mother would get home between 9 and 10 o'clock. Sometime I would be asleep and sometimes I deliberately would stay awake to hear her key in the door and to know she was safely home.

On the first day of school I was fearful about going to Main Street School, which was the main school in Springfield. I walked the 2-1/2 blocks and saw Cornelius waiting for me on the front porch of the 2-storied brick school building – which was new when Mother had attended school there in 1896. He was a welcome sight. He took me by the hand and led me to Miss Mable Ruffin's room and to the coatroom, where I hung my coat and left my lunch. Miss Mable led me to my assigned seat (double) with Bess Alice Clinard – who had been my playmate on Woodland Street and lived near Aunt Mamie's. People had gone to a lot of trouble to make me feel comfortable and at home. I appreciate this greatly, and more recently I have come to realize that Miss Mable was my cousin on the Featherstone family side through the Davis line.

Main Street School was more advanced than Woodland Street School. I was not a leader here; I was behind in all my subjects, which made me shy and hesitant. I think I still have some of these qualities left in me. I had not been exposed to the multiplication tables, but my class had, and they were into division. I went around for weeks saying the multiplication tables, which made no sense to me because I had missed the introduction to that phase of math. They had art one hour a week and music one hour a week. I did not know how to sing the scales. At the end of the year, students were exempt from exams if they maintained a certain average. I had never taken an exam and was not exempt. I had to sit on a frontbench with about 10 or 12 more students and be tested orally to pass the third grade. I was terrified – but I passed. I enjoyed the friendship of Bess Alice. I remember one day we were seated in school; Bess Alice pushed me with her body across the seat; I gave her a generous push toward the other end of the bench; she fell off; Miss Mable got mad and lectured to us. We took our lunch with two or three other girls and ate on the tree roots of a huge tree that was behind the girls' toilet building (there was no running water inside the school house, but the detached toilet buildings were large and contained a flushing system). A high board separated the grammar school from the high school, each in its own building.

Mother enjoyed raising flowers. The coal bin was at the end of the side concrete walk, which went into the hallway between our bedroom and kitchen. We used this method of entering our rooms, unless we had guests who were invited in through the living room. There was a slight rise in the land above the sidewalk. Mother always planted flowers in front of the coal bin and dahlias on the hillside. This created a mass of beautiful colors which otherwise would have appeared dreary. I played mostly on this sidewalk with my paper dolls and dolls.

Near "Aunt Johnnie's" was the Harris' family. Sue Ann Harris became my best friend all through school. Her father owned a drug store and was a cousin of my mother's. We would go from one house to the other without seeking permission – just a telephone call to each other. Near "Uncle Will's" shop was a small grocery store where we would go after school sometimes for chewing gum or candy. On this particular afternoon, Sue Ann bet me that, the following day at school, she would be able to keep more chewing gum in her mouth than I could. We each bought a 5-cent package of gum. Miss Mable caught each of us chewing 2 times. In front of the class on the second time she told us to throw out all of the gum we had in our mouths. Each of us had put a full package in our mouth at one time!

One day a pretty curly black haired girl was walking home from school at the same time I was. She was fun to talk too, my age, in my grade, and lived near me. I invited her to stop by "Aunt Johnnie's" and play with me. "Aunt Johnnie" gave us milk and cookies and allowed us to play dolls for about an hour. Then she told the little girl it was time to go home to her mother. Shortly afterward "Aunt Johnnie" sat me down for a lecture. I was not to invite this little girl to my house to play, not to walk with her from and to school and not to play with her at school. I was to always politely speak to her but never have any extended conversation with her. This was my first lesson in observing the town's social classes. The next day I saw her hanging on the garden fence separating "Aunt Johnnie's" house from the little girl's house. I immediately went to talk to her and I told her I could not invite her to play. "Aunt Johnnie" saw me;

evidently she got in touch with the little girl's mother because never again did she try to be friends with me. Several years later I found out the little girl's mother was considered the whore of the town. But happily the little girl moved away from Springfield when she was older and became successful in Nashville, succeeding in a career as a businesswoman in a legal profession.

And so ended my Third grade at Aunt Johnnie's. My circle of friends was selected for me from the better class, more socially prominent families in town. There were eight of us who would have slumber parties, birthday parties, swimming parties and play parties. I would keep the same circle of friends throughout grammar school and high school.

Chapter 6 – Summers with Auntie, Uncle Arthur, Aunt Effie and Uncle Clem

I would like to tell of my visits to tell of my visits to Auntie and Uncle Arthur Worsham in Nashville, starting with my earliest remembrances. I spent two weeks each summer with Auntie and Uncle Arthur, and mother and I saw them often at other times during the year.

Uncle Arthur and Auntie would come to Springfield to visit relatives. Sometimes I would ride back to Nashville with them. It was always a treat to ride in Uncle Arthur's new cars. They were Chevrolets, for he sold them at Capitol Chevrolet Company on Broadway Street. I would press my nose against the isinglass in the buttoned up window curtains. I would eventually learn the names of many of the people who lived along the Nashville Pike, through Greenbrier, down the ridge at Ridgetop, along Two-mile Pike to Gallatin Pike, and on to Fatherland St. Uncle Arthur always wanted to get down the ridge before dark in case they had a flat tire. We would stop to visit Uncle Arthur's parents, Uncle Will and Aunt Addie, at their home in Greenbrier and have a delicious supper meal. I remember the tomato preserves and hot biscuits, which were my favorites. Uncle Will had a grocery store in the corner of his yard and he always sent me away with a sack of candy.

Uncle Arthur and Auntie rented a front room and kitchen privileges from Mrs. Williams and her sister in an old brick home with a wonderful full-length central hall where people sat and congregated to talk, sew, and pass the time of day. The front door, side panels and overhead transom had glowing ruby etched glass, which made interesting patterns on the floor when the sun was shining. The bathroom was strange to me, for I had to pull on a long metal chain suspended from the ceiling in order to flush the commode. It was a challenge for me to reach the chain. When I went to Europe in 1968 I found the same type flushing arrangement in Trust Homes and older hotels. Under the back wing of the home was a summer dining room and kitchen with a brick floor and a covered brick porch where I spent many daytime hours. Several children in the neighborhood included me in their playgroup. African American servants lived in a house on the back of the lot. One night they had a revival. Never had I heard such clapping, shouting, singing, stomping, and noise. I wanted to walk across the yard to see what was going on, but Auntie said, "No."

There was a park, East Nashville Park, in which it was fun to play. One night a week they would set up a screen and show free movies. Auntie and I would sit on folding chairs. On our way back to her house we would stop by the drug store on the corner for an ice cream cone. On another corner was Tulip Street Methodist Church, where Auntie went to church. Across the street from that was Warner Grammar School.

When I was 7 years old Auntie and Uncle Arthur bought their home at 710 Porter Road. This was the last block in Nashville; the streetcar line ended near their front steps; the last street light was at the corner. Across the street was the Tillman farm (Mrs. Tillman was a Washington cousin to my grandmother Bell through the Davis line). Mr. Tillman rode horseback each day and would stop and talk to my grandfather Bell when he moved in 1932 to live with Auntie. Near Porter Road on the Tillman farm was a large springhouse and spring. Water from this spring was bottled in 5-gallon glass jars and used downtown in public and business places as drinking water. Each night we would go somewhere – Shelby Park playground, Centennial Park playground, where we would feed the ducks, downtown to a movie or a play at the "Princess," or to visit friends of Auntie and Aunt Susie – or they would have friends over. Uncle Arthur was doing well in selling cars so they lived well – a maid each day, good food and new furniture – until the Great Depression came along. Then the maid would have to go; but they would manage to hold onto their house. By this time, Aunt Susie had finished her business course at Draughon's Business College. She became the item control person for Castner-Knott; a job she held until her retirement. It was a joy to go with Auntie downtown and visit Aunt Susie in the business department. I knew everyone and everyone knew me until they expanded to stores in other cities. Aunt Susie and Auntie furnished me with my underwear (Vanity Fair), hosiery, slips, pajamas and gowns. They knew how I loved good underwear, so I always had lacey, pretty things. Later, when I was in the ninth grade girls started wearing silk stockings instead of the ribbed cotton stockings. One of my classmates, a paying student from the country, one day said to me, "Martha, you must be rich because you always wear silk stockings and have pretty clothes." I was surprised.

When downtown Auntie and I would eat lunch at Walgreen's at the corner of 6th and Church St. or at the tearoom in Loveman's basement, where I always got a pimento cheese sandwich and coke. She would see and talk with friends and neighbors, which made "going to town on the street car" a full-day outing. On our way home we would stop at H. G. Hill's Grocery Store at the corner of 3rd and Union Street. This was the first and only Hill's store for sometime in Nashville. The Hills were neighbors of Auntie and Uncle Arthur's and were good friends. Auntie would help me get onto a high stool at the luncheon counter and order me something to drink. Then she went to select meat in the meat department in the back of the store, where the floor was covered with straw. If she did not see any meat she liked, we would cross the street to the Market House where there was fresh meat hanging from racks, fresh vegetables and fruit, eggs, chickens (live and dressed), and all kinds of food common to a market. There was sawdust on the floor and a smell of blood and fresh meat in the air. I was too small and short to see the counters. This was never a pleasant experience. Then we would cross Union Street by H. G. Hill's and "catch" the streetcar home.

One night Uncle Arthur drove Granddaddy Bell to see his in-laws to his first wife, Amelia Fort. His brother-in-law, Dr. Rufus Fort, was having a family dinner at his home, "Fortland," on Riverside Drive just out of Shelby Park where he owned a large acreage which now is Amelia Fort Airport (she was the daughter of Dr. Fort, was one of the pioneer pilots of Nashville, lost her life in a plane crash and had been named from her aunt, who was my grandfather's first wife). Fortland was a beautiful

2-story antebellum Grecian type home. On our way back home to Porter Road there was a car pulled over to the side of the road; Uncle Arthur pulled over to stop and help the people in the car. I was seated in the back seat next to Aunt Susie and Auntie was in front with Uncle Arthur. I looked out the window on my side and saw a man standing at the door of his car with a gun in his hand, pointing directly at Uncle Arthur. Immediately, Uncle Arthur stepped on the gas and sped away. He wouldn't let any of us go back with him for Granddaddy later that night. Evidently the man with the gun was planning to rob us, thinking we had money since we had driven out of the palatial Fortland.

Another interesting place Auntie and I went was to Glendale Park – there was an outdoor zoo, a large open air dance hall, restaurant, smaller places to eat, picnic tables, play-ground for children. On one summer day we were at the park for an airplane drop of prizes for the young children. The airplane flew over, dropped prizes, and the large teenage boys ran over the small children to get the prizes. Uncle Arthur was angry that the boys had taken over – and, of course, I didn't get a prize. There was much in the paper about the roughness of the older boys who were not supposed to participate. Part of the fun of going to the park was the ride to Glendale Park. At the streetcar transfer station downtown in Nashville, Auntie and I would board the small open-air streetcar, south, down a tree-lined track to the entrance to the park. I have a picture of Howard, 2-year old, standing on the old concrete steps to the gate of the park, which was then being turned into a housing development. Some of the huge old trees are still standing in the area.

One summer Cornelius spent a few days with Auntie when I was there. I was on the concrete sidewalk playing with my Bye-Lo doll. Cornelius ran up behind to frighten me; the doll rolled out of my lap, and the head was broken open. I was upset; Cornelius was repentant. Auntie took my doll and me to the "Doll Hospital" on the second floor of the Transfer Station for a new head. So the present head is not the original; the body is original and one of the first purchased in Nashville. When the salesperson came to Castner-Knott's with samples for the Christmas season. Aunt Susie saw them and bought a sample for my Christmas present. Mrs. Carrie Orndolf Crossway (daughter of Aunt Johnnie) made a blue and white layette for the doll – a batiste baby dress; a knitted blue and white sacque, and a lovely quilted white satin receiving blanket. All of this was handmade. Somehow, the doll and clothes were left in an outside closet after I married and a mouse ate and tore up the layette. The body of the doll was not bothered. I regret that better care was not taken of the doll and clothes. I was 10 years old when I received my Bye-Lo.

About this time Billy, who was two years old, came to live with Auntie and Uncle Arthur. He was the son of Auntie's niece, who had died in the childbirth of her second child. Later Auntie and Uncle Arthur legally adopted Billy. They gave him much love and advantages in life. After Billy arrived, I was supposed to look after him when I visited Auntie. But I was a poor baby sitter, because I loved to read Auntie's books and magazines.

That summer I was going through the process of learning to cut my meat properly and eat with better manners. It was Uncle Arthur who announced that I had to learn to eat properly so I wouldn't be embarrassed later in life – for which I have been grateful.

In addition to the two summertime weeks spent in Nashville with Auntie and Uncle Arthur and Aunt Susie, I spent another two summertime weeks in Portland with Aunt Effie and Uncle Clem Lane, and their son Clem, Jr.

Aunt Effie Simpkins Lane was a strong, raw-boned, good-looking woman. Mother's sister, she was the only relative in the Simpkins family to make a significant effort to help mother and me. She enjoyed her garden, flowers, chickens, and cooking on her wood-burning stove. There was no running water in the house because Portland did not have a water system. Her home was in a closely-knit neighborhood of prominent people who took me into their activities. There 6 boys and girls my age who played together at different homes. Then as I grew older, the girls would have luncheons for me when I visited Aunt Effie, and she would have a luncheon for me. Aunt Effie was very conscious of social standing, so she made a real effort to give me a good social background when I visited her. She would plan a shopping trip downtown (one block long) and tell me whom I would see; to hold my chin up; smile when I talked; give a firm handshake; and hold my shoulders up. Grandpa Simpkins was living with Aunt Effie (he would live to be 88 years old). He used his knife and fork in the English manner, which I thought was so funny, but about this time Aunt Effie decided my table manners needed improving. She attempted to slow me down in eating. Uncle Clem owned a new wheat threshing machine, a new Buick, and an interest in a sawmill. All of this was lost in the Great Depression because people for whom he worked could not meet their bills, so he could not meet his bills. His bank account was wiped out. The president of the bank spent several years in the penitentiary for stealing money (his daughter was one of my Portland playmates) and the bank closed. Uncle Clem managed to save his house; but never recovered his trust in people nor enthusiasm for making money. Their son Clem, Jr. was 7 years younger than I, so we had different sets of friends. He loved ball games and played and lettered in high school football. Then he went into the army where he distinguished himself for his bravery. He was supposed to go into the funeral home business with his uncle and cousins in Portland, but when he returned from the army he wanted nothing to do with dead people. He lost a great opportunity for making money. He became a master tile setter for Blazer Company of Nashville.

As I grew older, I would go with Aunt Effie to pick strawberries at her brother-in-law's farm. He had two girls close to my age. I am afraid I did more eating of strawberries and playing than picking. We always ate with the family and other Lane relatives. It was a fun time. I always rode to and from Portland with Dr. Coles on a Wednesday, which was his office day in Portland for examining eyes. He and his wife were Presbyterian friends of Mother and Aunt Effie. My strawberry picking money always went into my savings account at the bank in Springfield.

Chapter 7 – The Remaining Grade School Years in Springfield

My grades improved in the fourth grade. I was "catching up" with my class and feeling that I belonged. Our music class was a new band class – I enjoyed striking the triangle with the metal rod – because I had a good sense of time. Singing the scales still gave me trouble and was my lowest grade. With some of the money from the sale of the rental house, Mother bought a piano (an old heavily carved oak upright). The couch in our bedroom was given to Aunt Effie, and the piano took its place in our bedroom. I enjoyed my piano lessons with Miss Johnnie Williams, who was organist for the Methodist Church. Twice a week after school I went to her studio and spent many hours at home practicing. No one ever complained of the noise and discord I made on the piano. My recital dress at the end of the fourth grade was a great excitement. Aunt Mamie designed and made the dress of pink silk georgette with a large bertha collar and tiered skirt with each edge of the fabric picoted, which had to be sent out of town to be professionally done. It was a beautiful dress and I had many, many compliments on it – it was worn for my fifth grade recital, also. At the end of the 4th grade I was given an IQ test along with five other students. Evidently my score was a high one because the school superintendent called Mother and offered to allow me to skip the fifth grade and go directly to the sixth grade the next year. Mother talked to a number of school people in regard to this. I didn't want to leave my friends of several years. So, the decision was made for me to stay in my class, which I led up through the eighth grade.

When Uncle Will Orndorf, became sick, his daughter "Miss Lillian" came often to be with Aunt Johnnie. After he died, Miss Lillian and her husband, and daughters, Ruth and Carabel, and son Ernest, lived with Aunt Johnnie. Mr. Duncan was a road-building contractor and was away on his job much of the time. Ruth was three years younger than I, and we loved to play paper dolls by building houses and furnishing them for our paper dolls. Carabel was a first year college student in Murfreesboro, so she was not at Aunt Johnnie's very often. Soon after arriving Ernest married. He lived in Springfield with his family and continued to work with his father in the contracting business. Aunt Johnnie made room for the additional folks by converting the dining room into another bedroom.

Aunt Johnnie was not well. She was confined to her bed most of the time and died soon after Uncle Will. Mother and I continued to live there because someone needed to look after me when Mother was at work. "Miss" Lillian took over that responsibility. I especially owe her a debt of gratitude for helping me with my homework. She was a scholar, loved math and literature and knew her grammar rules, so she was a great help to me.

The Telephone Company played a significant role in my life. From the time Mother started working with them, I had the run of the office (from 8 years until 18 years). The office was a full upstairs (1/2 block long) on Main Street. There was a large lounge room with bath for the ladies. They had a maid during the daytime. This old African American woman, whom I called "Aunt Odie," was my caretaker on many Sunday and Saturday afternoons and sometimes after school if "Aunt Johnnie" or Miss Lillian were away (her son would graduate from college and become principal of the high school which served Springfield's black community. One of my big treats was for "Aunt Odie" to order me a hot dog and fountain coke delivered from a small restaurant across the street – all of 15 cents worth. Then I would sit in a chair by the window watching the people pass on the street below. I wanted to sit on the broad window seat but she would not let me because of her fear of my falling out the open window to the concrete below. I never shared time at the telephone company with my friends because Mother only had permission for me to stay. When she started working on the "switchboard" (connecting calls) the old drop and plug-in method was used (1923). She let me pull up a high chair and plug in the cord to the proper number. When the caller rang off she would allow me to push the cover over the number with a long stick. This would occupy me for a little while. When I got restless she would send me back to the lounge to "Aunt Odie."

This was about the time Springfield got waterworks. Each household had to install a bathroom; privies became illegal in the township of Springfield. Before this, water for all usage was brought to the house in buckets from an open spring, which had been used since pioneer days. It was my job as soon as I got home from school to go to the spring and fill the water bucket, which stood on the table in our kitchen. I could not handle the large bucket, so I had two small buckets. This was a responsibility I enjoyed. The spring was down the hill, about 100 yards. It took two trips with two buckets to get the water we normally used in the kitchen. On clear days I would stretch out on the plank that crossed the center of the spring and watch the bugs skim across the surface of the spring and the crawly things in the bottom of the spring. On wash days, always on Monday afternoons, I had to fill three zinc tubs with water for Mother to start washing as soon as she came home from work (she had her choice of hours now so she chose to be home around three or four o'clock to prepare supper for us). It took five trips up from the spring to fill the tubs. Mother scrubbed clothes on the washboard; I rinsed them 2 times; once in clear water and once in bluing water. I would starch those items that needed it. Mother made starch by cooking bought starch powder in water to a thick consistency. Then Mother would hang the clothes on the lines to dry. In winter and bad days she would hang them in the kitchen and open hallway or in front of the fire in our bedroom. The fireplace burned coal; there was a coal bin beside the house. Mother tended the fire and I took care of the dusting.

Tuesday afternoon was Mother's ironing afternoon. I was supposed to sprinkle the clothes that needed ironing. As I grew older I would iron flat items such as cup towels, handkerchiefs, etc. Then Mother would take over when she got home. She was going to work early (6 or 7 o'clock). After Aunt Johnnie died, Mother would call me to awaken me and tell me what she had left for my breakfast; then she would call again later to ensure that I had left for school. Sometime Mother would call before she left the office to tell me what to start for supper – such as, potatoes to be peeled, to put something in the oven, etc. When the water lines were run, no water was piped into Mother's kitchen or Miss Lillian's kitchen. We filled our buckets from the bathtub faucet. This bathroom was installed in what had been an open porch between the hallway and the two kitchens. So my water responsibility continued to be an after-school job.

One of my interests was the Camp Fire Girls. I started at age 12, when the club was formed, and by my senior year I was assistant director. We had monthly meetings in each other's homes. hey were sedate affairs with reports, refreshments, and linen napkins. We had health charts for one month at a time which were supposed to be checked each day (this started me on drinking water early in the morning); we made beaded headbands on cigar box looms; we had brown canvas dresses which we decorated with our wooden beads; we had picnics; swimming parties, and participated in programs – all great fun and excellent habit and character forming experiences.

In the fifth grade not anything of great interest happened that I can remember, except I was "kept in" after school one afternoon. My teacher was Miss Blackburn, who was also my Sunday school teacher and a friend of Mother's. We were having something special in class, so she wanted us close together. I, with another girl, was seated at a front desk; Miss Blackburn was seated on the desktop in front of us with the class closely grouped in front of her. I was looking at her back, especially the large organdy bow located on her back at waist height. When she talked this bow would wiggle. I laughed. I touched the bow and it came untied. I took each end of sash and began to seesaw it back and forth. The class laughed. Miss Blackburn turned around and said, "Martha, meet me after school." I was frightened. At lunchtime the girls told me Miss Blackburn would probably whip me. All she did was talk to me and that she expected me to behave like a lady and not do silly things like that. When I ran out of the building my girlfriends were there to walk home with me.

The important thing for me in the sixth grade was winning a $5 gold coin. The local radio station had a contest. A hymn was played over the radio and each contestant had to write on paper the name of the hymn, the author, when it was written, and all the stanzas. Miss Lillian did not have a radio; but a neighbor, Mrs. Tomlin, did. She was also choir leader at the Presbyterian Church. She invited Ruth Duncan and me to her house to listen to the contest. Each hymn was familiar to her so she loaned a Presbyterian Hymnal to Ruth and me. We both entered the contest. We were the only two in town who knew each hymn (at least Mrs. Tomlin did). I won the contest and the $5 gold coin because mine was letter perfect and Ruth made some mistakes in copying the stanzas. I have always felt I did not deserve winning because it was partially someone else's work. The $5 gold coin started my savings bank account, which I added to over the teenage years. In our art class we had a traveling exhibit of prints of some great artist's work and studied a workbook of great artists of the world. In music we listened to classical records, identifying instruments and themes. These two things started my appreciation of art and music. Bess Alice and I were still seatmates and would continue to be through the eighth grade. She was one of the best spellers in class, and I was one of the worse. I did not lead my classmates this year; Russell Murphy now led the entire class, while I was second. This would continue through the twelfth grade.

I was attending Christian Endeavor at the Presbyterian Church on Sunday nights – a special time for children and teenagers. During this year I joined the church along with other friends my age. I attended classes for church doctrine and was baptized (sprinkled) when I joined the church.

During the school year, roller-skating was our entertainment – in the summertime swimming was our entertainment. We swam in the creeks. Aunt Bertha would take Martha Lou and me to Carr's Creek; Mrs. Harris would take Sue Ara and me to Sulphur Fork Creek. I had learned to float and take 2 or 3 strokes at Clover Bottom on Stone's River when Auntie and Uncle Arthur would take me swimming. Mrs. Harris left Sue Ara and me at the "swimming hole" with other children, while she visited her relative, Mrs. Wilks; I saw others, boys and girls, jump off an old limb head first in the water; I tried this. My body arched so that the back of my feet touched the back of my head – and my entire back hurt and was sore for a few days. Dr. Porter said I would get over it – just take it easy for a few days.

Another activity Sue Ara and I would enjoy was turning on the Victoria and doing the Charleston until the house shook. We were pretty good. Croquet was a game we could play, "even on Sunday." The wickets stayed up during the summer and the balls and mallets were stored in the storage area under the house so everything was handy for a game of croquet. I would play Jacks on the concrete front porch.

Next to our kitchen was an "ice house" dug into the side of the hill. This was the cooling place for vegetables, meats, etc. Mother had an ice chest (small, compact, sat on the floor) in which she kept ice to cool milk and other foods. She would "hang out" an ice card on the side door, turned to indicate how many pounds of ice she wanted – 10, 20, 50, etc. The "iceman" would then place the ice in this chest in the "ice house." I don't know how Mother paid him – by the day, week, or month. We always had ice because Mother liked her cold foods. She made the best pineapple sherbet I ever tasted, of beaten egg whites, pineapple juice, crushed pineapple, lemon juice and sugar. I would help her turn the crank on the one-half-gallon freezer. She then would place the container, with salted ice, into the ice chest, and it would stay frozen as long as ice was in the chest. The ice wagon, drawn by horses, would pull up in front of the house, and neighborhood children would gather around the end of the wagon to pick up the chips of ice from the 50-pound blocks from which the smaller amounts had to be chipped.

Mother enjoyed making divinity candy. She was asked to make "Miss Mrytle's Divinity Candy" in support of bazaars or any money making project. She would whip the egg whites in her mother's white iron stone meat platter with a wire beater until the whites were in beautiful peaks. She would then boil sugar and water to a dropping point. Here was the critical time. Slowly the hot sugar solution was gently, drop by drop, dropped into the beaten egg whites, beating them at the same time slowly and always in the same direction until all of the sugar solution was absorbed by the beaten egg whites and a beautiful white divinity mixture was ready to drop by spoonfuls onto buttered wax paper. Usually, Mother would add black walnuts to the mixture before dropping onto wax paper. Part of a red cherry would be placed on top. She made delicious chocolate fudge. She taught me how when I was 12 years old. Then I began to make my own fudge, which I dearly loved. Mother's mayonnaise was delicious. It was made in the blue-stripe crock, in which I now have my cooking utensils on the counter in my kitchen. When I was small she would let me stand in a chair and turn the rotary beater on the egg yolks while she gently poured in the Wesson oil, drop by drop. I realize now mother cooked by the French and German methods more than Scotch, Irish, and English methods. She wanted butter, rich cream, undercooked vegetables (still crisp), not too much bacon grease (she preferred butter), sour foods like peach pickle, beet pickle, vinegar on fish rather than catsup, no sage in her dressing or cooking.

Groceries were always delivered, regardless of the size of the order. I suppose Mother paid at the end of the week or month because I never remember any money being left out to pay for an order. She ordered from Weaver's store by phone. The outside doors were never locked in the daytime. If no one was home the iceman would go through the house to put ice in the ice chest, and the grocery delivery boy would place groceries in the kitchen on the table. At the end of the school day I never worried about going into the unlocked house.

When Mother had her day off from work we would visit friends and relatives – Aunt Mamie, Aunt Matt, Miss Lura Hancock, or friends of Mother's – and then we might stop by the cemetery. Mother enjoyed getting away from home and walking. Whenever she had flowers she would take an arrangement and put it on Daddy's grave. On some days off we would clean house, and I mean clean house from top to bottom. Mother would always say, "We may be poor, but we can be clean." Some of her German heritage came out in her zeal and desire to "clean." We slept on a featherbed, which had to be aired frequently (so Mother thought).

Visiting Uncle Pearl's was a special treat for mother and me. In my tenth summer, we made a weeks visit with Uncle Pearl, Aunt Betty and their children. Four of the girls were near my age. We spent many hours under the oak trees in the front yard playing with make-believe dolls and made outlines of floor plans with oak twigs and acorns. On Sunday we packed into their new Ford car and attended church in Charlotte, Tennessee. I remember wonderful home cooked garden fresh meals three times each day. The older girls helped in the kitchen while the younger girls and I played. There was also a creek wading time greatly enjoyed on a hot summer day by my mother and the Simpkins girls.

Thoughout the years my mother looked forward to her Christmas and in the summer her backyeard dinners of fried chicken and home frozen ice cream. Uncle Pearl and family would be invited.

Chapter 8 – The Junior High School Years in Springfield

In the seventh grade my classmates and I moved into the Junior High Building next to the grammar school. This was a newer building. The entire second story was a stage and auditorium, which was used by clubs, organizations, recitals, concerts, plays and school activities. The first floor housed the seventh and eighth grades and the cafeteria. The seventh and eighth grade girls played each other in town ball during recess and lunchtime. The game is similar to baseball, but requires a smaller field. We played with a red rubber ball and a 4-inch wide paddle. I was on the team, playing at 1st base. This continued through the eighth grade. When the ground was muddy, we played volleyball on the front sidewalk. I always took my lunch, as did most of the others, to allow more time for our game. A new girl came to town from Nashville. Her mother married a distant cousin of mine, Frank Bell. This girl automatically became a social member of our girl group. She was also smart, and she and I competed for first place on the girl's academic list from the seventh grade to the twelfth grade. Our teacher was Miss Thomas. She was a beautiful blond, fashionably dressed, young woman, who had spent some time in Europe the summer before she taught our class. She made a big impression on my life and opened my eyes to the world beyond Springfield, Nashville, Detroit, and Portland, which had been the limit of my travels. To her I am grateful.

All through school Bess Alice and I ate our lunch

together; we did not have the money to eat in the cafeteria as some of our friends did; Bess would bring the most delicious biscuits and country ham; I would bring store bought bread, peanut butter and "Hippolight" (marshmallow crème, as it is called now). We would often trade sandwiches and any other foods we liked.

Each year there would be a recital by Miss Johnnie Williams' students. I would have a new dress made by Aunt Mamie or wear last year's dress if it still fit. I often wonder what Uncle Pearl's children did with those old recital dresses of mine.

My eighth grade teacher was entirely different. An old maid, Miss McClellan, tried to rule the roost, so she thought, by loud, outlandish conduct; that did not impress me. One day she became angry with a boy seated behind me and threw a book at him, which barely missed my head. I had no love or respect for her, because I thought she was no lady. However, she did make us study. Her big interest was math. Algebra and Latin were taught the last six weeks of the eighth grade as an introduction to high school. I was the only student in her class who made 100 on the final exam in arithmetic in the eighth grade. She was so impressed she told Mother and everyone about it. She had charge of the cafeteria and we took turns helping there. Bess Alice and I worked together in the cafeteria for 2 hours for one week. We were shown how to make pimento cheese salad and then make sandwiches. We had to grate the cheese by inserting blocks of cheese into a large hand-turned grater. Once when Bess Alice and I were working away – she was turning the handle and I was pushing the cheese into the grater – the grater grabbed my fingernail, tearing away part of the nail and causing the finger to bleed. We were afraid to tell Miss McClellan, so blood and fingernail went into that cheese mixture without anyone else knowing. We often wondered who found the nail in a sandwich. We also made vegetable soup and mayonnaise. Burnett Miller worked with us.

For our eighth grade graduation, we had a printed program. The girls wore white dresses with white rayon or silk stockings and carried red roses. Florence Lee sang a solo and Marie Humphrey played the piano while the graduating class marched up the steps and down the aisle to the stage. The class sang a song. Our speaker was an inspirational one. After the ceremony, the girls cried – because part of our lives was over and we would be going to high school in a different building on a different campus. The girls in our group received wristwatches as graduation presents from their parents. My wristwatch was a white gold Bulova with engraving around the oblong edges; Mother had purchased it at McCord and Harris. Auntie and Aunt Susie gave me a white gold ring set with a ruby. These two pieces of jewelry I wore through high school and college. Our class had a picnic. We walked 2-1/2 miles to Wilkes' farm, ate a picnic lunch and walked back. I remember getting very tired and rode part of the way on horseback behind the Wilkes boy who was in our class.

In the summer between Junior High and High School Aunt Mamie noticed my hems were hanging longer on one side of my body. She and Mother determined I was leaning to one side and had developed curvature of the spine. Dr. Porter drove us to Nashville to see Dr. Duncan Eve, Sr. From then on, until his retirement, I was under Dr. Eve's care. He put me on a diet of one raw egg beaten in a glass of whole milk (Mother would add vanilla flavoring and sugar) each day, more cod liver oil, no lifting of heavy objects, sunbaths when possible, liver once each week, plenty of fresh fruits and vegetables, swimming whenever possible and working out on a bar to lift myself up by my arms. Each year I would go to Nashville for an examination. His office was on West End Street, opposite Vanderbilt, on the corner where Vanderbilt Plaza Hotel now stands (1992).

This was the summer for swimming whenever possible. A new public pool, dressing rooms and dance hall had been built at Miller Pike's Spring on what is now called the Old Nashville Highway, where it ran through what had been my great, great grandfather Bell's farm. This was called Perry's Park. There was a wooden float in the deep water – I could just make it by shoving off hard from the swimming pool side and taking three hard strokes. Sue Ara Harris and I would go swimming several times a week. Mrs. Harris would drive us out to the park and come for us later. I don't remember what the cost was. With Martha Lou I would go swimming in the creeks and with Eugenia Fisher I would go swimming at Sulphur Creek. So, with going to the "picture-show" once or twice a week with Sue Ara, my summer was full.

Mr. Harris bought Sue Ara and me tickets to a series of plays held under a tent by a traveling acting company from Chicago named the "Redpath Review." During that week we went to the Redpath teenage club in the mornings and learned a dance routine and songs, which we presented on stage for the younger children on the last morning. In the afternoons and nights we attended the Redpath plays and musical programs – so that was a full week of activities. All of this was held in a vacant lot under a large tent. With my visits to Nashville and Portland, my summer between 8th and 9th grades was full. I had not dated as of yet. One time Bess Alice's grandmother gave a party for the boys and girls in Bess Alice's classroom. We had date cards, which were filled in by the boys for 10-minute dates, and we played musical chairs and post office. The youth group at church had a similar party at the church. My Sunday school teacher gave a card party (this was a new thing for me – I don't remember what game we played, but I think it was hearts). Eugenia Fisher's mother gave a party where we played hearts; Mrs. Lyon gave a hearts party – both boys and girls were invited to all these parties. I had never been allowed to play with "spot" cards before. Now Mother allowed me to buy a deck of "spot" cards, and I learned how to play solitaire. Aunt Mamie gave a luncheon for me, to which she invited my special group of girl friends.

Chapter 9 – The High School Years in Springfield

Springfield High School was in the old Peoples-Tucker School building – a former private boy's school. Located on the north edge of town, this three-story stone building on a large campus covered with old trees was old and out-dated. The trip to high school was longer than it was to junior high or to grade school. I walked 7 blocks to and from school each day.

In my freshman year I took Civics, Algebra I, English, Home Economics, and Latin I. I maintained my average and took piano lessons. Sue Ara and all my girl friends went out for basketball and three of them played on the 1st team during their junior and senior years. I stayed after school the first day of practice my freshman year. Everyone was invited to stay so that girls of talent could be selected. I had a good sense of rhythm and balance in handling the ball; but, when I went out for basketball, my doctor, Dr. Porter, called Mother that night to say I was in no physical condition with my curvature of the spine to play basketball. So that left me alone in the afternoons – I missed Sue Ara going places with me after school. I continued my music lessons twice weekly; stayed in the Camp Fire Girl's group; belonged to the Music Club for teenagers; was active in the Christian Endeavor at church, and played the piano for the church youth group. At this time the church organist, Miss Bessie Banks, asked me if I would be interested in learning to play the pipe organ at church. I had no particular desire to do this, but since she was getting older she wanted to train someone who would take her place, and offered to give me free lessons. The lessons were fun. I was only fifteen and had to practice in the empty silent church by myself. The doors were always unlocked and I was constantly worrying about who would be around. Miss Bessie was disappointed when, after a while, I told her that I was no longer interested. She had been my grandmother Bell's friend when they were in school together.

My friends, Sue Ara Harris, Bess Alice Clinard, Eugenia Fisher, Martha Weakley, Mary Willard Chester, Carolyn Pearson, Charlotte Stark, Mary Harris Lyons, and I continued our slumber parties and birthday luncheons. As each one reached her sixteenth birthday, her mother would give her a big birthday luncheon. The slumber parties were more fun. Each summer during high school days we would spend a weekend at Bess Alice Clinard's home. They had a tennis court and horses to ride. Mrs. Clinard always had wonderful country ham and biscuits for me, and piles of whipped potatoes for Sue Ann Harris. I don't remember any other foods, but remember it always being delicious and plentiful. In the evening we would gather around the piano for songs. All this time Sue Ann Harris was learning to drive – I would ride with her to tell her about traffic. Mr. Harris was a pharmacist and owned two drug stores, so Sue Ara sometimes would have the drug store truck to drive. Now I realize it was dangerous, but Springfield was a small town. There was little traffic on the streets and everywhere we went was only a few blocks away. Another thing we loved to do was to go to the drug store; sit at one of the black wrought iron tables; order a coke or milk shake, and watch people come and go until all the tables were occupied. Then Mr. Harris would say, "You girls go on home, we need your table." When he bought a drug store in Murfreesboro on the square, he and Mrs. Harris had to go often to check on inventory. Sue Ara and I would go along and he would give us old boxes of powder, perfume, etc. – things he couldn't sell.

A big event happened to me in the ninth grade. A young, pretty teacher, directly out of college, was new at our school. She thought the young people should have more opportunity to be together. As the freshman class sponsor, she planned a school class party where the girls asked the boys for dates. I asked Dickie, who was on the football team; we had been in the same grade since the third grade. My Mother was horrified! He was a poor boy from a poor family on the "other side of the tracks." She called Aunt Mamie, who talked to Cornelius, who was back in Springfield working (he had been attending the University of Tennessee in Knoxville). Cornelius talked to Dickie. What was said I have no idea! But Mother informed me I could not go with Dickie and that Cornelius had arranged for me to go with Judson Edwards, who had also been in my class since the third grade. I realize now that this was a social arrangement between the two families. Judson was of pioneer stock (as my ancestors were); from one of the wealthiest families of Springfield; was the only boy in our class who had a car; wore expensive clothes; had excellent manners, plenty of spending money and had cultural advantages. I rebelled and said I was not going with Judson – he wasn't good looking like Dickie; but when Judson called me on the phone for the date and told me what time he would be there, I accepted him. Now, I would like to tell about this wonderful and true friend of six years, Judson Edwards.

Judson was my boy friend all through the four years of high school. He was musical and played in the school band. He drove me to Portland, to Nashville, to ball games, or we would just drive around town with a car full of my girl friends. During his freshman year he was making radios in walnut shells and boxes, and repairing old radios. This love of electronics and mechanical things became his life work. He attended Indiana Technical College, the only college in the United States that offered this type of degree. During his freshman year in high school he began announcing on WSIX radio in Springfield (WSIX would later relocate to Nashville). Later he announced ball games, tournaments, musical programs and made commercials. Sue Ara and I would sometimes go to the station after school and select the records to play.

Our relationship was more a brother-sister affair, consisting of holding hands, a little kiss on the lips, and a hug. Mother would trust me anywhere with Judson, and all the adults in town seemed happy over our dating and fully expected our marriage after college. I was "hands off" to every boy in town because I was Judson Edward's girl.

I was interested in my home economics class. Bess Alice was my cooking partner and I must admit she did the actual cooking, and I did the measuring, washing up, etc. – all of which made good grades for both of us. At the graduation exercise for the senior class, I won the Home Economics cup for having the highest grades in the two semesters of home economics. I had just completed my freshman year. Generally, the cup was awarded to a girl who was taking advanced home economics, so there were three or four older girls who were disturbed over my winning. I have the loving cup with my name on it. My son John had an arm replaced and replated in Atlanta. My home economics teacher expected me to continue with more home economics classes, but I wasn't interested. I wanted languages (Latin and French).

My cousin, Phillip Bell, was my Latin and American History teacher. I called him "Cousin Phillip" and he had called me "Martha." He was always at Granddaddy Bell's for family dinners. He told me that, in his class, I must call him "Mr. Bell" and he would call me "Miss Bell." He had graduated from Webb School and Vanderbilt, cum laude, and had taught at Webb School before coming home to teach at Springfield. He was a hard taskmaster, but I loved Latin and loved him as a teacher. He never let me slide by, but demanded perfection from me.

The summer between ninth and tenth grades were passed in the same way as the year before. I was expected to pick more strawberries than I ate when I went to Portland. Judson drove me to Nashville for the Nashville Symphony concerts at the Ryman Auditorium. We would eat at Shacklett's Cafeteria on Sunday afternoons during concert season. The Great Depression was underway, for it was the summer of 1931.
I was visiting Auntie when Granddaddy Bell died at the

age of 85 years. It was the summer of 1932. I was 17 years old. He had used Auntie's back bedroom and had died on the bed of which I spoke earlier, which had been in the "spare bedroom" at his farm, and had been used in Mother and Daddy's room. Dr. Fort Bridges, Granddaddy's stepson and son of Amelia Fort and her first husband, Mr. Bridges, was with him when he died of pneumonia. He was the first person I have seen to die. He lived with Auntie 2 years before his death. He lost all his money in the failed bank near the beginning of the Great Depression – all he had left were gold coins in the lock-box. His worry over money matters probably caused his death. Many years earlier, he had given each child payment toward a house; had supported the African American families that had been raised on the farm, and had paid all the doctor's bills for his large family. He died without money, and the president of his bank had to spend time in the state penitentiary.

In my tenth grade I took Latin II, English, Algebra II and Biology. During this year Mother and Aunt Mamie decided that they would rent a house together. Aunt Mamie's husband, Uncle Forrest, had died during the summer. He had lost a lot of money in the tobacco warehouse (1930) at the beginning of the Great Depression. He had a heart condition that had probably been aggravated by the economic loss. Aunt Mamie was left deeply in debt. She sold her large house and many of her furnishings. Cornelius was working, but not making much money; Aunt Mamie now did sewing and alterations to add to their income. This was a big letdown for them – going from wealth to poor. Uncle Joe (Granddaddy Bell's brother) went to live with his nephew in Savannah, Tennessee; Granddaddy Bell and Aunt Susie went to live with Auntie and Uncle Arthur. So there were no more large family gatherings in the big house with a cook in the kitchen. The house they chose to rent was a two-story frame house on 7th Ave. It was closer to the high school, church, and mother's work.

Upstairs there were two large bedrooms for Aunt Mamie and Cornelius, a hall, and bathroom on the stairs landing which extended out over the roof that covered the downstairs utility room. Mother and I, and Aunt Mamie and Cornelius lived together until the fall I left for college. This was a very good move for me. Mother bought a living room suite and some tables and lamps for the living room. Judson gave us a cabinet radio, which he said he had repaired and, at last, my piano had a room for itself. Aunt Mamie made ruffled curtains with tiebacks for Mother's three rooms. They were made out of 3-cents-per-yard tobacco netting. They were beautiful and sheer, covering the new shades at the ceiling-to-floor windows. The house featured 12-foot ceilings, high baseboards, dark oak flooring, mantels, and woodwork. This old house had been used as a private school to which my grandmother Bell had attended. It had been moved from its original lot and updated by adding a bathroom and kitchen. Mother and I enjoyed this house. She could have her flower garden, and she had grapes, apples and pears for canning and preserves. Aunt Mamie was at home in the afternoon when I returned from school because she was working at home, taking in sewing jobs. Cornelius was clerking at J. C. Penny's and dating. Since his bedroom was upstairs, I remember seeing him little during those years of sharing the house.

After I left for college, Mother kept the house and rented the two upstairs bedrooms to single ladies.

My life in the tenth grade continued as usual. In the spring, Eugenia Fisher and I attended the Presbyterian Youth Conference of Middle Tennessee at Lebanon. We stayed with the Seagram family for two nights. I had a wonderful weekend with the young people and enjoyed staying in such beautiful surroundings.

During the summer between tenth and eleventh grades, Eugenia Fisher and I were delegates to Ovaca Church Camp for one week. In the mornings we had lessons and lectures. During the afternoon we went swimming or hiking, or just enjoyed free time. Not far from the edge of Lake Ovaca was a wooden float on which the young people gathered to sun. Eugenia wasn't much of a swimmer; I thought I was. I tried to swim to the float; I got there – but completely winded and a little frightened. That was my only trip to the float. During the week Andrew Thack and I became a twosome with some other young people in various activities. He was the brother of Martha Curry, who would become a good friend of mine in adult life in Nashville. Their father, Dr. Andrew Thack was camp doctor. Andrew and I wrote several letters to each other but Judson took preference as my boy friend. The week was climaxed with a candle light walk from the lake to the assembly hall where we had a vesper service. The church in Springfield paid the tuition for Eugenia and me to attend the camp. It was a rewarding and beautiful week for me. Each summer our church would have a family picnic at some mill, pond, or historic site in the county. Mother and I would ride with someone, or when she couldn't go, I would ride in a truck with straw on the bed floor with other young people my age. The places that interested me most were: Sycamore Mills, Hills Mill, Washington Mill, and the lock on the Cumberland River.

Mother continued to work at the Telephone Company on the day shift. The Telephone Company did not play as large a role in my life as it did when I was younger. But I continued to occasionally stop by after school, but I no longer needed someone to look after me by the time I reached high school. Over the years I saw technology change in the telephone system. Each change was dramatic to Mother. She would remain with the Telephone Company for 42 years, until her retirement. It was a great influence in her life and she had the respect and admiration of the town people and the people with whom she worked. The ladies had a big picnic each summer at someone's house – and parties for each other's birthday and special occasions. After Mother moved to the large rented house on 7th Avenue with Aunt Mamie, she always had her own big picnic in the backyard with fried chicken and home made ice cream. Also, the entire telephone staff of Robertson County would have picnics in the summer and sometimes Davidson County staff would join in having picnics. Mother was furnished free telephones and long distance calls, which she never abused. When she moved into her apartment the telephone company installed three telephones over her insistence she didn't need them or want them (the kitchen phone was about 6 feet from the phone by her lounge chair and there was a phone by her bedside). This was in the time most people had only one phone in their house.

All during these years Mother was buying telephone stock out of each paycheck. The stock dividends (quarterly) were always spent on something special for us or for the house. At this time Mother would go to work at 6 o'clock in the morning and be home for supper. The first thing she would do in the mornings at home would be to make her bed and sweep the front sidewalk. It was said a person would have to get up mighty early to beat "Miss Myrtle." Each house occupant in Springfield was responsible for keeping the sidewalk clean in front of her house. I never remember trash, debris, or leaves on any sidewalk in Springfield – nor an unmade bed in our house or the house of friends. Mother would cook cereal for my breakfast or get out dry cereal – then go to work and call me on the phone at 7 o'clock. I knew I had to get out of bed to answer the phone. She would tell me what was available for my breakfast; I would make my bed, dress, eat breakfast and clear the table. Again, Mother would call me to see if I were ready to walk out the door for school. It would take me about 6 minutes to walk to school for classes at 8 o'clock. This was our regular routine during my tenth, eleventh, and twelfth grades, while we were living on 7th Ave.

Everyone in town knew Mother as "Miss Myrtle". There were so many "Mrs. Bells" that each was known by her first name. Aunt Mamie was called "Miss Mamie," etc. This was a Southern custom in small towns to refer to an adult white woman, married or not, by "Miss" and her first name. An adult African American woman was referred to by "Aunt," followed by her first name. When the Springfield Woolen Mill and the dark fired tobacco industry brought in more strangers from different parts of the world, Mother would laugh and say she wondered what these strangers thought about so many of these "Misses" living in our town, all of whom had children, homes, and husbands. The blankets made at the Springfield Woolen Mills were considered first and best in the nation.

The Springfield tobacco warehouses and associated tobacco auctions represented the second-largest dark-fired tobacco market in the world. From all over the world, buyers came to Springfield to buy dark-fired tobacco. The auctions, held once per year, lasted two weeks. Dark-fired tobacco, not used in cigarettes, was difficult to make well. It was prized for use in snuff and medications, and much was sold to buyers from the Far East. For these two reasons there was more wealth and more strangers in Springfield than in most small towns.

My responsibilities continued to be on Monday afternoons to get the wash water hot on the coal oil stove during spring, summer and fall. During the winter, there would be a fire in the stove in Aunt Mamie's kitchen, so I would heat water there. Then I would fill the tubs and begin to soak the white clothes, make the starch and prepare the bluing water. On Tuesday afternoon I would sprinkle clothes to be ironed and press the flat items. Mother would call me about the time I was expected home and tell me what to do about supper. Other afternoons, or on Saturday, I would clean house. When there were coal fires in the bedroom and living room there was always a lot of ash dust. I remember using lots of Cedar Oil furniture polish trying to keep furniture shining. I only helped clean house – Mother did the greater amount of work. It was my practice to get my homework as soon as possible after I would get home. We had a study hall period of 50 minutes each day and usually had a short study period in each class. My homework consisted of special projects or unusually long assignments. In the tenth and eleventh grades I helped my English teacher grade the grammar and punctuation of daily homework. We had only 33 students in our class, so it didn't take long to do this – I brought the papers home and only marked the errors.

In the eleventh grade my subjects were English III, Geometry, Latin III, French I and typing. In English class we began to do more writing of stories, themes, etc. I would help Judson with his papers. He would help me in French pronunciation. Because of the larger tissue between my tongue and palate of my mouth I have great difficulty in making some sounds. Both Howard and John had this tissue clipped at birth so they do not have this difficulty, which we all inherited.

The Campfire Girls decided to have a moneymaking project – a play was decided upon. The girls decided who would take which part. I played the role of the mother of a group of girls – this was a night play in the town auditorium and everyone was invited (they paid of course). For me it was a terror! I couldn't project my voice in that large place – no microphones – and, because of my soft speaking voice, I almost drove the director crazy. This was one time I was very mediocre; however, our group did make some money. Miss Carver did not choose me to be in the school senior play. I wore a new long dress and gave out programs with Eugenia

Fisher, who had difficulty speaking loudly as well. Some of the others who were not in the play worked behind the scenes, controlled the lights, curtains, music, etc. At least I had an interesting job and a new dress.

In the fall Eugenia Fisher and I attended the youth conference in Nashville and stayed two nights with a family near East Presbyterian Church. This was not a very interesting weekend – nothing new. In the spring we attended the youth conference at Hillsboro Church directly across from Peabody campus. We stayed in a lovely home in the community and had fun with the young people. There was a banquet at the church, a concert in Wright's Chapel at Scarritt College, and I met Kenneth Duke, a most attractive boy who was a leader in the conference. He was three years older than I, and attended Cumberland College in Lebanon. He asked me for a date Sunday afternoon after the conference. He wanted to pick me up at Aunties' house, where Eugenia and I planned to spend the afternoon before taking a bus to Springfield in the early evening. But Uncle Arthur said, "no," so he called Kenneth to tell him that I was too young to go out with him that afternoon. Kenneth got his law degree from Cumberland; became a Vice Admiral in the navy, and had a ship named for him after he was killed in service. Before he went into the Navy he owned Duke Insurance Company, which his widow still operates in Nashville.

Sunday nights were my date evenings with Judson. He was a full-time announcer with WSIX Springfield radio station after school. He announced all basketball games held in the Springfield gym. I would sit in the booth with him and follow the players' numbers with a pencil so he could keep up with names and plays. The tournament games were especially hard because we did not know the players. Judson was my date to any special occasion in Springfield. During the eleventh and twelfth grades he helped Mother and me decorate our Christmas trees which he had bought and set up in the living room for us. Occasionally he would go to church with me or I would go to the Baptist Church with him. One Sunday I especially remember. After church I was invited to have dinner with him, his mother, father and brother, four years younger than he. Although we had dated for three years, this was the first time I visited with Judson's family in his house. I realized the difference in our life styles. For the first time in my life a white maid with a frilly maid's cap and apron served me from beautiful silver serving dishes. It opened my eyes to another way of living. I had always been accustomed to African American women in the kitchen and serving in the dining room, but never before in frilly maid's uniform. Never did Judson refer to my poor way of living and his moneyed way of life. That year, for my birthday and Christmas presents, he gave me a red compact with my name engraved across the front and a silver drop necklace with black cameo-type decoration in the drop.

Judson was interested in airplanes. One Sunday we drove to McCabe Field in Nashville, which was where the McCabe Golf course is now located off Murphy Road. The two of us went up in a small open cockpit airplane – we were the only passengers other than the pilot. I do not remember being afraid. We flew over the Cumberland River, and the pilot dipped the plane sideways so we could get a better view of the river and the town. It was thrilling! Another Sunday we went up over Nashville in a small four-passenger enclosed airplane, but that was not as much fun. After the second flight, my mother had a fit when we told her what we had done, and she made Judson promise he would never take me up in an airplane again.

Springfield had a small landing field used by airplanes, which would take people on rides over Springfield. The summer between my eleventh and twelfth grades, someone had a contest. Whoever guessed how much gasoline would be used to go so many miles in this airplane, which was being used to take up sightseeing passengers, would get a free plane ride. Judson filled out two contest answer forms – one for me and one for him – my guess won on the exact amount. Since I had promised Mother I would not fly again, Judson got to take the trip.

Judson's love of airplanes continued in adult life. He became a licensed pilot and owned his own airplane. But he sadly lost his life and the life of his third wife while flying across the Gulf Stream from Miami to Nassau, The Bahamas. He had a home on one of the islands. This occurred during 1957 or 1958. At that time he owned a chain of radio and television stations. He had worked at WSIX station after they moved to Nashville, and later had bought a station on Catalina Island, off the coast of California, where he had lived for a number of years.

In the fall of 1932 Judson's mother and father invited me to go with them to the State Fair in Nashville. We sat in a box seat with the dignitaries and had a delicious dinner in the dining room that was reserved for the dignitaries. Everything was first rate and first class – so different from my previous trips to the State Fair.

The onset of the Great Depression frightened my Mother. On the day the banks closed she came home from work extremely upset, because everything we owned (money-wise) was in only one bank. For money she had only her one-week paycheck ($10). The banks opened one week later. Many people had lost everything. We were fortunate in not losing anything. Mother had no debts called in. And she refused to sell her Bell Telephone stock at the depressed price, for none were margined. Aunt Effie and Uncle Clem, Auntie and Uncle Arthur, Aunt Mamie and Granddaddy Bell lost almost everything they had. Auntie and Aunt Effie saved their homes from mortgage foreclosure by the hardest. It took Springfield several years to recover. Houses needed painting; people reworked old clothes; did a lot of canning and preserving; people ate inexpensive foods and saved every penny they could. I remember eating a lot of potatoes, cornbread, soup beans, and hamburger meat.

My senior year was full of physical discomfort. Before I reached my eighteenth birthday, Dr. Eve planned to put me in plaster casts to prevent hump shoulders as my bones began to "set up" and "firm-up" with adulthood. This was done in the fall of my senior year at St. Thomas Hospital. A heavy plaster cast was applied from under arms to the bend of my legs (I remember it being three inches thick). Because of the tightness of the cast I had to learn to shallow breathe in my chest rather than deep breathing from my abdomen. I could not reach over, stoop over, take a bath in the bathtub or take any physical exercise. I had to roll out of bed and into bed. Not any of my clothes fit. I remember a jacket dress (an old woman's type) that I wore a lot. Aunt Mamie made me several blouses, skirts and beautiful collars to wear with a sweater. These I also had to wear in college, because during my freshman year in college I was wearing a heavy metal brace to finish the correction. Under my cast my skin became dry and would itch in places I could not reach.

During the months that I wore the cast, people were nice, kind, and considerate, so I never felt like an outcast. I continued my music lessons, dating Judson, helping him in the broadcast booth, slumber parties and luncheons with my girl friends. In our homeroom my girl friends and Judson sat in the back of the room. Someone always walked with me to class; so I had protection from falling or being bumped into by other students. One of the streets near the school was being paved and was closed to traffic but open to skaters. So Sue Ann, Martha Weakley, Carolyn Pearson, and I asked Judson if we could hang onto the back of his car on our roller skates and he would drive very slowly and give us a ride. It was fun – until he rounded a corner and all of us fell. My clothes were torn where I had landed on the road and rubbed against the cast. Judson was frantic. We were only one block from my house, so they all went with me home and put me to bed. No one was home – Mother was working and Aunt Mamie was not at home. Judson called Mother, who called Dr. Porter. Both of them got to me about the same time. Judson stayed with me to get their blessing out. I believe that was the last time I ever wore skates in Springfield.

During my senior year my subjects were English IV, American History, Latin IV and French II. Latin was my easiest subject – as a class of twelve students, we met at lunchtime 10 minutes before class and Russell Murphy read (translated) our assignment, and we discussed any rules that might be involved. One Monday morning I could not meet with them, so I went to class without any preparation, thinking I would have time while Mr. Bell called on someone else. But this day he selected me to be first! When I stumbled around on my translation he immediately launched into a tirade about boys and girls who dated on Sunday night instead of studying (Judson was in the class). Mr. Bell turned to me before the whole class and said, "Miss Bell, I drove by your house last night. There was a light on in your living room and Mr. Edward's car was parked in front of your house." That was small town for you! For my Christmas present Judson gave me a small leather suitcase fitted with mirror, comb and brush – just the right size for me to handle.

During the school year I went to Nashville to have the casts changed out. First the thickest cast was taken off and replaced by a thinner cast. By graduation time I had a still thinner cast. My clothes had to be altered to fit my cast and body each time. Aunt Mamie always did that. For graduation I had to have two evening dresses, which created a problem for Aunt Mamie. One was my recital dress; the other was for class night, where the will, prophecy, jokes, and stories – all relating to the class – were told from the stage before parents and townspeople.

For this I wore a white-eyelet cotton dress embroidered in pale green. Around the waist I wore a crushed green satin belt with a large bow in front and streamers descending to the floor. My shoes were dyed a matching shade of green. For my recital I wore a white eyelet cotton dress embroidered in pink with a pink bow at the waistline and with streamers descending to the floor. I wore pink shoes dyed to match the ribbon. I well remember, my piano selection was a fast one, and I got into the long runs and panicked because I had forgotten which notes came next. I repeated the runs until, unconsciously, I came out of my difficulty. Miss Johnnie was grateful that I didn't stop playing when I panicked; she gave me a big hug and kiss when I came off the stage. Judson was my date for the evening and he grabbed my hand with a big squeeze because he had heard me practice the selection so many times that he realized what had happened. I think they were the only two people in the audience who knew that I had panicked and repeated and repeated until I had recovered myself. That was my last recital.

And, of course, on class night there was a takeoff on Mr. Bell blessing me out for dating on Sunday night. I had been elected as having the prettiest eyes and smile in the senior class. I won something else, but I can't remember what it was. Eugenia and I gave out programs before we went on stage.

In our school we had only two clubs – YMCA and YWCA. These met one time each week for a short program. Each student had to go. I was elected president of YWCA my senior year. All I did was preside at the meetings, because the teacher sponsor got the speaker and programs together. It was good practice for me.

In American History we had to write a term paper from selected subjects. I chose Thomas Jefferson. I did quite a lot of reading on the subject. One morning at homeroom Mr. Bell brought me my term paper, which he had finished grading, and asked me to read it in assembly that morning. Although I had written the paper, I had not practiced reading it out loud, so I asked my French teacher if she would let Bess Alice and me go to a vacant room so I could practice (Bess Alice was good at pronunciation). At the time there were several students around the teacher's desk who were upset about their grades. She would not listen to me and was getting angry. I would not sit down until she hollered at me, "Martha Bell, sit down!" I knew I couldn't read that paper well without practice. I told Mr. Bell before assembly began that I would rather not read it. He patted me on the shoulder and said I would do all right. I read it before all four grades of high school – mispronunciation and all – and made a mess of it. Following assembly the French teacher came to me and apologized over and over. She said she was so angry in class with the others she didn't comprehend what I was saying. Mr. Bell was provoked with the French teacher who apologized to him over and over. But no one ever (faculty or student) said anything out of line about my ordeal – everyone blamed the French teacher.

Another way Mr. Bell would give me an opportunity to learn was to ask me to substitute for him in Latin I class when he had a meeting or had to be out of the classroom.

I knew everyone in his class and they all knew me (only about 125 students in the 4-year school). When I walked in the first time as a substitute, everyone was quiet as a mouse. I thought something is wrong. On the desk there was a box with a small frog in it. When I sat down in the chair at the desk, the frog hopped out; I had never touched a frog in my life, but I picked him up and put him back in the box and said, "at the end of this class will the person to whom this box and frog belong please take him because I don't think Mr. Bell will want him in the next period class." So I put the top on the box and left him there. I never again had trouble with that class whenever I filled in for Mr. Bell.

I did not particularly care for typing – I couldn't build up my speed. Bess Alice was excellent with the typewriter. She represented our school in a regional contest and won an award.

My friend, Eugenia Fisher, was a beautiful girl and won the beauty context in Springfield. She represented Robertson County in the state beauty contest held in Nashville at the Princess Theater. Judson and I went and clapped and clapped for Eugenia, but she did not win.

Our senior picnic was held at Perry's Park. I was unable to swim, but with girl friends we played bridge. The senior class had a big weekend at someone's camp on Red River with the chaperone being a young couple from our class who married soon after graduation. I didn't get to go, nor did Judson go. Mother would not let me. I don't know why Judson didn't go – probably because he was announcing at WSIX.

At our high school graduation we wore caps and gowns on the stage in the auditorium of the Junior High School. Our commencement sermon was at the Springfield Baptist Church. Both places were hot as "Hades" – there was no air conditioning then. And remember I was wearing a cast from under my arms down to the bend of my legs from my hips.

We were still in the Great Depression. Out of our senior class only four girls went to college: Bess Alice Clinard (Murfreesboro), Sue Ara Harris (University of Tennessee Pharmacy School), Mary Willard Chester (Peabody College for Teachers) and me. For a while it had been decided that I would go to Draughon's Business College and stay with Auntie and Aunt Susie. Then I was offered a scholarship to Cumberland College through the Presbyterian Church; the representative came to see Mother and me. Mother was not familiar with Lebanon or the college and would not agree. Dr. Porter heard I was planning to go to business school. He called Mother and said he would do all he could to get me a scholarship to Middle Tennessee State College in Murfreesboro. That suited Mother because Bess Alice was going there and we would be roommates. Dr. Porter said I was not well suited for business school because I couldn't work at a desk all day without aggravating my health problems. With my back problem I needed varied positions and activities during the day. I got the scholarship for tuition, books, and room. Mother had to furnish meal tickets (money for food). That decision to go college at Murfreesboro was the major turning point in my life.

Soon following graduation Judson went to Indiana to a

college that had a prominent radio program. I don't remember where any other boys went to college, or how many did.

The summer between high school and college was uneventful. Friends were traveling, getting jobs, going to school, etc. My best friend in Springfield, Sue Ara Harris, moved that summer to the most elegant house in Springfield (formerly owned by the president of the bank, which had failed, and who was at the time in the penitentiary). She was busy getting clothes ready to go to UT where her older sister had graduated that year. Mrs. Harris was sewing constantly for Sue Ara – the closet in their guest room was completely filled with evening dresses, with shoes to match on the floor under the dresses. For the first time I felt left out. I had no one interested in my clothes, and I was going away to college. Aunt Mamie became critically ill that summer. She stayed in the hospital or at Auntie's most of the summer. Mother didn't sew and had never bought or planned clothes for me. That was left up to my Bell aunts. Many times in later life Aunt Mamie expressed her regret at not being able to help me with my wardrobe for college.Each day I received a letter from Judson from his college. He was lonely and in a strange situation.

That summer, several times Sue Ara and I rode to Dunbar Cave with Mr. and Mrs. Harris when they were going to Clarksville on business. We would take our lunch, tour the cave, go swimming and sun until Sue Ara's parents would come for us.
My Sunday School teacher said she would help me cut out a dress if I would buy the material and pattern. I had

never selected either by myself – the plaid material I bought was not suitable to the pattern. My Sunday School teacher didn't know much more than I did about sewing. A pitiful looking dress it was, but I wore it, for it was my only new dress.

In the early part of the summer I had the last cast cut off. A brace was fitted on me, which I wore in the daytime and took off at night. Dr. Duncan Eve of Nashville wanted me to swim as much as possible, which I enjoyed doing. So ended my summer.

Chapter 10 – Ray White and Middle Tennessee State Teachers College

In August Orman and Mrs. Clinard drove Bess Alice and me to Murfreesboro. Bess and I each had a suitcase. A trunk was sent by train for each of us. Two 18-year old innocents went to Murfreesboro to Middle Tennessee State Teachers College. We had never been on a college campus, and did not know what to expect.

Mrs. Clinard and Orman drove us to the main building – the administration building. As we went into the front lobby, we saw a boy from Springfield and a member of the Presbyterian Church, Joe Peyton. He was a senior, so he knew how to register and get around the campus. Bess and I took the usual classes for freshmen – English, Biology, Home Nursing (an elective), French I and American History. I was exempt from gym class because of my heavy back brace. This I took off at night and on special dress occasions. Dr. Porter had made special arrangements for me regarding scholarships, and he requested I stay in Rutledge Hall, the old dormitory, to be near my classes, the cafeteria, and the housemother, who would give us special care.

When Mrs. Clinard and Orman left, Bess and I were on our own for the first time in our lives. We met the young women who lived in the room next to us – Ruth Hines and Frances Shanfer of Shelbyville. They were totally unlike. Ruth, a pretty natural blond, wanted to meet young men. Frances, a short, fat, old-maid-type person, was interested in her studies. We four decided not to eat in the school cafeteria, but to walk across the street for a sandwich at "The Rosary," which, we had been told, was run by two men students.

This meal was the greatest turning point in my life. A senior man came to our table for our order. He was tall and handsome, with brown eyes and dark brown hair. His name was Ray White. My heart turned over for him and remained true and faithful to him for 49 years – two of courtship, 42 of marriage, and 5 after his death until my second marriage. Along with a football player named, Leonard Mansfield, Ray owned "The Rosary." They operated the eatery only for one school quarter because they did not make money – the football player was a big eater and shared food with his friends.

I talked Ray White into selling me a tomato sandwich for 10 cents – if I had had a hamburger on the bread it would have cost me 5 cents more. I was very short of money – food was the one thing my scholarship did not cover. I was a small person – weighing 89 pounds – but I should not have scrimped on food. I knew Mother was sending me to college on a bare necessity of money, so I felt obligated to be saving.

Ray did not pay me much attention because he had a girl friend on campus and was writing each day to a girl in Monterey, Tennessee. Whenever I saw him I did my share of flirting. In the early spring he asked me to walk with him to a game room for some ping-pong. I had never played, but with his help, and with another couple, we spent many early evenings after supper playing ping-pong.

I made the honor roll and my name headed an article in the *Robertson County Times* about college students from the county. For English I took bible as literature, and I read the *Bible* from *Genesis* through *Revelations*. My brace came off most of the time. Aunt Mamie reworked my old clothes and made me a new blouse. We went to all the ball games and school activities; read the best sellers (Anna Karenna, etc.); started gym in the 3rd quarter of my freshman year. Occasionally I had dates to school activities; but I was always on the lookout for Ray.

When Ray gave up his restaurant work he became the lab assistant for biology and chemistry (paid by the school). When I came to the dissection of the worm and frog, I was partner to Bill Threbeld who did the messy cutting and I did the writing. All the time with one eye on Ray White, who helped the students.

I learned later that Dr. Davis, Head of the Science Department, was a schoolmate of Ray's father, John Andrew White at King College. Ray continued his lab assistant job work until he graduated in August 1934.

My first real date with Ray was on a hayride to the school's farm on Stones River. He kissed me for the first time, and from then on I was interested only in him as a boyfriend. Our next date was attending a concert (a concert by symphony musicians from Nashville) in the school auditorium. We sat on the back row. Ray would make little remarks to me about the music and the musicians, and I would giggle. Both of us knew better. His mother had been a piano major at Randolph Macon

College; I had 9 years of piano and had spent many Sunday afternoons with Judson listening to Symphony concerts at Ryman Auditorium. In front of us was an old maid teacher, Miss Monihan, Ray's history teacher. The next day in class she lectured on the proper conduct of college students at a concert. We received a lot of teasing about this from students who saw us giggling, laughing, and whispering in the concert. So by the end of the third quarter of my freshman year, we were a twosome on campus. And thank goodness I was totally free from having to wear the body brace. Ray had stopped writing the Monterey girl and had stopped dating the campus girl. I continued writing to Judson each day and always got a letter from him. Each day, Ray would walk to the post office with me to mail a letter to Judson and I would usually also receive a letter from him. His mother sent me a box of cookies because Judson was afraid I was going hungry. I had not met any of Ray's family and knew very little about him, except I knew that I wanted to be with him the rest of my life. My family was upset that, by giving up Judson, I was passing up an opportunity for money, easy living, and prestige in the town of Springfield. However, they had not met Ray at this time and knew nothing about him.

I stayed in Murfreesboro during the summer quarter and took tennis lessons. I ate supper in a little restaurant across the campus with Ray each night; he would walk me back to the dorm – the long way by the science building steps and the library steps so we would escape the campus security guard and be in the dorm by nightfall.

I was selected to represent the college in a beauty contest at the movie house downtown for the title of "Miss Rutherford County." There was much excitement about my dress. I borrowed a short evening dress in rich pink georgette from a classmate. It was a disaster! We were not given a routine to follow – no practice, or instruction. We were told to walk out on the stage, turn around, and walk off. Of course, I did not win, nor do I remember who did.

I had planned to major in French and English. I had no trouble reading or writing French but my pronunciation gave me fits. My roommate, Bess, was also majoring in French – she later taught it for many years in Robertson County. One night I had read, translated, and explained the sentence construction to her. The next day I was called upon to read in French – then the teacher turned to me and said "Have Miss Clinard help you with your pronunciation, Miss Bell." At that moment I dropped the idea of majoring in French and turned more to English, in which I had always made an "A."

At Ray's graduation in August I met his father, John Andrew White, and two sisters, Margaret and Polly. Mr. White was a native of Avery County, North Carolina. He was the son of William Burleson and Sarah White, and had been reared by his grandfather, Moses White, and his step-grandmother Elizabeth, who was a Wiseman. His childhood had been extremely poor, but he had pursued education with dogged determination and had achieved moderate success. Mr. White had met Ray's mother, Catherine May Wood, while he was attending King College in Bristol, Tennessee, and she was attending a nearby Baptist school, where she was majoring in music and piano. Catherine May was from Doyle, Tennessee. Her parents were Dr. Jesse Matthew Wood, a physician, and Mary Story Wood. John and Katie May had married and taught a few years at Doyle College. They had relocated to Hohenwald and then to the farm on Asbury Lane outside of Murfreesboro. They had six children. Ray was the youngest boy. But Katie May died when Ray was 12 years old, and the White family had struggled thereafter.

Bess and I returned to college in the fall of 1934. She got a school job in the school cafeteria, which threw her with the football and basketball players because their work scholarships had them working in the cafeteria. She dated several – nothing serious.

Ray got a good job at $80 per month teaching Algebra and Industrial Arts at Central High School, Davidson County, Tennessee, his alma mater. Each weekend he would ride the bus or ride with Mr. Maples back to school to see me. He would stay with someone in the men's dorm.

Bess and I moved into a new dorm, Lyon Hall, for upperclassmen. We still had to be in by dark; our rooms were checked. If we went off campus during the daytime, we had to sign out, and sign in on our return.

I needed additional money for food. Ray went to the Dean and asked him about giving me a job on campus. I filled out an application blank for a job. I was offered a job being house matron to a group of orphans at a downtown settlement house, but I refused it. I could never have handled that job, being only 89 pounds, having never been around small children, and having no experience in management. Then I was given a library job, which I accepted. The previous summer I had had a course in library science, so I met the requirements. I thoroughly enjoyed this job. I was on the book repair group. Then I was given the job of completely reworking and organizing the files and the catalogue files in the main reading room. I worked behind the stacks. The next job I kept until I married. Each day for 2 hours, I had charge of the history room and magazine room, which included checking up and locking up at the end of the day. This additional money, 10 cents an hour, gave me money for more and better food. I made about $1 per week; a tuna fish sandwich cost 10 cents, so I could eat lunch all week on this one dollar.

Ray wrote me from Nashville each day, and I wrote him each day. He lived in Nashville with a fellow teacher and his wife, Mr. and Mrs. Hall, near Central High School. I had told Judson about Ray – but Judson still had hopes that I would come back to him.

 At Christmas time Judson came home to Springfield, and he came to Murfreesboro to pick me up for the drive to Springfield. Judson had told me earlier he wanted to meet Ray, so he could judge him for himself. So they met beside Judson's car, as I was packing to leave for Springfield. On the way home I told him I had chosen Ray. This was a difficult thing to do to a true friend of so many years. Judson continued to keep up with me through Auntie, Aunt Susie and Mother. I never saw him again after the day he drove me from Murfreesboro to Springfield. I shall always carry a bright memory of his thoughtfulness, goodness, kindness, and caring acts toward me. I gave up a well-mannered gentleman (my age and classmate through third grade) who was accustomed to the finer and better things in life, had a new car, his own money, and bought his own radio and TV station. I gave all of this up for a farm boy who had milked cows, never owned a car, borrowed money to go to college, no social graces (never learned how to properly help a lady with a coat or open a door for her and pull her chair up to the table), had difficulty evaluating a social situation quickly – but a man of integrity, honor, kindness, and talent, a hard worker, and we loved each other passionately.

In the spring I did some practice teaching at the demonstration school across from the campus and in the summer quarter I took as many teaching courses as I could. My thought was to start teaching in the fall of 1935. I applied for a job in Robertson County, but did not receive one at first. Mother borrowed some money from the bank to buy me some clothes (now my brace was off and I desperately needed clothes) and spending money for supplies, etc. On the day I left Springfield for my third quarter junior year (fall 1935), Mr. Fisher, the County Superintendent, came to the telephone office to tell Mother he had a teaching job for me. But I would be limited to teaching grammar school with two years of college. She told him I had left for college and that she had borrowed money to carry through the quarter. He apologized that he hadn't had a job earlier for me. But mother and I were glad of it, for I could continue in college to complete my degree.

Ray's salary went up to $110 per month. We decided to marry at Christmas time, 1935. You must remember these were Great Depression days. Jobs were extremely hard to come by. In order to get his raise, Ray went to the Davidson County Board meeting with a councilman, Mr. McMahon, who had known the White family for many years. Ray and Mr. McMahon successfully convinced the Board to grant the raise of $10 per month.

Immediately Ray went to a jewelry store and bought a wedding set of rings to be paid for in 1 year, month by month. Of course, I did not get the diamond ring until our engagement was announced on the front page of the Sunday *Banner*, Thanksgiving weekend, when I went home for the holidays. I do not remember when my family met Ray. It became the usual thing for Ray to ride to Springfield with Auntie and Uncle Arthur when I was in Springfield for a holiday and he would share a meal at Auntie's when I was over there for a holiday. The people of Springfield gradually got to know Ray, but there was always a slight coolness toward him on the part of those people who thought I should have married Judson, especially Dr. Porter.

Life went on as usual. I was Bess' roommate (she became Bess, not Bess Alice in college); we had to be in the dorm at nightfall; on Saturday nights Ray and I dated; typically we (sat) in the large dormitory reception room with some other steady couples (there were 8) and talked and held hands. The men had to leave at 9 o'clock. We went to ball games, student activities, ate at the College

Inn (across campus) and played cards; I continued my work in the library. I was elected a member of the Girl's Student Council, representing the junior class. I had completed my English classes for my major and started taking Home Economics classes as electives.

Ray was busy in Nashville with his teaching job at Central High. To make more money he was also making cedar chests and other pieces of furniture to order in the school shop. No one ever mentioned he was not supposed to use school equipment for gain or money. On Friday nights he would work the ball games at Central High to make additional money; then he came to Murfreesboro on Saturday morning. He did not have a car, so his transportation was still by friend, bus or train. He was paying room and board in Nashville, paying on the wedding set of rings, and paying on the loans he had obtained for past tuition. He also had to have new shoes, a suit and 3 shirts. The suit cost $17.50. He was so proud of his new clothes.

I don't remember any new clothes for me. I remember Aunt Mamie made me a green tweed wool skirt that I wore with a white shirt and tan jacket. Aunt Bertha gave me an old dress of Martha Lou's. Aunt Susie and Auntie kept me in underwear, hose and gowns. Ray gave me for Christmas an "Evening in Paris" perfume set – I still have the small blue glass purse flacon – no perfume, however.

Mother was having a hard time coming to the idea that I would not come back to Springfield. She had imagined that I would teach there and live with her. During my first year in college, Uncle Melvin, mother's brother, had retired from the telephone company and had come to live with her. He had several jobs while he lived there, including clerking at a store and working in a tobacco warehouse. He kept the grass cut, the leaves raked, maintained a good vegetable garden, brought in coal, kept the fires going in the house, and was a protection for Mother. She had rented the 2 large bedrooms upstairs to 2 single elderly ladies. In this way, Mother was making ends meet rather well. There were pear and apple trees on the property. Mother enjoyed making pear honey and apple jelly, and canning apples, pears, tomatoes and beans by the new hot-pack method. She had a flower garden – enjoyed cutting flowers and arranging them for the church service in her beloved Presbyterian Church. Mother continued her big family dinners, sometimes using Aunt Odie, the maid at the telephone company, to help her.

Ray gave me my ring in Springfield at Thanksgiving. Mother had a big Thanksgiving dinner. We had already told Mr. Nat Langford, the *Banner* reporter for Robertson County, about our engagement and given him permission to put it in the paper. We made our wedding ceremony plans with Rev. Van Wyke and his wife, "Miss Lucille," (my former high school English teacher for whom I marked home-work papers). Mother would not have anything to do with the wedding plans, and said she would not go to the wedding. But she said would not prevent my marriage to Ray. The Van Wykes said we could be married in their living room and we set the date and time, Dec. 26, 1935 at four o'clock, and planned for two attendants, Martha Lou Simpkins and Jimmy

Durham. If our marriage plans were mentioned during these days Mother would start crying.

On this emotional note, I left Springfield on Sunday afternoon with Uncle Arthur and Auntie, and then caught the bus to Murfreesboro, finally taking a 5-cent taxi ride to the college.

However, the next weekend I met Mother and Auntie in Nashville to buy my wedding clothes. Mother had sold some of her telephone stock to have money to buy me some good clothes. I bought a tunic, crepe silk, street length dress in a soft brownish tone at Tinsley; at Cain-Sloan, I bought French kid gloves, an envelope-type leather pocketbook and medium-height-heel leather shoes; Miss Carrie, who always made my hats, made a small silk twill peaked hat, dipping slightly in left front. At Cain Sloan I bought a stroller length mouton coat (real fur – most likely rabbit). This was a beautiful outfit for many occasions – I shall forever be grateful to Mother for her thoughtfulness. I also bought a pure silk, peach-colored gown. Most likely Auntie and Aunt Susie gave me some new underwear – I don't remember.

When I got back to school everyone was excited over my ring and the announcement being on the front page. Bess and two classmates gave me a bridal shower. I don't remember much about it except there were a number of people there, including my art teacher, who gave me the oval framed floral print that I have hanging in my bedroom (1993). I had to take exams because we were still on the quarter system, and the quarter ended with Christmas Holiday. I packed my trunk and had it sent to the apartment Ray had rented on 8th Avenue. It was just in front of Reservoir Park – a back bedroom, a small kitchen, and a bathroom shared with 3 other apartment dwellers. I sometimes wonder when and how often that bathroom was cleaned; however, I was never afraid to use it.

Mother had her usual big Christmas dinner – Uncle Melvin, Aunt Mamie, Cornelius, Auntie, Uncle Arthur, Aunt Susie, Aunt Effie, Uncle Clem, Clem, Jr., Grandpa Simpkins, Aunt Bertha, Uncle Buford, Martha Lou, Mary Ruth, and Ray. She was too busy to cry, but I was told that when her hair was done at the beauty parlor that week, she had cried constantly. The person doing her hair had known me all my life and she begged Mother to go to my wedding – that she was not fair to me. I still can't understand why Mother would not go to my wedding. It has been hurtful to me all these years. The big Christmas dinner was my wedding dinner, but it was not put in the paper as such. The report in the paper said it was Christmas dinner and listed everyone there. Aunt Bertha Simpkins and her daughter Martha Lou gave us a luncheon on Dec. 26, a few hours before our wedding. The only people at the luncheon were Ray, me, Martha Lou and Jimmy Durham. It was a beautiful party in their morning room, using a small table. At that time Uncle Buford, Aunt Bertha and Martha Lou were renting the Dowlen Mansion – a beautiful home (1890). Aunt Bertha begged Mother to let her have the wedding in their living room, and have me come down the lovely steps to the hall and have an invited guest list – but Mother said "no, we did not have the money." I realize now that Mother didn't want Aunt Bertha, her sister-in-law, to have anything to do with my wedding. We could have managed, and it would have made such happy memories for me, because I was hurt immensely by not having family and friends at my wedding. Ray never fully realized that my family and friends did not want me to marry him. They were always nice and friendly toward him, and I never told him how they really felt.

Leaving the luncheon, we rode with Jimmy Durham and Martha Lou Simpkins to "Miss" Lucille and Rev. Van Wyke's home, a few blocks from Mother's. They were so kind to us; Miss Lucille gave me a hug and kiss (she knew how I wanted my Mother there); both were kind and friendly toward Ray. Miss Lucille had fresh flowers in the living room and stood by during the simple ceremony. It was December 26, 1935. Following the ceremony Jimmy drove Martha Lou home (a few blocks away); we stopped by Mother's to say goodbye (remember, she had worked at the telephone office all day). After a tearful goodbye Jimmy, Ray and I drove to Nashville to the small back apartment. There, Jimmy left us about 9 o'clock.

So, my life with Ray White began! I had no regrets in my decision; I did what I wanted to do. That night was my first look at the apartment. Ray had furnished it. The bed he had made in the Central High School shop according to his own design. For Christmas and my wedding present, he had made a matching walnut blanket chest – a beautiful piece of furniture. The remaining pieces of furniture in the bedroom were his cedar chest, a dresser belonging to Auntie, two rocking chairs of Auntie's, and a bridge lamp. In the small kitchen were a kitchen cabinet, a wooden breakfast table, and four chairs, which had been bought from Ovalina and Angus Maples, who had moved into a new house. The gas stove was furnished with the apartment; we shared the use of an electric refrigerator, placed in the back hall, and we shared the bathroom, which had a door leading from our kitchen. There was a small, shelved closet in the kitchen and a clothes closet in the bedroom. We had so few possessions that this was plenty of room. Ray had rented the apartment in the fall and had been living there while teaching at Central High School. To reach school he walked down Wedgewood Avenue from 8th Avenue to the Fairgrounds and on to school – a distance of about 1-1/2 miles. The apartment was opposite the reservoir on 8th Avenue; then nice people and nice homes were there. A shopping area on the corner of 8th Avenue and Douglas was handy – H. G. Hill's grocery, drug store, barbershop, beauty parlor, dry cleaning, and the streetcar came by the house and stopped at the corner. We had no car so our transportation needs had to be met by walking or by taking the electric streetcar, which ran on tracks.

This was our first night spent together. Very little sleeping was done – much love and a complete feeling of belonging to each other.

The next day we went to Second Avenue to buy a few pots and pans, and a skillet. This took a big part of Ray's money. We ate at B & W's cafeteria downtown. The next day we rode the bus to Monterey – our wedding trip – to visit Ray's aunt, Auntie Bates (his deceased mother's sister). Her son Harold and his wife Jean were visiting also. They were newly wedded, so we had three or four interesting days with them and with Auntie Bates, who was an excellent cook. Then it was back to Nashville for Ray to start teaching at Central High.

Chapter 11 – A Young Married Couple

The day Ray started teaching I took the streetcar to the Rehabilitation Commission office in the State Office Building to ask for a continuation of my college scholarship at Peabody College. Dr. Porter may have given an important recommendation on my behalf. The person at the office asked me one question: "If they granted me a scholarship to Peabody would I promise to teach in the public schools of Tennessee for five years?" Of course, I said yes. I had promised my mother that I would get my degree if I married. Therefore, I had made two promises, and I would keep both.

On registration day at Peabody (winter quarter, 1936), I presented my credentials to the head of the Home Economics Department. She was impressed with my grades and suggested a schedule for the next year (fall of 1936 and winter and spring of 1937) to complete my Smith Hughes BS Home Economics degree. Smith Hughes was a national science-intensive Home Economics program, but Davidson County was not a participant. I had enough hours to graduate at the end of the spring 1936 quarter with an A. B. degree, English major. But I was truly interested in the harder B. S. degree and, since I was on a scholarship, very little money had to be spent in obtaining it.

The first three months of my marriage were spent in a full schedule, 8-to-5 day, with streetcar transportation to and from Peabody College, transferring at 8th Avenue and Broadway. My hardest subject was organic chemistry, which was taught from 3 to 5 in the afternoons. It had been 2 years since I had had inorganic chemistry – so I really had to study hard for organic. Ray helped me in the evenings. This was the same organic chemistry class in which pre-med Vanderbilt students were enrolled. In the spring I took food chemistry, which was a "snap" after having endured organic.

Ray would cook breakfast, pack my lunch, go to the grocery store, cook supper and take as much responsibilities off of me as he possibly could, to help me to get through that first quarter at Peabody. I realize now Dr. Wilson, head of Home Economics Department, was testing my ability to cope with difficult studies, marriage, and life; thus preparing me to be a better teacher. Other studies gave me little trouble, except for cooking class with Dr. Wilson. She entered me in an advanced cooking class, because I had had a basic cooking class at Middle Tennessee State Teachers College. This gave me difficulty because it was based upon notes and work techniques from her first course, which I had not taken. But I soon caught on.

Winter of 1936 was extremely cold – the Cumberland River partially froze over. I did not dress warmly enough for the chilling winds when waiting for the streetcar and the transfer. I had the warmer clothes, but did not realize how terribly cold it was. As a result I developed a severe sinus infection, the first in my life. When I was waiting for the streetcar, I knew I did not feel right, but it never entered my mind I was sick! My first class was the cooking class with Dr. Wilson, who was teaching cake decorating. I chose to sit on a high wooden stool next to the radiator during the demonstration. She was making white icing and tinting it in different delicate colors – turning the icing over and over to distribute the tint evenly – I felt dizzy and the next thing I knew I was falling from the stool. Someone caught me and stretched me out on the floor. I remember Dr. Wilson saying in her kind voice, "Martha has a cold and I believe has fever." Of course, a newly married woman was thought to be pregnant by most people. Her gracious words were kind and thoughtful at that particular moment. She led me to her office and had me lie on the couch. I asked her to call my Uncle to give me a ride to the apartment and to call my husband at his school to meet us at the apartment. I stayed out of school several days. My fever went so high that I was incoherent at one time; I came to and found Mother sitting by the bed. I could not raise my head from the pillow because of extreme dizziness. I remember the doctor coming to see me – but do not remember what medication or treatment was given me.

When I was over this, I went back to my old schedule at Peabody and made my grades. This was the longest and hardest quarter of my entire college life. Each succeeding quarter became less difficult, and involved fewer hours of class.

I missed my girl friends – no one to go anywhere with except Ray. I had no time to make social friends at Peabody, because I was in class, or I needed the time to get my assignments. I took my lunch, which I ate in the reception room of the Home Economics Building while studying. Sometimes there were other girls in my class doing the same thing.

Ray's friends on the Central High School faculty were friendly and became our social friends. Ovalina and Angus Maples were dinner friends; Billy and Walter Hall were dinner and bridge friends; Madeline and John Koen were dinner and bridge friends. John was also getting his master's degree at Peabody so we four went to the Peabody dances. These friendships were very meaningful throughout our marriage.

Summer of 1936 was spent at Med Ransom's summer camp out from McMinnville on the Caney Fork River. We had given up our apartment to save money, and had stored our furniture at Central High School. This was my first camp, and my first out-doors experience! The camp was at the site of a hotel on the side of a mountain. There was a swinging bridge across the river to the road to McMinnville. The hotel was in bad condition and much of it was not safe for habitation. Ray and I had a room that was on the first floor and safe (floors not rotten or falling in). A bed, a chest of drawers, a table with water pitcher and washbowl, and a closet were the furnishings for the room. There were no chairs, and everything was old. This was our living quarters for 6 weeks.

Med Ransom was a teacher at Central High School and he lived on Lynwood Blvd in Belle Meade. He and his sister owned this decaying hotel site. It used to be a fashionable spa – probably had seen its glory days in the 1890's. They lived in a nice, neat house on the camp property. The campers (20) lived in other cabins. The dining room and kitchen were in a basement room under the hotel, which opened onto the side of the mountain. The campers were ages 9 to 16. They loved the outdoor life. Ray was program director – which meant being with the campers every waking minute – and I went along for all activities – swimming, boating, hiking, games, and outings. Each night after supper, Med Ransom would have a story and vespers program. That was the extent of his participation. I never saw his sister enter into any camp activities. She stayed in her cabin; she and Med Ransom ate their meals in their cabin.

The camp food was of poor quality and of limited quantity for active growing boys. No milk was served. Ray complained and finally Med Ransom began to buy fresh vegetables from the farmers to round out the nutritional value of the meals. Each morning, by each person's plate was placed a small square of margarine on paper. If the person did not use all the margarine it was placed on a shelf to save for the next meal – everyone had to remember which was his margarine. I remember one lunch consisted of crackers, mustard, and Vienna sausage – not as much as you wanted to eat; each person received a measured amount! Terrible! After that meal Ray complained!

Ray was working the six weeks for only room and board for the two of us. And both benefits were insufficient and of poor quality.

After supper and before vespers Ray and I and the campers would cross the swinging bridge and walk down the road to a country store. The campers would buy all kinds of food and cold drinks. Ray and I could not because we did not have the money. For the first and only time in my life I was hungry to the point of almost starving. My weight was 85 and I was brown from being in the sun everyday and wearing either shorts or a bathing suit with a blouse each day. This was the time the woman whose husband owned the store called me to one side and said, "you are hungry?" I said, "yes." She said, "I know the cook at Ransom's Camp, and I know you people are not getting enough food." She gave me a glass of buttermilk. Never have I tasted anything as good. To the end of camp she always gave me a glass of buttermilk when we walked the campers to her store.

Another trying time for us was when we drove the campers to McMinnville to go to the picture show and a stop at a restaurant for hamburgers, ice cream, cokes, etc. This occurred three afternoons a week (we had to divide the group so that everyone could go 1 time per week). Ray and I had no money to go to the show and we kept our restaurant food to one item – ice cream cone or coke. While the campers were in the show we would do some shopping for the camp or Med Ransom, or sight see around town.

A mile from camp, through the woods on a wagon trail, was a small settlement. The campers heard there was a "Holy Roller" meeting in progress. They wanted to go. So one night after supper we hiked out to the church. It was daylight when we got there. Soon it was dark and a terrific storm came up. The wind was bending the branches on the trees around the church to the ground; lightning was flashing; thunder was shaking the building. The church people were shouting; crying on their knees; speaking in unknown tongues, while the minister walked up and down the aisle preaching and calling on the "Lord to save us." He stopped by Ray and said, "These are fine boys you have here – a fine family." There were 2 rows of us; the preacher must have thought we were mass-producing boys! And that experience was one never to forget.

Word came to camp that a field had recently been plowed and arrowheads were showing up in the dirt. That afternoon we made a river hike (shallow water) up to the freshly plowed field. We found arrowheads; the same ones I have at my house, displayed on a green felt mat in a wooden frame.

I enjoyed swimming in the river. I was proficient with the backstroke, sidestroke and breaststroke, but never mastered the crawl. I had been accustomed to a swimming pool, so the currents in the river strengthened me. I tried kayak boating – but was not successful. I turned over, with my body and head dangling down in the water – my only try.

After camp we went to Auntie Bate's in Monterey for a one-week visit. To get bus money Ray had written Polly in Nashville for a $10 loan. She had completed her nurse's training and was head nurse in the pediatric ward at Vanderbilt – therefore, she was making a good salary.

This was an enjoyable week. Auntie Bates had a wonderful garden of fresh vegetables, which Ray and I helped prepare for cooking. She was a wonderful cook. Conrad Bates was there and several of their friends had us over to their houses for visits and dessert. Outside of Monterey there was a lake of several acres. Mary and

James Bates were camping there with friends from Nashville (Dr. Burch and family). They had a boat on the lake which Ray and I enjoyed with them.

Our $10 was running out. I rode the bus to Nashville and Ray hitchhiked, both of us getting to the bus station in Nashville about the same time. We went to Auntie's and Aunt Susie's until Sunday. Then went to Springfield with Auntie and Uncle Arthur for a visit with Mother. We stayed a week with her; again we had to borrow some money from her to carry us over until Ray's first paycheck, at the end of September, which was $120 per month. We enjoyed our visit with Mother and Uncle Melvin. He had raised a garden and the apples and pears were ready for cooking. These fresh foods were delicious. One day Sue Ara Harris, Ray and I rode to Dunbar Cave for swimming, while Mrs. Harris drove to Clarksville to visit relatives.

At the beginning of the fall 1936 school session, Ray enrolled for a few hours at Peabody on his master's degree at the same time that I enrolled. We rented a Peabody College apartment on 18th Ave. (Larry and Edna Willis and their daughter Suzanne lived in the house next door, but were not social friends. They would have a second daughter Judith, who would marry my first son Howard. This was also near where Howard and Judith would spend their first months of married life in the fall of 1959 and the spring of 1960.) We moved back the furniture that had been stored at Central High, borrowed some more furniture from Auntie, bought a refrigerator; and had our own private bathroom. This was a wonderful time in our early, married life.

Ray walked the one-and-one-half miles to Central High School. I could come to the apartment for lunch and shop for groceries on 21st Avenue, across from Peabody. I also washed all of our clothes in the bathtub; hung them outside on a clothesline and did the ironing. I had time to do this because I was taking fewer and easier class hours – interior design, psychology, American history and dress drafting. To add to our income Ray did small jobs for some faculty members and friends; but the cost of the apartment became more than we could handle financially. We moved back to 8th Avenue to the smaller apartment, where we shared the bathroom with other renters. I started riding the streetcar again. In the winter quarter of 1937 I did my practice teaching at Peabody Demonstration School and took bacteriology and catering. Ray enrolled again in Peabody for a few hours on his master's degree. However, he allowed other activities to interfere and never completed those courses – receiving incomplete grades. He never enrolled again and lost all interest in getting his master's degree.

In the spring 1937 I had only one course, children's sewing, which took a lot of my time. This completed my courses for a Smith-Hughes B. S. degree in home economics. There were only a few classmates to graduate with this more difficult degree – 10 or 12. Ray and I went to the senior dance with Corinne and John Judd and had a lot of fun. We had double dated at MTSTC before they had married and moved to Nashville. They were our close personal friends – dinner, bridge, badminton, and picture shows – until John became interested in other women and Corinne divorced him.

Ray and I went to the Peabody College breakfast on the campus the morning before graduation. Then on Graduation Day, Mother came over from Springfield by bus, planning to spend the weekend with us in our apartment. Auntie was bringing over a canvas cot so that Mother could sleep on it in our kitchen. My invitations were limited. I had invited Mother, Auntie, Aunt Susie, and Uncle Arthur. When my name was called, and I was walking to the podium for my diploma, I glimpsed Ray's father, Mr. White, standing next to a column in the walkway of the Administration Building with tears streaming down his face. What a shock! I had not invited Mr. White, who was living by himself in the tenant house on the farm he owned outside of Murfreesboro. Feeling unable to make a profit farming the place himself, he had chosen to rent out the farm and the main farmhouse. He had never shown any interest in Ray and my life, nor had he given us any help or encouragement. He rode back to our apartment with Mother, Auntie, Aunt Susie, and Uncle Arthur. Immediately, Auntie and Mother took me aside and said they thought Mr. White wanted to spend the night with us, so Mother ought to go with Auntie and spend the weekend with her and Uncle Arthur. I don't think either Ray or Mr. White were aware of this change of plans. Of course, I wanted to be with my Mother on this special occasion. Mr. White stayed with us that weekend.

Ray had taken a summer job with Webb School Camp for six weeks or two months (I don't remember which). This did not start until the middle of June so we moved out at the end of May, stored our furniture at Central High and moved in with Auntie for about one week so we would not have to pay the June rent on the apartment. Ray and I slept on a featherbed mattress on the floor, upstairs between Bill's room and Aunt Susie's room. Uncle Arthur and Auntie were sleeping in the dining room because they had rented out the 2 downstairs bedrooms for additional income. Remember this was still the Great Depression!

Ray was hired to replace Mr. Maples on the Webb School faculty. He and Ovalina, who had a three-month-old daughter, wanted more children. Ray helped with the sports activities in the afternoon and taught math and algebra in the morning school program. This was a remedial summer school for children who were behind in their studies. I had no responsibility and did not participate in the program, except for swimming and keeping baseball scores in the afternoons. We lived in a tent placed over a wooden floor, which was 3 steps up from the ground in front and even with the ground in the back. Ray and I slept on adjacent camp canvas cots. There was a primitive table, which held a pitcher of water, washbasin, soap dish, and towels. A "chamber pot" was furnished. Each morning a black servant would bring fresh water and fresh towels, a clean "chamber pot," and would take the used one to empty. Ray placed upright wooden poles forming a framework for cheap (3 cents per yard) cloth to partition off part of the tent as our dressing room, bathroom, and clothes closet, where we hung our clothes on nails driven into the wooden poles. In front of this enclosure he placed a plank, which I used as my dressing table for my make-up, brush and comb, etc. Above this we hung a cheap mirror. Folding chairs completed our living quarters. We left the tent flaps up all day to receive the breeze and closed them at night for privacy.

Webb School camp was at a permanent campsite with substantial buildings. There were only two tents for married couples; the boys stayed in cabins with single male adults as supervisors. The superintendent of the school and camp lived in a nicely furnished house on the grounds.

The dining room was well ventilated with eight people at each table and with an adult supervising. Ray and I were together at the same table. We enjoyed generous, delicious and well-balanced meals prepared by the African American kitchen staff. Each meal was complete and hot. The same kitchen and dining room employees were used at the school during the regular school term. We did not have to bring food to the table nor help clear the table. Hired help did all of that. It was a joy for me.

After our mid-day meal we had rest time – campers had to remain in their cabins until the bell rang. Then we walked to the swimming place on the Caney Fork River. There was a float in the middle of the river, but I did not go to it for it was reserved for the boys. When the life-saving tests were given, I swam the full mile down river with a group of boys, passing the tests, while Ray rowed the boat alongside us. I stayed close to the boat and came back to the dock in the boat. That summer I gained a lot of strength in my swimming.

After swimming we took our coldwater showers from several spigots along a long water pipe, while standing on a wooden walkway. After supper there were baseball games, table tennis, mail call, shopping at the camp store, songs and programs. When these activities were called off because of rain, Ray, I, and two other faculty members would place a suitcase between our beds in our cabin and play bridge by lantern light.

During this camp session I once rode out of camp to Sparta with the superintendent's daughter to pick up mail and get supplies. His family did not eat in the dining room nor participate in activities except for an occasional swim.

At the end of the camp season, parents came for the campers, a festive dinner, and some speaking. Uncle Arthur, Auntie, and Aunt Susie came for Ray and me. We stayed a few days with them; then we went to Springfield for a few days with Mother.

In Nashville Ray's salary went up to $125 a month; we had the money he had made teaching at Webb Camp, and I had no college expenses. We had decided on starting our family rather than deferring until after I had worked off my five-year teaching commitment. Later, after the children started school, I would teach for 27 years.

Chapter 12 – Our Two Little Boys Howard and John

On Allison Place (2 blocks from Central High) we rented the front room, bedroom, kitchen, breakfast room, back porch and front porch of a small bungalow from a mother and her adult daughter, who also lived there. They kept one bedroom and had their kitchen and dining facilities in the basement. We shared the bathroom. Ray and I bought a sofa, chair, cabinet model radio and two lamps. Auntie loaned us rocking chairs and old curtains.

This was a small three-block community of families who had children in Central High School. We knew most of our neighbors; everyone was friendly; I would sit on the front porch in the swing and before long a neighbor would come to sit with me. I did the housekeeping and cooking. We had our friends over for dinner and bridge, eating economical meals since we were striving to pay off Ray's college bills from MTSTC. I washed all our clothes on the back porch using washtubs that belonged to the landlords, and I did all our ironing. My big deal was walking to the Wedgewood streetcar, catching the bus to town at Douglas Corner, window shopping and buying a coke and pimento cheese sandwich – all of 25 cents worth.

But these lazy days did not last long. Mr. White had to have a prostate operation (Ray and his brothers and sisters paid for Mr. White's surgery). Ray offered to let Mr. White stay with us during recovery, and he occupied our bedroom. Ray slept on a folding canvas camp cot in the living room beside the couch on which I slept. I could not straighten full length on the couch. Mr. White stayed with us three weeks. During that time it was my job to wait on Mr. White, cook for him, and wash his linens and clothes. This was during the fall. At this time Howard was conceived, though we did not know it for a few weeks.

My first indication of pregnancy was on Christmas holidays in Springfield. Mother had had her family Christmas dinner, and Aunt Mamie had had one as well, so we were at Aunt Bertha's for her family Christmas dinner. Just before dinner was served I became sick at my stomach, was dizzy and suffered some stomach cramps. Ray and I went to Mother's before dinner was served, while everyone else stayed for the dinner. I continued to be sick after going home to Nashville. We decided on Dr. Thomas Zerfoss as my doctor. He examined me, said he thought I was pregnant and gave me some medicine for my sick stomach. This medicine would not stay down. Then we knew I was pregnant.

As my pregnancy progressed I started sewing. I made some clothes for myself, for I looked like a big fat barrel. I truly looked as big around as I was tall. I made day gowns for "the baby" out of batiste, lace, small single thread embroidery, entre deax lace, and tatting made by Mother. Sitting on the porch in the swing when the weather became warmer, I hemstitched and embroidered sheets and pillow cases for the walnut baby crib that we had brought from Aunt Mamie' house – her son Cornelius had slept in it as a baby, and I had slept in it as a baby, so I wanted my children to sleep in it as well. Latter my grandchildren, Howie and Keith would also sleep in it. I went to the baby department at Cain-Sloan and talked to Mrs. Johnson about a layette. She suggested 3 of each item and showed me the different brands, prices and types. So I bought the "Carter" brand knit sleeping gowns that tied around the bottoms and sleeves, under shirts, belly bands (which are not used today), three dozen cloth diapers, a large bath towel and a small wash cloth (soft white knits), sterilizer with bottles, nipples, washer, olive oil, baby powder, baby pins, rubberized pads and Q-tips. All of these items were placed in the walnut baby chest, which was mine as a child. My father had purchased the chest at his grandfather's estate sale for 50 cents (people outside the family who attended the auction had refrained from bidding against a family member). Grandfather had used the chest. And my great, great grandparents Bell and my great grandparents Bell had used the chest in the loom house to hold yarn or raw wool for weaving. Therefore, we had gathered the basic baby supplies and a baby crib some months before Howard was born.

About this time Auntie Bates (Ray's mother's sister) had surgery in Nashville. Since she had no children in Nashville, she spent her recovery time with us during the spring. Again I had the responsibility of caring, cooking, and washing linens for her, but I felt it was a pleasure because she had been so good to Ray and me following our marriage. She made a crib quilt for the new baby – blue on one side and pink on the other side, which I still have.

After Ray and I decided we had to have a car for transportation, Uncle Arthur looked for a used car for us. We borrowed $300 and bought a used, four-door, beige

Ford, which we used until 1945, the first year that new cars were available following the war. This car was a major purchase for us, for we still owed money for Ray's college education. That year bananas were 3 cents per pound, a loaf of bread was 10 cents, 3 pounds of bacon cost 25 cents, so we worked at economizing on food. We obtained all the food we could get from the farm, we frequented the Farmer's Market and I began to can some foods. I cooked everything from scratch to save money. In these ways I helped to pay our debts and to provide for the new baby. The doctor's fee of delivering Howard would be $25, but there would be hospital bills and other expenses.

Grandpa Simpkins had lived at the City Hotel until his health would not allow him to continue working. Then he had moved to Portland, Tennessee, to live with his daughter Effie. He died of pneumonia in Portland in June 1938 at the age of 88 years. He is buried in his family plot in the Elmwood Cemetery in Springfield, Tennessee.

In the early summer Margaret Shands (Ray's sister) paid us a visit, bringing her daughter Anna K., who was a toddler. Margaret used our house as a base of operations from which she visited and lunched with old friends from Central High and St. Thomas Hospital – leaving me to take care of Anna K. Margaret had her own car and plenty of spending money, but never took me shopping or to lunch with her. And she didn't help me cook dinner at night either. I had hoped for more consideration, especially since I was seven months pregnant. After about four days of being a servant to Margaret I became furious over her attitude. I packed my bag, and, when

Margaret came home that afternoon, I walked out the front door, caught the streetcar and went to Auntie's. It was a great surprise to Ray when he came home and found me gone. He called Auntie to find out if she knew where I was. I told him why I had left, and that I would return when Margaret left. We never discussed it – but Ray found out I was no one's servant unless I wanted to be.

For the cradle I had made a quilt top appliquéd with dog print cotton fabric. I spent a day with Aunt Mamie in Springfield to finish the quilt with her help. She had made several receiving blankets for me and had made a small pillow out of fine goose feathers. Mrs. Hall, wife of a Central High faculty member, made a bedspread. Corinne Judd made a net carriage cover. And other people gave us baby items. Margaret gave a sterling silver baby cup. Mother refurbished my tatted baby cap, which she had made before I was born. Several beautiful baby dresses were given. So, all in all, Howard was a well-dressed baby.

Ray spent the summer doing construction work. He worked for Mr. Maples and he did some private jobs. Ray made more money at construction work than he did teaching school – but this was hard on his heart, which had been damaged when he had suffered rheumatic fever as a child. This is when I learned that Dr. Tom Zerfoss warned Ray not to do such hard physical work and that his heart had been damaged as a child. We had another problem, our landlord had told us we would have to move after the baby was born. We decided on a nearby duplex, three houses up the street, on Allison Place.

There, we had a living room, bedroom, kitchen and breakfast room, and we shared the bathroom and telephone with a husband and wife and his mother.

The baby's birth time arrived. He had matured in the womb correctly – not causing any trouble and very little pain during development. Since I was so small (weight 89 pounds, height 5' 2") Dr. Tom was concerned that my birth canal might be too small to give birth. He took measurements and sent me to another doctor for more measurements and consultation, to decide whether to allow me to give birth or do a cesarean section. There was great concern among members of my family that my heart murmur and those past years in a body cast might also cause problems for the baby and me. However, everything went smoothly.

The labor pains started in the early evening hours. Ray took me to St. Thomas. A nurse with a wheel chair met us at the door to take me to my room – a four-bed ward – where I stayed until the contractions were close together. I was moved on a stretcher to a small, sterile white room where a nurse stayed with me, but she would not allow Ray to stay. I was begging for medicine and screaming with pain before Dr. Tom thought it was the correct time to sedate me. Then, I remember being moved to the delivery room. The next thing I remember is feeling pain when the nurse and Dr. Tom were taking stitches in my torn vagina. The nurse was saying how brave I was and that my husband was not in the building. Dr. Tom agreed, and said that I was a "beautiful woman." I wanted to tell them that I had a husband who loved me dearly, and I wanted to ask them where my husband was.

I moved slightly and immediately I felt a needle go in my arm and I was unconscious again. This all took place between 4 and 7 o'clock in the morning hours of August 4, 1938.

My next clear remembrance is waking up in a large private room with a private bathroom where Ray was sitting in a chair by the bed, holding my hand, as my eyes fell upon a beautiful arrangement of pastel gladiolas. Then a nurse came bringing in our baby for nursing – my first baby! And I was afraid I would hurt him, drop him or break him. It took many weeks to find out he didn't "break" easily. I also learned that Dr. Tom had insisted that Ray go home for some sleep during the night, and that's where he was when Howard had been born. I stayed in the hospital five days and did not get on my feet. I went home in the ambulance with Howard by my side. Mother was at our house to wait on Howard and me. He was a perfect angel of a baby. He slept; he nursed; he learned to take his bottle; he did little crying and looked adorable in his little walnut cradle when friends and relatives came to call and bring him presents. When Mother left, Aunt Susie stayed for two or three weeks, for which we paid her. She loved to cuddle and rock Howard while he was taking his bottle.

During pregnancy my metabolism had changed my assimilation of food nutrients. I could not wear any clothes I had worn before pregnancy – shoes, underwear, dresses, etc. were all too small. That meant more money spent on a few clothes and reworking my old clothes where possible.

Our first outing with Howard was a trip to Springfield. Mother had a big family dinner to introduce her first grandson. We did not have a basket for Howard. I carried him on a pillow in my arms while Ray drove the car (this was before protective car seats for babies). Mother had borrowed a baby bed and a baby basket from Mrs. Ashbrawer. Mother had made the baby bed so attractive, lovingly preparing it to receive her grandson. I brought the basket home for carrying Howard.

Immediately upon returning from Springfield we moved up the street into the duplex to be in by September 1. Ray started teaching at Central High School, drawing a salary of $130 per month, on a nine-month basis, which he supplemented with outside jobs, including repair work, painting, and making furniture.

For one day a week I had the luxury of an African American maid. She was Nancy, Felix Haynes' daughter. Felix's family lived across the road from Mr. White's farm outside of Murfreesboro, and they had worked for the White's since Ray had been a young boy. Felix's wife did our washing and ironing in her home on the Central High School campus, where Felix was custodian. She had been a nurse and housekeeper for Ray's mother at the Murfreesboro farm, so the Haynes' took a special interest in us. Nancy cleaned the apartment and the bathroom, and she ironed Howard's baby clothes. Ray paid Nancy $1 for each day she worked for us. On this day I would go to town or someplace special.

On pretty days I would place Howard in his baby buggy, push him around the block, and talk to our neighbors. We kept a rigid schedule: his bath in the kitchen sink (in a baby tub), feeding, then nap time, during which I washed the diapers and his baby clothes, feeding again, nap time, and finally a trip around the block. My breast milk was insufficient for Howard's needs, so we put him on the bottle completely by the end of his first six weeks.

We continued our social dinners and bridge games with friends, and added two more couples to our group. Henrietta Lawrence and Jimmy Durham had married and were living in Donelson. He was with American Airlines, and they were expecting their first child. We had double-dated in college. Across the street from us lived Blair and Steve Stephens, who had their first baby during Howard's first year. Together, Blair and I would push our baby carriages around the block and enjoy each other's companionship. Steve worked in the post office near us and made a fine salary. We enjoyed exchanging dinners and playing bridge.

I still felt insecure caring for Howard – afraid I would hurt him in some way. He had a stopped-up nose and a low-grade temperature when he was 6 months old. Dr. Tom told me to crush 1/4 aspirin in some milk and feed it to him from a teaspoon. I had never given Howard any medicine. When I tried, Howard pushed his tongue out and the milk and aspirin ran down his chin. I called Ray's sister Polly, who was an RN and head of the pediatrics ward at Vanderbilt Hospital, to ask her how to get Howard to swallow his medicine. Polly said, "Oh, Martha, just hold his mouth open and poke it down his throat."

During this year, Ray's brother Ed ran into difficulty with his insulin problem. He was diagnosed as a diabetic at the age of 18 years – the same year insulin became available for treating diabetics. During 1939 he was living in Detroit where he owned a transport truck that he drove between New York and Detroit. One day he was found unconscious in his truck, parked on the side of a street in Detroit. He was placed in a hospital where they thought he was in insulin shock but didn't know enough about the condition of a diabetic and were placing him in deeper shock. His friends with whom he lived located him in the hospital, called his father, who called Ray. It was decided Ray would go to Detroit – a drain on our finances. Ray moved Ed to a different hospital where there was a knowledgeable staff and they brought him around to normal. But Ed could no longer drive a truck. He sold his truck, and came back to the farm in Murfreesboro, which had been leased out for several years. Ed and Mr. White then moved back into the big house and began to personally operate the farm and build up the herd of milk cows.

Before settling down at the farm Ed stayed with us for 3 or 4 weeks to be near the Vanderbilt diabetic clinic. There he established a doctor relationship and his condition was stabilized. Once during this time, when Ray was at school, Ed went into insulin shock. He would not take orange juice from me and became so argumentative and angry with me that I became afraid for Howard and me. I called Ray at school. He came home and took Ed to Vanderbilt for more testing. Ed was a dear and thoughtful brother-in-law, but this could change quickly when his insulin was not balanced. Ray loved Ed dearly because he was the brother who always took up for him and helped him fight his battles when they were children. Often, instead of helping Ray, John A just egged the fight on. Ray would remember Ed's kindness all his life.

Howard outgrew his cradle and began sleeping in my iron baby bed, which is painted white. That winter I dressed him in a pair of little boy's button-on pants and a little boy's shirt. For his first Easter I made him a white pique buttoned-in-front coat and bought him a white cap. We have several pictures of him in this outfit. During his first summer he wore one-piece sun suits that Aunt Mamie made. He loved his swimsuit and would help his Dad wash the car by holding the hose.

The first and second summer of Howard's life was spent mostly at home. Ray was doing construction work building "Berry Hill" housing project and helping Mr. Maples. He was exhausted by the end of a hot working day. There was no air conditioning in our apartment and I do not remember a fan. We would spread a quilt in the backyard, turn on a small radio, get Howard to sleep, and rest on the quilt until the night cooled off. Our neighbors were the Archers. Mr. and Mrs. Archer worked and Mr. Archer's mother was a "germ nut." She used Kleenex to open doors, talk on the telephone, etc. She never came into our side of the house, and hardly spoke to Howard – a very unusual woman.

In the fall of 1939 Ray got a teaching job with Nashville City Schools at Bailey Junior High School. He taught math. His salary jumped by $10 per month on a 10-

month yearly contract. He was not as good at teaching math as he had been at teaching manual arts because he was too impatient. When he graded papers he couldn't understand why some students did not understand the math process. He stayed at Bailey 2 years, and then moved to Howard High School, where he was a full-time manual arts teacher – a subject he taught well and successfully.

Ray, Howard and I went downtown for dinner at Shacklett's (across from the old Cain-Sloan). I bought whipped potatoes for Howard, who was about 2 years old. He got a lot of smiles and pats on the head as he sat in his high chair and ate his potatoes with his thumb. He was a darling handsome little boy. Another outing we enjoyed included Auntie, Aunt Susie, and Uncle Arthur. We all went to Cascade Plunge, which was at the end of Wedgewood Avenue, on the State Fair Grounds. This pool was large, with 3 diving boards, a tall slide into the water and a child's play pool, complete with swings and slides for under 6-year-old children. Howard took to the water wholeheartedly, swinging and going down the slide with fun sparkling in his eyes.

John was conceived during August 1940. My morning sickness was not as great as it had been with my first pregnancy. I had learned that ice-cold cokes and salted soda crackers would alleviate the sickness. Dr. Tom was my doctor as well as Howard's. His office was in one of the old resident houses on the Vanderbilt University campus, where he was the student and athletic doctor. He was a good family friend and doctor until his death – a fine man.

In good weather I continued my walks around the block with Howard in a stroller. Blair Stevens and her son Virgil would sometimes go with me. Dickinson McGavock had built a small new house at the end of Allison Place. His wife had a baby boy during this year, so we enjoyed walking together. Her son Dick became a counselor at Boy's Club Camp, and later married a former Peace Corps Volunteer who had served with John's group in the Philippines. They divorced. Then she remarried and has been a guest in our home on Lynwood, and she occasionally calls me.

I received several comments during this pregnancy. An older friend said I was a good and pretty mother. Another friend said I was so big that I looked like a barrel rolling along.

Each morning during the week a fresh produce truck would stop on the street, and I would buy fresh vegetables. We were still paying off the car notes, and Ray made the final payment on his loan from Middle Tennessee College. Then he did what I considered a foolish thing. He bought from a friend, John Judd, a set of encyclopedias to be paid off by the end of the 1940-41 school year. So the red covered set and 2 large dictionaries were bought at a cost of $50 – at a great hardship on us.

In the spring 1941 we got things ready for the new baby. I filled out my layette needs from Cain Sloan's with Mrs. Johnson's help. I placed Howard's clothes in a drawer in my chest of drawers and filled the baby chest with layette items. We brought the walnut cradle from Springfield and continued our routine of home life – there was very little socializing at this time. I was busy making day gowns, a special dress for John and receiving blankets. I had been told in my March examination that Dr. Tom could hear two hearts beating and thought I would have twins – earlier he said because of the fast heart beat of the fetus that the baby would probably be a girl. Also he said the fetus was growing breach. Labor began about 2 weeks before the expected time of delivery, in the spring, while I was trying to do some spring-cleaning. I had taken down the living room sheer curtains, washed them, starched them and placed them on stretchers. I had just finished hanging them with Ray's help when the pain started – an intense pain. Howard was asleep in his bed, so we asked our next-door neighbors, the Archers, to look in on him and left ajar the door opening into the hall. Again, I went to St. Thomas Hospital. I was immediately taken to the delivery anteroom. Then Ray went home to be with Howard. Again, I was left to give birth without my husband waiting in a nearby room. A nurse stayed with me. I was crying and screaming for sedation. They said they could not give me any because they wanted the baby to right itself into the proper birthing position in the canal. He was doubled up and trying to get into the canal feet first and with crossed arms. I did not stay long in this anteroom, for they took me into delivery room. It was a white room; I was facing two windows with a clock between them: it read 6 o'clock. There was a thunderstorm with heavy lightning and rain sharply hitting the windows. A nurse placed a gas mask over my nose. I could feel myself slipping into a nice sleep with pain lessening; then two nurses on each side of me at the head of the bed started slapping my face, telling me to wake up that I had to cooperate and bear down. I could distinguish Dr. Tom and two other gowned men at the foot of my bed. Dr. Tom said in a tense strained voice that they had to get the umbilical cord from around his neck or the baby would strangle himself. They also were trying to straighten his legs, but John was born buttocks first with his legs up against his body, which resulted in a pulled muscle in the upper part of his right leg. His cries were a relief to everyone. Dr. Tom said to me several times in after years how grateful he was that John was a live baby because he felt sure he was going to lose him in birthing. Immediately, they put me out like a light. My next memory was later in the day in a private room with Ray sitting beside me and a vase of gladiolus by my bedside. I asked about the baby; Ray appeared to be evasive in answering me. The nurse brought John into the room for his first nursing. I held him in my arms and he screamed bloody murder. I was frightened and the nurse said Dr. Tom would talk to me about why John was in so much pain. This gave me more fright. I checked for all his parts – he had all fingers, toes, legs, and arms. Dr. Tom came in about that time. He explained the pulled muscle. Already doctors had examined John ruling out nerve, vascular, and bone damage he could have sustained in birthing. Dr. Tom explained they had circumcised John and clipped the excessive connective tissue between his tongue and the palate of his mouth. Howard also had this done at birth. Both boys had inherited this physical trait from me, which is the reason I cannot make certain sounds and combination of sounds. Howard had been circumcised 6 weeks following his birth, which had been standard practice then.

I stayed in the hospital 5 days. Mother and Aunt Mamie came over to stay with Howard. When I came home Aunt Mamie stayed one week longer than Mother, who was still working. After Aunt Mamie left (we paid her for her work), a practical nurse stayed for 3 weeks, sleeping in the living room on the canvas cot.

Every time John moved his leg he would cry; we would rock him night and day for 6 weeks. I could not give enough milk, so he was put on a formula soon after birth. Dr. Tom suggested we place both Howard and John under the care of Dr. Overall, the leading pediatrician in Nashville. I carried out his instructions carefully and minutely to the best of my ability, because my boys and my home life were the core and center of my life. I worried that Howard might feel left out because of the constant attention that John required. One day I missed Howard. I called and called, ran outside, looked up and down the street, asked the neighbors if they had seem him, went back in the house calling Howard by name, he answered in a small frightened voice from the kitchen pantry. Only 2 years 8 months old when John was born, Howard was sitting on the floor eating sweet pickles from a jar. About this time we realized his hearing was not accurate; sometimes he would appear not to hear us. One day we were talking to Auntie on the phone and placed the receiver to Howard's right ear. He did not respond to Auntie. We changed the receiver to his left ear and immediately Howard's face lit up and he responded to Auntie. This we knew was wrong. He could hear only out of his left ear. Dr. Overall examined Howard's hearing, as did a hearing specialist, Dr. Bill Wilkinson, also of Nashville. They concluded that no nerve had been formed in the right ear – therefore, no hearing. Dr. Wilkinson recommended that, when Howard was 4 years old, he undergo X-ray treatment in hopes that might stimulate growth of the hearing nerve in the right ear. We went along with the recommendation; it did not work, and we later realized that subjecting Howard to X-rays was a mistake.

When Howard was 5 years old his tonsils were removed in hopes that would help generate the hearing nerve, but nothing happened. We were told everything possible had been done. Dr. Overall and the Bill Wilkerson Hearing clinic continued to follow Howard's hearing until adulthood, but no further treatments were attempted. The hearing in his left ear remained very good. But he could never tell the direction from which sound was coming, and in a noisy situation he had difficulty hearing conversation from people on his right. Because of his hearing deficiency he was not drafted into the armed services during the Vietnam War.

By the time John became about 2 months old our life became routine again. No longer did I have to rock him most of the night so the neighbors and Ray (with cotton stuffed in his ears) could sleep. Howard had accepted John and I was trying to again spend more time with Howard. We resumed our walks. I placed Howard's toys (small cars and trucks, etc.) in the breakfast room and spent more time reading to him. Both boys had their baths each morning; John, in the small baby bathtub, followed by Howard in the sink – a large white enameled sink with large enameled drain boards on each side. This made an ideal bathing facility. Naps, both in the morning and afternoon, for boys gave me enough free time to cook, wash clothes, iron, clean house, etc. Nancy, the daughter of Felix Haynes, still came one day a week to clean and Mrs. Haynes still did laundry for us.

For Easter that year, at Loveman's, I bought for Howard a navy blue coat with brass buttons and a navy cap. He had graduated into real boy's clothes. I bought shoes at Armstrong's Specialty Store. Everything else was bought at Loveman's, in the boy's department on the balcony: knit shirts, underwear, socks, pajamas, etc.

Both boys had the proper shots, food supplements, etc., as recommended by Dr. Overall.

Summer 1942 was the time for me to have my wisdom teeth out. Dr. Boyd was in the Medical Arts Building downtown and chose to take out the upper two, which were crowding my teeth. Blair Stephen's sister, Jim Lee Allen, visited her at this time. I missed a bridge luncheon for Jim Lee but went to a dinner party for her the night before my wisdom teeth came out. This was the beginning of a pleasant friendship, which lasted until her death in 1991. She was teaching at Hillsboro High School when I started teaching. I was taken into the ladies faculty bridge group and invited to their luncheons and parties – this was a select group of 8 ladies – all lady faculty members were not invited into the group. I replaced Dot Moss (Mrs. J. E. Moss, who had stopped teaching when her husband became Superintendent of Davidson County schools).

After John was born he had many gifts from relatives and friends. One thing he enjoyed was a small wooden horse (given by Ovalina Maples) that he could bang onto the floor causing the horse to change position. He did not like to stay in his playpen. When he began to pull up on his feet he was constantly trying to climb over. At that age Howard had played with his toys in the playpen, but John wanted out. Howard especially liked a little wooden stand and hammer, where he could hammer pegs into the proper size holes. Both of them liked a canvas swing that I hung in a doorway. Both Howard and John met their age achievements on their growth and development charts – having had courses in child care and child play, I was keeping up with their progress in my course books.

Auntie, Uncle Arthur, and Aunt Susie liked for us all to go to Centennial Park with a picnic lunch, feed the ducks, play in the playground and sit in the old horse-drawn streetcar, which the park had turned over to children to crawl in and out and over. This was something they had done for me when I was a small child. Occasionally, we would go to Shelby Park, rent a pontoon boat or rowboat and play in the children's playground. We would have a picnic at the community center on the Cumberland River. We would walk down to the riverbank and skip rocks on the water.

Chapter 13 – The War Years

One summer day in 1942 I decided to spend the day at Cascade pool with Howard and John, who was 16 months old. I walked to the pool, pushing John in the stroller. I dressed them in their tight maroon stretch swimsuits, which were alike. John didn't like his. We walked to the baby's pool. Howard walked down the steps. John balked. So John and I sat on the top step – then we moved down another step until we were sitting on the bottom step with water up over John's tummy. Only then was he ready to walk in the water and swing on the swing. Since then John has enjoyed water sports and become proficient in swimming, skiing, and diving. We ate our lunch at a picnic table and walked home for afternoon naps. This we did several times.

John was a beautiful little boy with his golden curly hair, blue eyes, fair complexion, and a ready smile for everyone. When he was learning to walk and keep his balance steady Ray's sister Margaret Shands and her children, Anna K. and Robert, came to visit. Anna K. was 2 or 3 years older than Howard and Robert was about 6 months older than John. They stayed several days sleeping on the canvas cot, sofa, and a pad on the floor. The children got along well with the exception of Robert, who was walking with perfect balance. He would walk up to John, place his open hand on John's chest and push him to the floor. This would cause a commotion, which all the children enjoyed, except John. I remember Margaret went to Cain-Sloan and bought for herself a lot of new clothes. This was a major purpose of the visit, for their home in New Albany, Mississippi, a small town, had minimal clothing stores. While Margaret shopped and visited friends from her college days, I kept the children in our apartment. I remember being very disappointed that she did not show any appreciation toward me – she did not give me a personal gift, a hostess gift, or buy any food or take us out to eat.

We always celebrated birthdays of Howard and John. I either made them a cake or bought one. Howard's big birthday, at 4-years old, was celebrated on Allison Place by inviting the neighborhood children. There was a picnic table in the back yard, many balloons, and presents. We have good pictures of this party. His other birthdays (1, 2, 3) were celebrated at Mother's with family present. John's first birthday was celebrated at Mother's in Springfield.

Polly often visited us for a meal, often bringing a nurse friend or her boyfriend, Bill Clark. As a nurse she was doing very well. She had an efficiency apartment near Vanderbilt and had bought a new Chevrolet. She would bring gifts to Howard and John, but never to me. I was disappointed that she did not help with the food when I was cooking for her and her friends.

 We would drive to Springfield once a month on Sunday to have dinner with Mother and sometimes go to church. She would invite other family members over as well. At other times, about once per month, we would drive to the farm near Murfreesboro to visit Mr. White and Ed. When going to the farm I would always take food, already prepared, for a meal. Mr. White and Ed were beginning to garden, which was great, for we brought home fresh vegetables. Another time Jean and Harold Bates and their son Paul spent a few days with us.

In the fall of 1942 we were asked to move. Mr. Maples suggested we look at a small two-bedroom house near Central High School, which was selling for about $3,000. But Ray and I were not interested in the location or house. Howard would, within 2 years, be going to school, and we did not want him to go to Fall's School. Ray said he wanted to build his first house with Mr. Maple's help. War was threatening at the time. We made a big mistake not buying that house because prices of houses went sky high during the war, and we could not build because of shortage of materials. Blair and Steve Stephens and their son Virgil had moved that summer to Abbott Martin Road, so Virgil could go to a better school. The family next door to us, with a little boy and girl, had moved to a better school area for their children as well.

We rented the downstairs half of a 4-unit home on Eighth Avenue. This was a nice large building, but it had the same living arrangement as the one on Allison Place; we had a private bath and, in the basement, a full paneled room with a shower and toilet. This downstairs area was reached by going down stairway and through the storage area in the basement. There was no direct connection to our apartment. I was afraid to go down there by myself or to let the boys go without me. So it was used for storage. The owner of the house did not live there, and at all times he kept the basement doors unlocked in both directions for safety in case of fire. By erecting a wire fence between the side of the house and the fence next door, Ray built a protected outdoor play area along the side of the house for the boys. And he installed a sand box and placed other play equipment, including tricycles, trucks and a swing. A back porch connected with this play area and our kitchen. This made an excellent place for the boys. We continued our walks with John in the stroller. Ovalina Maples sold us their maple baby bed for John. During our stay on Eighth Avenue Ray made the cherry drop-leaf dining room table and the coffee table. We had placed newspapers in the floor in front of the sofa and drew the outline and size of the coffee table so it would be in proportion. At the farm Ray found an old picture frame that was coming to pieces. He glued it together, refinished it and built in two shelves. We hung this above the table in the living room. Mr. White said the frame was one of 12, which he and Mrs. White received as a wedding present from her uncle, Flem Story, the lawyer.

There was one drawback to moving to this part of town – I did not know anyone. I was lonely for lady friends and friends for Howard and John. I did not drive and Ray used the car every day. By this time he had been transferred to Howard High School, where he taught drafting and manual arts. He was an excellent woodworking teacher. The principal, Mr. Gruber was a friend. He owned a farm on Nashville Pike, near the White farm, outside of Murfreesboro. We occasionally got together for diner and bridge. Mr. Gruber made no objection to Ray using the shop after school hours and on the weekends. Ray made new fence gates (bought material himself) for the farm. He made beehives, took them to the farm and settled bees in them. For Castner

Knott's he repaired damaged merchandise. He made items for other people. For Howard and John, he made a wooden seesaw, wooden guns, a swing with back and sides, a wooden train, and small toys. He made the wooden cabinet (now painted red) to hold linens and dishes in the kitchen, for we had an old-fashioned kitchen without any cabinets and with a gas stove.

The war was on in full force. Gas and sugar were rationed. The couple next door (across the fence) did not drive out of town often, so she offered me gas ration tickets, which we used to go to Springfield to visit Mother and to the farm to visit Mr. White, Ed, and John A. We would bring back home lots of vegetables. I got my start in canning, making pickles, chow-chow, etc. Thus, we were able to have plenty of food throughout the winter.

Doug Jeffords had opened a locker building for frozen foods in the Melrose section of Eighth Avenue South. We rented a large locker. John A., Ed and Mr. White rented a similar type locker in Murfreesboro. The three of them and Ray bought a beef to split and freeze. We continued sharing beef and pork for many years, which was a great help to our finances and health.

During the summer of 1942 Ray was in charge of the YMCA outdoors program for teenage boys (8 to 16 years old) on the Central High School campus and inside the gym. After this program he worked in the Central High shop making items for other people. And it was during this time that he made our gate-leg table and our cherry coffee table.

During 1943 I did spring cleaning early because Nashville's soot was into everything. After one month of hard work I had just finished cleaning the curtains, the windows, the bathroom, and the kitchen. At this point the manager told us he wanted our apartment for a nephew who had married. This was terrible. Because of the war there were no houses or apartments for rent at a reasonable price, and we couldn't afford a down payment on a house purchase. But the manager did give us until late summer to find a place to live.

During the spring we invited my cousin, Martha Lou Simpkins, for the weekend and, for Saturday night we invited Ray's brother John A. for dinner and Michigan poker. Martha Lou and John A. hit it off right away. They would begin dating and would marry. Ray, I, and Martha Lou drove John A. back to the farm later that evening. On Sunday, Martha Lou rode the bus back to Springfield. Before she got on the city bus at Douglas Corner, we went with Martha Lou to the drug store, where she bought her mother a box of candy.

During the winter months we started going to Blakemore Methodist Church on Tenth Avenue near Falls School. Dr. Anderson had visited us and invited us to church. He had been a pastor in Springfield and knew about my Bell background in the Methodist Church, although Mother was a Presbyterian. The White family had a Baptist background both on the Wood and White side. The first time we went to Sunday School, John was about 22 months old. He went into the nursery. He cried when I left him, but Mrs. Sheridan, a sister to Ann Moss, said she could quiet him. But she could not quiet him, and finally she sent someone to come for me. After that first Sunday John calmed down and seemed to enjoy going to Sunday School and being with Mrs. Sheridan. Her son Bill would go to Central High and be in Ray's class. He had been at Ned Ransom's camp with us the first summer Ray and I had married. Now Bill Sheridan is a medical doctor and a member of the Centennial Medical Association, which from its first year has been very successful. Howard had no trouble in his Sunday School class. I went to the Young Married Ladies' Class. Mrs. Fischer was our teacher. Each month we had a social gathering at someone's house. Also in this class was Mattie Pearl Regen who taught at Hillsboro High School when I went there as a teacher and was a member of the faculty bridge group into which I was invited. Pearl and I continued playing bridge with other faculty members until her death in 1989. She was a special friend. At one Sunday School class gathering I was hostess with several other ladies, and we decided to serve grape juice and ginger ale with cake and ice cream. A young missionary on sabbatical leave who was visiting our class was there. She was very upset over the fact we were serving "wine." Even after we explained that it was grape juice and ginger ale, she wouldn't drink any. Pearl and I had many a laugh over that. Ray went to the Young Men's Class. His class was never invited to our monthly socials.

During the early part of the summer I took Howard to Falls School for a summer check-in for upcoming first graders. He needed more clothes for school, so I made him and John several pieces of clothing. Mother gave me her sewing machine, which she had bought after I married. She thought she would learn to sew, but was busy working at the telephone company and with her flower garden and canning, preserving and fruit drying. My aunts gave me old woolen pants and jackets belonging to the men in the family, especially some of Billy Worsham's old clothes. I ripped these old woolens open at the seams, washed the cloth, steam-pressed it and made short pants and Eton jackets for Howard and John. I made white shirts for the boys out of the good tail end of the old men's white shirts. I bought camouflaged print cotton cloth at the downtown army surplus store for 3 cents a yard and made pajamas for the boys. I bought Carter's knit underwear, socks and polo shirts from the boy's shop at Loveman's on Fifth Avenue. From the same store I bought a brown reused-wool overcoat and a cap with earmuffs for Howard. One-hundred-percent-new wool cloth was unavailable because of the war. John wore Howard's navy blue overcoat with leggings and a cap with earmuffs, which I had bought earlier at Loveman's.

In our bedroom John, who slept in his bed on Ray's side of our bed, would say, "Pat me Daddy" to get him to sleep. Howard slept in his white iron bed on my side.

Dr. Overall decided that Howard should have his tonsils and adenoids out the spring of 1943. He went to Baptist Hospital for surgery. He and I spent the night in a semi-private room with another lady and her daughter. Howard wanted some juice, and when the doctor visited the next morning, he asked for some. Dr. Overall asked Howard what kind of juice he wanted. Howard said "orange juice." The doctor agreed it would be good for him, but the acid in the juice hurt Howard's throat as it went down. I have wondered why the doctor would have agreed with orange juice rather than suggest something not so acid. Howard got along fine with his surgery; however, several weeks later he developed a high fever. This temp was over 104 degrees. It frightened me. Dr. Tom gave him a prescription medicine over the phone about 8 o'clock at night. He said to take his temperature each hour all night long – if it did not start down, to call him again. There was a chance Howard might go into convulsions. Dr. Tom also told me to sponge Howard's body with a damp cloth each hour. We filled the washtub with tap water so that we could put Howard in the bath water with any signs of convulsion. This was one night that I got no sleep. The next day his temperature was normal.

To celebrate John's third birthday, I made a chocolate cake and decorated it with white icing. We invited the girl and boy who also lived in the apartment. They were older than Howard and John. We had a picnic lunch, cake and ice cream on the picnic table in the side yard.

One evening John fell in the kitchen, hit his head on the edge of the cabinet, and cut a gash in his forehead. Blood began to flow from the cut. All the neighbors in the apartment came and stood in the kitchen doorway to look at the screaming child. Ray was trying to find the pressure spot to help stop the flow of blood. I was on the phone trying to call Dr. Tom, but no one answered his phone. Ray said to call Dr. Lucius Caldwell – a friend of the White family. When Dr. Caldwell answered the phone I was so relieved that I had found a doctor, I started crying almost hysterically. This elderly kind man said, "Just give me your address, I will be there as quickly as possible." When he came in he understood who we were and stayed about an hour. I have forgotten whether he took stitches in the cut, but I suppose he did. His presence and kindness calmed both of us. John still has the nail shaped scar on his forehead.

The Caldwell home place was in the Nolensville community, in which Dr. Caldwell's brother and sister lived. Dr. Caldwell and his wife had built a beautiful brick house there when that community had first begun to build. This was about a mile from where we were living. Throughout their lives we visited the Caldwells and had dinner with them several times. Dr. and Mrs. Caldwell moved back to the home place following his retirement. One day Mrs. Caldwell brought out family scrapbooks for me to see. She explained that she thought that Mr. White's family was related to them through the White's who founded Knoxville. I wish I had been interested in family genealogy at that time. Ray and his brothers and sisters called Dr. Caldwell, "Cousin Lucius." His son, Sam Caldwell, had a radio program called "The Old Dirt Dauber" on which he answered questions regarding raising flowers, garden vegetables and trees. Once I called Sam to find out what to do with the three money plants that one of my students had brought me. Sam talked about one hour on raising money plants; said they were very difficult to grow; told me about their life cycles; asked questions about the family, and seemed to appreciate my call. The family is dead now, the old house has new owners who have renovated it.

During the summer of 1943 we had the same visitors as

previous years: Margaret Shands and her children, Anna K. and Robert; Polly and Bill Clark and their son Billy; Ed and John A.; Aunt Effie and Uncle Clem; Auntie, Aunt Susie and Uncle Arthur; Mother; Mr. White and his lady friend, Miss Lura Williamson, and our dinner and bridge friends.

Mr. White had started dating Miss Lura some time following Mrs. White's death. The Williamson farm and the White farm were approximately 2 miles apart. Their friendship had continued when he worked in Detroit at the Ford plant before Ray and I married. He had given her a ruby ring as a Christmas present when he was in Detroit. This is the large ruby ring I now have, which she wanted me to have. Miss Laura was a grade school teacher in the Nashville City schools and boarded with the Beasley family, who lived not very far from Ray and me. When Mr. White would visit us Ray would drive him and Miss Lura to a movie, a lecture, or a community affair. When visiting they would often have dinner with us, and Mr. White would spend the night with us. They made a gracious, educated and good-looking couple. History, English literature (especially Shakespeare, which Mr. White could quote line after line to suit the occasion) and the Bible made up the topics of their discussions.

In 1942 we made an automobile trip to North Carolina with Mother, Mr. White and Miss Lura. Aunt Susie took care of Howard and John. Of course the car was not air-conditioned. We went to Knoxville, and then up the valley to Johnson City, where Mr. White had attended a boy's private high school. Here we found only the gym still standing, for the school had long since been torn down. Then we went to King College, which Mr. White had attended for 2 years, before he started teaching. Then we went over the mountains to Plum Tree, North Carolina, where we spent the night with the Burleson family. The Burlesons were first cousins of Mr. White's. The family operated a "bed and board" place at Plum Tree in the summer. We visited a cemetery where his sister was buried, and visited his boyhood friend, Dave Vance, President of the Mica Company. We also visited another first cousin who owned a clothing store in Spruce Pine. We visited an aunt. All this time Mr. White and Miss Lura talked about history. I have a few pictures of this trip. Sadly, it was about this time, 1943, that Miss Lura discovered she had cancer. It caused her death soon after 1943.

The war moved on. Three of my first cousins were in the military: Cornelius Bell, Billy Worsham and Clem Lane, Jr. Ray received his notice to go before the draft board. It placed him in 4F because of his heart. Bob Shands, Margaret's husband had been called to service as a surgeon. This was difficult for them. They had bought a small hospital in New Albany, Mississippi, and had built a house there. With the help of the staff, including the doctors still in the area, Margaret ran the hospital. She was a Registered Nurse, having been trained at St. Thomas Hospital in Nashville. Mr. White and Ed went to live with her for a year to provide protection and help with her property – leaving John A. at the farm. John A. married Martha Lou Simpkins the following year. Polly and Bill Clark had moved to Baltimore, Maryland, where, with a partner, he opened an air conditioning company. They received contracts for air conditioning Navy ships that were based in Baltimore Harbor. They were successful in their business, but Bill would die young, leaving two boys, Billy and Tom, for Polly to raise. Following Bill's death, his partner and Polly would continue the business for a while. Then, Polly sold her partnership and became a nurse supervisor in a Maryland State Nursing Home.

In the summer of 1943 I lost the household services of Nancy and her mother. They had moved back to their home across the road from the White farm in Murfreesboro. We started sending our clothes "damp wash" to White Way laundry with flat wear ironed (sheets, towels, pillow cases, etc.) and Ray's shirts finished. Ray would take our laundry to and from White Way, located on Sixteenth Avenue. Mr. Sofgee was the manager.

We continued to get together with our social friends – exchanging dinner and bridge, but with children present. One night John and Madelain Koen, and their son, were having dinner with us. Sitting in his high chair my John leaned over and grabbed the cord to the electric percolator that sat on the sewing machine, which I was using as a serving table. Hot coffee went everywhere but no one was severely burned.

John loved his night bottle of milk. He would quickly finish it in bed, stand up, throw the bottle on the floor and demand more milk. Then he would pull himself up to the top railing and roll himself over, falling to the floor. After he did this twice, we knew we had to do something. So Ray built a top for the bed using wooden slats, which provided lots of opening for light and airflow. This prevented John from falling out. At this time he was only 13 or 14 months old. To help him go to sleep each night we patted him and told him stories or read to him.

There was another thing John did that caused me much worry. Between 2 and 3 years old he learned to climb up and fall over the top of the wire fence separating the house next door from our play area. One time I barely caught him before he headed out to the street. He had run down the alley toward Eighth Avenue. My only solution to that problem was to stay with him at all times when he and Howard were in the playground. Being close in age, they were good playmates and loved each other in a wonderful brother relationship. This continued throughout childhood.

During the summer of 1943 we were forced to move again. In August we moved to a small four-room frame house on Stewart Ferry Pike in Donelson. It had no running water and no telephone. We drew water from a well by hauling it up in a bucket using a hand winch. There was only an outdoor toilet. Except for camp and my childhood days with Aunt Johnnies house in Springfield, these were the most primitive living conditions I had ever lived in.

Howard entered the first grade at Donelson Grammar School. The teacher was Mrs. Emily McDonald, a native of Springfield, whom I had known all my life and whose parents were friends of Mother's. She gave Howard special attention and was considerate of his hearing disability. I had taken interest in teaching Howard and John numbers, reading, concepts, etc., to prepare them for school. Each night I read to them after they went to bed. An elderly friend had given them a large picture Bible for children. They had books of all kinds and games suited to their age. So they were ready for school – more so than the average child.

The owner of our little house lived across the street. They had a little girl John's age. Up the street was a girl a year or two older than Howard. The children had to walk two miles to the bus stop. Mothers usually walked with them in the morning and afternoon. Ray drove Howard to school when his schedule fitted in. In this way we made friends with two families – but were never social friends. I used the telephone across the street for emergency calls. I could tell she became aggravated if I made a social call to a friend and talked too long (remember there was a war and telephones were hard to come by. We had had a telephone in Nashville, but a transfer to Donelson was not permitted). John and our dog, Brownie, always walked with me if no one else did. Ray was offered Brownie as a puppy. Her mother was a trained war dog at Vine Hill Army Camp. Brownie grew into a large guard dog, protective of the boys and me. She was a German shepherd with long curly brownish-red hair. She did not snap nor show any anger with Howard and John, nor any of their friends. While we were living on Stewart Ferry's Pike she had her first litter of puppies: beautiful little balls of brown fur. We gave them to the pet shop on Eighth Avenue in Nashville.

The days were long for me. Total control of the house and the boys fell upon my shoulders. Ray taught at Howard High School, leaving home before 7 o'clock. After school until 6:30, 2 days a week, he had the Boys' Club physical education program at Martha O'Bryan Methodist Center, not far from Howard High School. Three evenings a week, from 7 to 9 o'clock, he taught drafting at Watkins Night School. That left Saturday as our day to grocery shop, run errands, etc. Each night I read to the boys at least an hour before they went to sleep. We kept Brownie in the house with us for protection. I felt very lonely and cut off from people: no telephone, newspaper, family, friends or transportation. The only house in sight was the one across the road. I don't believe Ray ever fully realized the extent of hardship he had imposed on the boys and me. He was accustomed to country living, but I was not. During the winter only the boys' room and the kitchen were warm enough. I was always afraid of the little coal stove in the boys' room – fearful it would start a fire.

This is the year Ray made the two cherry beds – one each for Howard and John. We gave John's baby bed to Clem Junior's baby, and Betty Lee Cotter of Springfield borrowed Howard's baby bed for her son Charles, and later for her son Ray. Then the bed was stored at the farm until we used it for the grandchildren, Howie and Keith.

I was so lonely that Mother insisted I move my piano from Springfield to the little frame house. I taught Howard and John the notes on the piano and simple melodies. We sang together with the two neighborhood children. This was great fun.

We attended the Methodist Church in Donelson. Mrs. Fischer, who had moved from the Nashville community to Donelson, taught the ladies class. They had parties each month, but I did not go because there was no one to stay with Howard and John, nor did I have transportation.

Howard and John had mumps this year – during the winter months. That is the only illness I remember during our stay on Stewart's Ferry Pike. During the summer I canned or preserved 500 cans of food. Ray built a special set of shelves to hold the glass quart jars in the kitchen. This is now antiqued black, set up in the basement, and used to hold books, etc. I took pride in my food preservation – this added a decorative note to the yellow walls in my kitchen.

That summer my friend of Allison Place, Blair Stephens, had a serious kidney disease. Her husband, Steve, had a short nervous condition. To get their children away from them so they could have some peace and quiet, I kept Virgil and his little brother for one week. They were not accustomed to country living. Each time I put the younger boy in the zinc metal round tub in the middle of our kitchen for a bath he would scream bloody murder. I solved that problem by putting bathing suits on the 4 boys, walking them to the creek, and bathing them in the creek. They thought that was great fun. Blair Stephens died a few years later.

The social circle of friends we had developed in Nashville was slowly ebbing away. The Maples had moved to their family farm in Rutherford County. Angus ran his own construction company and managed the farm. He had once offered to partner with Ray in the construction business, but Ray declined. Jimmy and Henrietta Durham and their boys had transferred to Maryville, Tennessee, with American Airlines – a big promotion for him. Walter and Billie Hall were getting a divorce – he had gone back in the army when war started and afterward married a girl in Germany. He died soon after marriage while playing tennis in Germany. His ex-wife, daughter, and son moved to Nashville, where she went back to teaching. That was a sad situation. John and Madeline Koen were having marital problems. She had had a nervous breakdown and they were living on a family farm in Williamson County. John Koen had become principal of Hillsboro High School. John and Corrine Judd had built a larger home off of Tyne Blvd., and he had opened his own insurance office, but soon he was in trouble, financially. There were marital problems that led to divorce.

So you can understand why I was at loose ends – having always had a close circle of friends. I decided it was time for me to learn to drive. Ray saw no need for it, but I was determined. We would drive out in front of the house and I would try to shift gears going up and down the hilly gravel road. Ray would get angry when I would kill the engine. He lost patience with me. I gave up trying for a while. Eventually I would learn to drive at Boys' Club Camp, going to and from the store, in a war surplus car.
 One summer day the boys disappeared. I called and called, but there was no answer and our dog, Brownie was nowhere in sight. I was afraid they had run into snakes because we had been told there were rattlesnakes on the hills back of our house and on both sides. Finally,

I heard a weak answer. John and Howard were hiding in a dip in the ground next to the driveway. I was so upset, and relieved they were fine that I got a thin switch and switched their legs. This I regret. I believe that is the only time I struck them in anger. I hope they have forgiven me and understand my reason.

At the end of the school year Ray took a new job as Executive Director of Nashville Boy's Club. He worked from a desk on Church Street in the Whitsitt Real Estate Office, where Ann Whitsitt provided secretarial services. At that time the Boy's Club operated in various community centers in the Nashville Housing Authority projects and at church-sponsored locations, including Centenary Methodist Institute, the Martha O'Brien House, Teen Town at Woodbine, St. Luke's Community House, and the Lucy Holt Moore Gymnasium. His job included hiring personnel, overseeing the activities in each center, budgeting, working at fund-raising with Community Chest (later United Giver's Fund), liaison with the churches and the communities, seeking donations for operating a summer camp, and getting out a monthly newsletter to the members of the Board, to whom he was responsible.

He enjoyed this work and the companionship of people downtown. Our first convention was in the latter part of May 1944 in New York City. This was a great adventure for me. Expenses were paid for both of us. Mother and Aunt Mamie stayed with Howard and John. Ray and I rode the train, sitting up all night. I remember our stop in Pittsburgh – we passed several steel mills, lit up with bright lights, and saw white-hot iron being poured into molds. I enjoyed eating in the diner car – especially the orange marmalade at breakfast. (I had never seen nor heard of it before.) We stayed at the Commodore Hotel on Forty-second Street, next door to Central Station. It was a beautiful hotel – my first. If I remember correctly we stayed on the seventeenth floor. I had done a lot of reading on New York, and Ray and I had selected some of the places we wanted to see. There was a hostess desk in the lobby. Each morning I would talk with her about our plans for the day. She was most helpful, giving me maps, illustrative material, etc. On our last day there she said to me, "You are not afraid to get out on your own and explore. I admire you for that. Most wives stay in their rooms and won't get out on the streets by themselves." Ray attended his morning meetings, sometimes the luncheons, and one evening banquet. That left us considerable free time. I walked "miles" window-shopping by myself. I went through Macy's, Bloomingdale's, several art galleries, and explored the shops under Grand Central Station and the Commodore Hotel. I ate meals in the automats and little snack bars.

Ray and I saw a show at Radio City; rode the ferry to the Statue of Liberty; rode the subway to Coney Island and the zoo; walked through Chinatown and ate a great dinner in a Chinese restaurant; saw Wall Street; "Little Church Around the Corner;" Trinity Church (the oldest cemetery in New York), Frances Tavern where George Washington took the oath of office as the first President of the United States; St. Patrick's Cathedral, and Central Park. One morning I met Una Waddell at the hostess desk. She was going to buy lace and ribbons and wanted to know where to go. I spent the morning with her in shops. Her husband was Executive Director of the Eldorado Boys' Club in Arkansas. This was the beginning of a great friendship between the Waddell's and Ray and me. At future conventions we always shopped together and shared tables in restaurants. Occasionally we visited each other's homes as well.

Getting together clothes for this trip was an ordeal, for we had little money and a small selection of clothes – I only had two suits. I made a pillbox straw hat from the crown of an old hat and put a bunch of flowers on it. For Christmas Margaret had sent me a length of pure silk with a small geometric monochromatic design in a beautiful shade of soft brown, which I made into a two-piece dress suit using a Vogue pattern. That really looked great! With several old blouses, my wardrobe was complete. I looked as well dressed as the other ladies. I had my brown mouton jacket, my leather bag and gloves, and the shoes in which I had married.

The boys were fine when we got home. The only complaint Mother and Aunt Mamie made was that the boys wanted to climb under the house. They had feared there were rattlesnakes under there. Not long afterward Ray found a little green snake and introduced snakes to Howard and John, explaining the difference between poisonous snakes and good snakes.
 This summer, the little frame house was sold by the couple across the street. Again we had to find a place to live. I wanted to go to Springfield and live in the big house on Seventh Avenue with Mother, but Ray would not hear of it. In the early summer we moved to Oleshine Camp near White House, Tennessee. We thought this

would be a temporary move, but it lasted a full year, and Howard spent his third grade at White House Grammar School.

The camp belonged to the Jewish Community Center. They did not plan to open a camp that summer. We paid rent for the camp; lived in a large log house with two small rooms, a bath, a hall, a large recreation room with a massive stone fireplace, and a front porch. Part of the recreation room was curtained off as a storage area. We placed Howard and John's beds in the recreation room on either side of the door leading to the short hall. Ray and I slept in one of the small rooms. The other small room was used as a kitchen. We had running water in the bathroom, which was between the small rooms. The house was cool in the summer time, but it could be cold in the winter. To combat the cold Ray bought a kerosene stove for our bedroom and converted it into our living room, moving our bed into the large recreation room next to Howard and John's bed. On extremely cold nights Ray would build a fire in the fireplace. Again, we would be spending a lonely, uncomfortable year – no telephone, transportation, or friends for me, Howard or John.

For entertainment the three of us would take nature walks with Brownie, wade in the creek, and occasionally talk to the neighbors (1/4 mile to 2 mile away). These people expressed fear that we would run into rattlesnakes and cautioned us to be very careful. However, I never saw a snake the entire year. An older couple lived about 2 miles down the gravel road. They had a telephone. Occasionally, we would walk to their house, sit in the swing and I would call Mother (we were in Robertson

County). This couple knew my Bell family well and was extremely kind to us.

Two men and some women lived about one-quarter-mile up the graveled road. Ray learned the two men had served time in the penitentiary, so I was told to be cautious. Once the boys and I were picking blackberries on the roadside near their house. A lady who lived there invited me to go to the back of the house to pick berries because there were many clean large blackberries. Out of these blackberries I made jam, pies, and I canned some. But I was not comfortable in her presence because I had been told the family was noted for stealing. However, I was always polite to her because each school day Howard had to pass her house on the way home. Ray would take him to school; John, Brownie, and I would meet him at the bus or on the road. There were other children getting off the bus also.

We hardly had time to settle in at Oleshine Camp when it became time to start the Boys' Club Camp. That summer of 1945 was our first Boy's Club Camp. Before camp started we invited the Boys' Club staff to Oleshine Camp for a picnic. Ray cleaned the badminton court, got a boat out of storage and placed it on the little lake. I don't remember anyone going swimming. I doubt that anyone did because the lake was dirty looking with a lot of green growth (algae) in it. We enjoyed the day. Because the court was cleaned off Ray and I played badminton during the summer, teaching Howard and John something of the game.

Boys' Club Camp was held for two weeks at

Montgomery Bell State Park, Camp Site Two. At that time we stayed in the old barracks used by the WPA men who had built the park. Our food was excellent. Our cook, Mr. Barton, was on vacation from the police department, and by profession he was a chef. He had opened and managed the Noel Hotel for many years. He had been in charge of the cooks when the Alaskan Highway had been built. By this time on retirement, he worked some with the police department. By night he was a "beer drinker." A staff member would take him out of the park to a beer tavern on the highway and return for him at bedtime. In spite of this, he was an organized, good-natured excellent cook and manager. Ray, I, Howard, and John slept in one room on bunk beds. Very uncomfortable, but we did have a bathroom that we shared with Mrs. Miles, our camp nurse, whose room and first aid station were next to us. We went swimming each afternoon. Swimming classes were in the morning hours. John loved to ride on the shoulders of the swimming instructor, Jason, down to the lake. His wife, Mrs. Miles, and I were the only women in camp. I began to learn to drive on the park roads when Ray and I went to the store, the park office, or to Dickson for medicine.

World War II ended the day before camp was over. An adult staff member, having heard it announced over the radio, came running out in the open yelling: "The war is over." There was much excitement – a wonderful way to end our camp session.

Chapter 14 – On the Farm in Murfreesboro

Ray had ordered a new car when they became available, as no personal cars were made during the war. Our Ford was 10 years old. We were lucky: a member of the Boys' Club Board owned a dealership and put Ray's order at the top of the list. In the fall of 1945 we bought a new Mercury car, paying cash for it. It was beautiful. I thought we deserved it because we had been working so hard to save money.

Now we knew we could begin to think about building our new house. The previous year Ray and Uncle Clem had selected choice trees to be sawed in his sawmill in Portland, Tennessee, to use in our future new house. This was prime oak lumber. Mr. "Red" Jamison, President of Jamison Bedding Company, had allowed Ray to store this lumber in his kiln dry for seasoning – it generally took a year for proper seasoning.

The next step in our project was to buy a lot, for which we had money in our savings account. Mr. Maples had several lots off of Harding Place Road and Trimble Road, near Belle Meade. We were also interested in a lot on Woodmont Lane, across from Woodmont Country Club. We looked at them all – but couldn't get excited over the small lots, but we liked the area because we wanted the boys to go to the area schools. Mr. Coile, a member of the Boy's Club Board, heard Ray was looking for a lot in this vicinity. His daughter had planned a house at 410 Lynwood Blvd, dug the basement and planned to get married. But her future husband, a pilot in the army air corps, had been killed in the war. The family wanted to get rid of this property, and he offered the lot to Ray for $1,800. It was one acre and contained many large trees. We accepted his offer. Next we began to think about plans. Ray wanted to draw his own plans. We drove around the community many times. I saw a large picture window in one house and wanted a copy of it in my living room. Instead of a detached garage, the new thing in house building was a connecting breezeway between the house and the garage. We decided on that, but it was a mistake because the lot was too narrow to accommodate a breezeway without sacrificeing other space. He brought home books and magazines of house plans. Finally, we decided on our plans, and Ray drafted them for construction. But the plans violated the building zoning laws, because they placed the house too close to the property lines. Not familiar with the Belle Meade zoning laws, Ray had been thinking in terms of the Davidson County rules, which permitted building up to the property line. Consequently, the whole width of the house had to be made smaller. This resulted in the smallest house I have ever lived in, and it was a great disappointment to me. This planning work was our project for the year we spent at Oleshine Camp.

Howard was involved in a serious accident one day while Ray attended a Boy's Club Conference. We had gone to Springfield to spend the weekend with Mother. Because the house she had rented on Seventh Avenue had been sold, she had moved into an apartment across from Springfield Junior High School. While we were there Howard and John were playing on a large trailer with other neighborhood children. Everyone jumped off the back of the trailer together, except Howard, who may not have heard the others holler, "jump." Alone on the back of the trailer, Howard was thrown up into the air and came down hard onto the ground, breaking his arm at the elbow. It was a bad break that threatened to cause permanent injury. By this time John A. and Martha Lou had moved to Springfield. John was driving to Nashville each day to paint for Mr. Maples, and Martha Lou was teaching school in Springfield. (Martha Lou and Mr. White had argued, and I understand that was the reason they had left the farm.) So John A. drove Howard and me to St. Thomas Hospital in Nashville where Dr. Porter, my Springfield doctor, wanted him to go. I remember holding Howard in my arms and telling him over and over that everything would be all right and that I loved him. Oh, how my heart ached for him and all I could do was hold him in my arms. He was placed in a ward with other children after his arm was set. It was around 11 o'clock at night. They would not let me stay with Howard, who was sedated. Someone got me a place to sleep in a rooming house across from the hospital on a canvas cot in the living room. I was so tired; I slept in my clothes. John A. went back to Springfield after Howard's arm was set. I spent the next day (Sunday) with Howard in the hospital ward. Ray came in the afternoon. John A. had called him.

Some time after Howard went back to school he caught chicken pox. He had to stay home for several days. The sores that developed under his cast gave him fits. The teacher sent his assignments home by a child who lived up the road. I did a lot of reading to Howard and John those winter months. Ray always got home past dark. His supervision of the Boys' Club activities were from the time school was out until bedtime. His drive was 30 to 45 minutes. He was home very little except Saturdays and Sundays. It was always a great relief to hear his car pull up to the back door.

We would visit Mother on Sunday and go to Sunday School and church with her. She was always so happy to see us.

One night Howard and John were asleep. Brownie started snarling, growling, and hair bristling. He was on the porch outside the front door. I looked out the window and saw a car pulled up at the bottom of the hill. Two men were coming up the steps on the path leading to our porch. That was the only time I ever heard Brownie be on her killing guard. The men stopped, turned around, ran to the car and drove away. It was about 10 o'clock at night. Ray drove in some 30 minutes later. I was grateful for Brownie and her training, which I feel was a life saving benefit to us that night.

Mr. White asked us if we would consider coming to the farm to live while our house was being built. He offered no rent and plenty of garden food. Compared to Oleshine Camp, it would take Ray just about the same length of time to drive to work, and Howard, John, and I would have protection while Ray was in Nashville. I agreed. I knew it would be a difficult year for me – so much work, the cooking, and still no friends for us, but we would be able to save considerable money.

When the school year was over at White House (June 1946), we moved to the farm. The downstairs rooms were clean. Martha Lou and John A. had painted and papered them. The hall and upstairs rooms had not been cleaned. There was no bathroom, but there was running water in the kitchen sink. That was an improvement over the last two places we had lived.

Arrangements had to be made for Howard and John's schooling. The school bus that came by the house carried students to a county school. We wanted the boys to be in the city school so they would be prepared for Woodmont School in Nashville the following year. We went to see the county school superintendent, Bealer Smotherman, who had been in college with Ray and me. We explained our situation. Bealer agreed. He worked out a situation that was pleasing to us and to him. The school bus picked up our boys at the farmhouse driveway, took them past the Federal battlefield graveyard with its 6,000 gravestones, and delivered all but Howard and John to the county school. On the way back, the driver left John, a first grader, and Howard, a fourth grader, at Crichlow Grammar School, a Murfreesboro city school. Coming home in the afternoon, he reversed the run. I later realized that passing the 6,000 gravestones every day made a deep impression on Howard.

Howard was behind in his work and still in a weakened condition from his broken arm and chicken pox. I read his assignments to him each night and spent much time helping him "catch up" to his grade level to be prepared for the fifth grade the following year at Woodmont.

John had no difficulty with the first grade. His teacher, Mrs. Rogers, said John was smart enough and talented enough to do anything he wanted to do. Her daughter had been in college with me. She was related to one of my good friends, Mary Willard Chester, of Springfield, and I had been to parties in Mrs. Roger's home while at college. She especially encouraged his artwork, and asked him to do a mural for the parents' open house, the nural was done on 15 feet of brown kraft paper, John still remembers drawing the coconut trees and nepa huts. There was a special assembly at the gym/auditorium of Crichlow, it required a dime to go see the magician. John did not have the dime but was allowed go go anyway, this one performance affected his life with magic.

The only difficulty encountered in riding the bus was during a terrific rainstorm, which closed some of the roads. I had heard on the radio that some school buses could not get the children home. But I had no transportation to go for Howard and John. It was beginning to get late in the afternoon and I was frantic. Then a car pulled into the drive. Howard and John came running down the driveway. I never could find out who had met the school bus on the road, transported the children around the water and drove each child home. My boys did not know the people. I feel grateful to them.

It was another year with Ray not home in the evenings. He left home about 7 o'clock and returned between 9 and 10 o'clock in the evening. He missed a lot of Howard and John's growing years, their companionship, and a total lack of social interaction with us, now even on weekends. He was working hard – making a name for himself in the social work profession. Mr. Whitsitt presented his name before the Rotary Club to represent the social work profession in Nashville and Ray was accepted. Being a member of the Rotary Club gave Ray an excellent opportunity to meet and talk with top men in every profession and business segment within Nashville. And Ray made good use of that opportunity! Also, he was overseeing the building of our house, which took up most Saturdays and Sundays. He was using many of the workmen from Mr. Maples' construction company.

I got my driver's license in Murfreesboro while we were at the farm. I never had the car for a full day, but occasionally I would use the car when Ray was at the farm.

April 4, 1947, I gave John a birthday party, inviting all the members of his first grade class. The day before John had tried to catch a bumblebee in a morninglory flower.He was successful! But the bee stung him through the flower and his arm was double size on his birthday. We played games in the yard and had cake and ice cream in the living room. It was a beautiful spring day, John was in pain, even when holding hands with Marsha Littlefield, his favorite – I don't remember how many came or anything about the presents.

Country living was new to me, for I had grown up a small town girl. The first night spent at the farm was a revelation. I started to lock the doors for the night, but I could not find the key to the large brass box-shaped lock on the front door. I asked Mr. White about the key. He laughed and said, "Martha, there hasn't been a key to that door since the Civil War." The house was used as a field hospital by a Federal surgeon during the Battle of Murfreesboro (Stones River). It is identified on all the battlefield maps as the "Widow Burns" house. There are dark bloodstains on the wide plank floors of the upstairs bedrooms, which had resulted from amputations that were performed while blood dripped into the very core cellular structure of the wood. Sanding, painting, staining would not remove these dark stains because they had become part of the wood. The amputated body parts were thrown out the window into a wagon positioned on the ground below. The bloodstains would be the inspiration of Howard's four volumes of history, which are titled, "Bloodstains, An Epic History of the Politics that Produced the American Civil War."

Felix Haynes lived across the road. His parents had been slaves on what was then the Burris farm. Felix was born soon following the Civil War. It was a joy to talk to this elderly black man about the farm and its history. According to him, during the Civil War, the house consisted of four large log rooms (two up and two down) with a dogtrot in the center. It faced the old Nashville road. When the Nashville Pike was built before the Civil War, this road became the farmhouse driveway and the farm cow path. After the "Widow Burrus" sold the house, the new owners made major renovations to the old house. They tore down the southern half of the house, which must have been damaged by cannon fire during the war. They enlarged the house greatly by moving a frame house from across the road and attaching it to the remaining two-story log house. They enclosed the dogtrot, making it a hallway. The frame house section consisted of a large main room with a bedroom above, a kitchen, a small dining room and a kitchen with porches. The kitchen was attached to the house by an open porch and there was a wide porch to the side. They built a two-story front porch across the front of the frame section, enclosing the upper level with a turned-post railing. The front of the enlarged house faced Asbury Lane. Cedar trees were planted in the front yard, and along the driveway to Asbury Lane. Behind the kitchen was the log smoke house with the original salting log (hollowed out of a log) where meat was cured, and then hung from the rafters on hooks. Behind this was the outdoor toilet. Behind this was the chicken house. Behind this was the large garden site. To the right of the back of the house were two large log cabins where slaves had lived. The original rock-lined hand dug well was to the right of the front of the house. This well would furnish water to the community when other wells would run dry in late summer. Before city water lines were run, an electric pump was put in the well to pump water into the kitchen. When city water came to the farm, the well water was used for the livestock, the milking barn and garden. After Mr. White sold off some of the land, the remaining farm consisted of 115 acres. That was the size of the farm when we lived there.

The remains of the old Nashville road went through the hallway of the large barn, which Mr. White had built. The old cow lane intersected this old road. The big cold spring in a sinkhole in a nearby grove of trees was a favorite stopping and camping place for the pioneers and travelers of late 1700s and early 1800s. When the

Nashville Pike was upgraded to the Nashville Highway, Asbury Lane was rerouted a short distance where it intersected with the highway. For this Mr. White donated an acre of land in the bend of the road. Before the Pike was upgraded, the farm fields and the outlying boundary lines were enclosed by rock fences, which had been built by the slaves who had lived on the Burrus farm. These fences must have been beautiful, but Mr. White had sold them all to the highway contractor to use as foundation rocks for the new roadbed. He had wanted to modernize the farm with wire fencing.

Felix Haynes enjoyed telling old stories about buried treasure from the Civil War era. Years later John and some other grandsons of Mr. White would go over some of the ground (cemetery, under house, etc.) with metal detectors, but they would find no treasure. But the farm was a good place to find shells, bullets, buttons, etc. from the Civil War battle. I have framed some articles the family has found on the farm. Felix Haynes also told us that, in front of the large sink hole near the Big Spring, there had been four Federal soldiers and 4 Confederate soldiers buried in a cross configuration. Later they were exhumed and placed in the Federal Stones River Battlefield Cemetery.

When Ray and I went to see Bealer Smotherman about the boy's schooling, I made application for a substitute teaching job in the Rutherford County system, requesting that I be called the night before so I could make transportation plans. Soon after the school year started I was called – not the night before but about 8 o'clock in the morning. I had gone to Nashville that day with Ray to shop and visit Auntie and Aunt Susie. Mr. White answered the telephone. He got angry with the person who called me – saying not to call me again, that I didn't have time to substitute teach. When I came home with Ray that evening, Mr. White and I had our first and only argument. I said I was going to teach; that I would make time; that I wanted my own money; that I had given a promise to teach in the schools of Tennessee for five years as a payment for my scholarship. I feel Mr. White was surprised at my veracity, because he never said anything more about it. But I did call Bealer Smotherman and asked him to take my name off the substitute teacher list. And I began to make plans to apply for a job teaching in the Davidson County system or the Nashville City system. Ray began to talk to people about getting me a teaching job. By the end of that school year I had been hired and placed at Joy School (Davidson County) as a second grade teacher for the coming year. I was told this was a start – that I would get a home economics teaching position as soon as one was available.

Mr. White wanted us to sell the house we were building on Lynwood and settle on the farm. One day he walked me over the farm and told me he would give us any section of land on which to build a house. I said "No," I wanted to be nearer to Ray's work so we could have a closer family relationship. Ray did not want to farm either.

One day, soon after we moved to the farm, I could not find Howard and John. I called and called. No answer. Time went by. I began to think they were hurt and couldn't answer. I rang the dinner bell. Was that ever a mistake!! At 10 o'clock in the morning! Mr. White, Ed, and the farm hands came in from the fields to see what was happening. Several neighbors in their trucks and cars drove up the driveway. Mr. White had to explain to everyone that there was no emergency – that his city-reared daughter-in-law did not know the dinner bell was never rung except in an emergency, like fire, death, or accident. Mr. White did get mighty red in the face trying to hold his temper, but he did not bless me out. I suppose he felt sorry for me for not knowing any better. Howard and John did come to the house – they had not heard me calling for them, so they said.

Food preparation was always a major activity – picking beans, corn, okra, squash, turnip greens, and tomatoes; canning and making pickles, preserves and jams; canning pears and peaches from the orchard; making grape juice and jelly; canning the stolen honey from the bee hives, and separating the cream from the milk, both morning and night. The milking vessels had to be sterilized twice daily, seven days a week. Furthermore, all three meals had to be put on the table daily. Because Ed was a diabetic, he required nutritionally balanced meals – not too much starch, sugar, or protein. From early rising at 6 o'clock in the morning to about 2 o'clock in the afternoon my day was spent in food preparation. Then I served leftovers with a few additions for the supper meal. The farm hands did not eat with us except when wheat was thrashed. A tenant family lived in the little house that Mr. White had built in the cedar glade when he retired from Ford in Detroit (at that time the Lewis family was renting and living in the big house and farming the land). I rarely saw the tenant family.

One day a week a sister to Nancy Haynes cleaned house and ironed for me. We had the washing done at Whiteway in Nashville – damp wash, with Ray's shirts finished. She was a kind woman. Her mother had been nurse and housekeeper when Mrs. White was living. She had been a nurse to Ray's older sister, who died of a heart condition following her first year of teaching at Millersville, Tennessee. She lived in a rock house on the Nashville Highway, located just before the entrance to Asbury Lane.

My Mother worried that I was moving to the country and would never see anyone. I saw people each day, coming and going to the farm for various reasons. Of course, many of them were black people who wanted to get garden produce such as turnip greens; to borrow a farm implement; permission to fish in the pond; to buy or be given milk, or to work for wages. One afternoon I had finished in the kitchen and decided I would rest on the bed for a few minutes. I went to sleep. I was awakened by a knock on the window opposite my bed, and I saw a black elderly man looking in on me. I was alone in the house – even Brownie was away from the house with Mr. White. This elderly man had his family outside and they wanted permission to go into the field and pick turnip greens for their own use. Mr. White had started for the house when he had heard the car approaching. He gave his permission. He knew this family but asked them not to spread the word about the turnip greens because he didn't want people trampling down his fields.

There were chickens running all over the backyard. One day I thought chicken for the next day's meal sounded good. I asked Ray to kill a chicken before he left for the office, but he replied, "Ask Dad to kill one." I did. Mr. White said, "Oh, you select any chicken and just kill it." I asked Howard and John if they would chase down a chicken by feeding them. That part was no problem. I gathered the chicken under my arm and placed her on the wood chopping block outside the kitchen porch. I told Howard to hold one end of the chicken and John the other and I raised the axe. Chop! I only cut half through her neck. That old chicken got up and started running around with her neck hanging to one side dripping blood. Then we went chasing after her with Brownie barking on the sideline. We caught the chicken and finished chopping her head off; let her flop around in the backyard dirt for the blood to drain out; dipped her in hot water to loosen the feathers; plucked the feathers; scraped off the pin feathers, and placed her in cold salted water to season and whiten her. What an operation! All for fried chicken for one meal! That was the first and last time I killed a chicken. Howard and John were our egg gatherers – from the chicken house, the barn, or any other place the hens decided to lay.

When we were at the farm I had my yearly physical with Dr. Tom Zerfoss. He found a lump in my breast – cystic mastitis. I went to Vanderbilt for the removal. My surgeon was Dr. Ralph Larsen. We decided not to tell Mother I was going to have the surgery until it was over. That was a thoughtless mistake, which I regret. Everything turned out well – except one breast was larger than the other.

Ray's bees had multiplied to five hives. The clover

honey was clear, bright, beautiful, and delicious. The beehives were in the orchard to the right of the house. Ray had a facemask, gloves, heavy protective clothing, a bee and honey separator, and a bee wax cutter. We canned the honey in one-quart glass Mason jars. In some jars we would place a slab of bee wax with honey in the cells. These quart jars of honey were sold for $1 each. And we gave some away and ate lots of honey. It would take all day to rob the bees and fill the sterilized jars. Another day was required to clean honey from the floor, counter tops, table, and to wash the cloths used in canning. I remember mopping the floor three times with hot detergent water and still feeling sticky stuff on the bottom of my shoes. When John A. bought the farm, Martha Lou did not want the bees, and Ray did not want to move them, so Ed sold them. As far as I know Ray never got any money from the sale of his bees, hives and equipment.

The telephone at the farm was on a party line. The first night we spent at the farm the telephone kept ringing at various times during the night. This disturbed our sleep. But Mr. White and Ed were sleeping upstairs and could not hear the phone ringing. Ray investigated and discovered that a nearby "motel" on the Nashville Highway, in the black section, had been put on the farm party line. The manager of the Murfreesboro office took the so-called "motel" off our line after we explained that we had too young boys at the house.

J. P., an adult son of Felix Haynes lived with his parents near the farm. J. P. was a construction worker for Mr. Maples and did farm work for Mr. White. He would get his check on Friday night. The weekend was spent gambling and drinking. The first weekend at the farm, he scared the daylights out of me. I was awakened by J. P. calling "Mr. Ray, Mr. Ray" and the loud noise of drunken men laughing. The front door was not locked. To placate me, Ray had nailed a hook on the doorframe, but I knew a big strong man like J. P. could have pushed it opened with his shoulder. I did not know J. P. and his relationship in the community. Ray went outside. J. P. wanted a certain amount of money to pay his gambling debt to the men in the car. Otherwise they were going to beat him. Ray gave him the money and the car of men drove off in the night. This happened several times during the year; finally Ray told J. P. never to come to the farm for money, but go to the police instead and have them lock him up for the rest of the night for his own protection. J. P. would call Ray from the police station and he would go to the jail to get J. P. out the next morning. We never lost any money on these dealings with J. P. because Ray would tell Mr. Maples, who would withhold the money from J. P.'s pay check and give it to Ray. Even when we moved to Lynwood, J. P. would call Ray from a Nashville jail. The second time J. P. called, Ray decided not to get him out of jail and told him and the jailer never to call him again because J. P. no longer worked for him. J. P. was a hard worker, congenial, courteous, kind to children and animals – but other black men took advantage of him because he always had money on Friday nights.

There was another time I was frightened, but the situation was of my own making. I had ridden the bus to Nashville, and Uncle Arthur, Auntie, and Aunt Susie had met me at the bus station. I rode with them to Springfield to have Sunday dinner with Mother. Later in the afternoon I rode with them to Nashville and caught the bus to Murfreesboro. It was dark. Ray had said he would meet me at the end of Asbury Lane. Evidently he had forgotten what he had said. I pulled the bus cord to get off at the lane. I saw no car lights; even the store a block away had no lights showing. I remember hesitating before stepping off the bus. The thought entered my mind that Ray's car was in the lane with lights turned off. The bus pulled away. There I was in the dark in the middle of an all-black community about one mile from the farm. There was nothing to do but pick my feet up – one after the other as fast as I could – and walk that mile in my high heel dress shoes. About half way to the farm a car full of young black men passed me and laughed. I was so angry when I came into the kitchen and found Ray, Ed, and Mr. White laughing and talking that I began to cry. They had forgotten me! Bright and early the next morning Felix Haynes came to talk to Mr. White. Felix told him never to allow me to walk anywhere after dark or on the road by myself in the day or night. He said I had been lucky Sunday night that the carload of young men knew who I was and did not follow me or harm me. After that the men in the family were better guardians of my safety and welfare.

During the years at the farm several relatives came to visit us. Ray's sister Margaret, her husband Bob, and their two children, Anna K. and Robert, spent one weekend. Mother spent part of her vacation with us during the summer when garden vegetables and peaches were "coming in." I remember, during Mother's visit, spending a lot of time on the back porch preparing food. Mother, Ed, and I were peeling and slicing peaches when he began to go into an insulin reaction. He talked louder and louder, waving his sharp knife all the while. I tried to give him orange juice. He refused and got mad, pushing away the orange juice and me. I was afraid he would hurt himself or one of us with the sharp knife. I went for Mr. White who finally got orange juice down him and the knife away from him. By the time we left the farm Ed was becoming more and more belligerent toward his father during these episodes. But he would take orange juice from Ray.

Ed would take 6 year old John on the tractor rides around the farm and while doing the work of the day. John loved this activity. He asked his grandfather if he could drive the tractor up and down the driveway, permission was granted.

I looked out the window and saw my son, John at the wheel of the farm tractor riding down the driveway and turning into the main road, Asbury Lane. I screamed at him. Mr. White heard me and came in from the fields, John had the tractor turned around and back in the driveway. John had heard his grandfathers shouts from the house 100 yards away and over the sound of the tractor engine. Mr. White gave John a switching. I asked John how he knew how to operate the tractor. He had watched his Uncle Ed drive and had shifted gears for him when driving in the fields.

Ed had a difficult time balancing his insulin and food intake in the hot summer time. He needed to lead a quiet sedentary life. Cutting hay, riding the mower, being in the hot sun would often bring on a reaction. The neighbors were good about looking after Ed when he was away from the farm. Ed was cutting hay in Stone's River Battlefield Park when a neighbor drove by and saw him slumped over the wheel of the tractor and the mower still mowing and cutting hay. The neighbor got to Ed in time; he cut off the motor and brought Ed home to the farm. Orange juice soon brought him to consciousness. That was a close call for Ed. That's when Mr. White laid the law down: Ed was never to get on the tractor or the mower again.

Polly and her family spent a few days with us. So did John A. and Martha Lou. Auntie, Aunt Susie and Uncle Arthur visited the farm. He died during that year. Uncle Arthur had suffered a stroke in 1942, which had left him impaired. Afterward he spent time in and out the hospital until his death. While we were at the farm Bill Worsham came home from Japan. Aunt Effie died that year. Little by little my family was slipping away from me into death.

Brownie died in the spring while having her third litter of puppies. She was greatly missed. Ed had a little shorthaired dog called "Bingo," but it was not much of a guard dog. We also had barn cats and yard cats of every description and size to hold down the mice population.

Howard and John were in good health during the year. But Howard did have one accident. He and John were running down the hill toward the Big Spring. Howard tripped over a root, falling to the ground with his weight on the arm that had been broken before. Fortunately the elbow was not involved. This was a simple break a few inches from the wrist. When we moved to Lynwood his arm was still bent slightly out of shape because of the earlier elbow break. He had little feeling in some fingers on that arm. For a long time, especially while living at the farm, he spent some time each day carrying a heavy metal iron around the house to lengthen and stretch the tendons and muscles of his right arm.

While we were at the farm Mother and Uncle Melvin moved from their tiny apartment in front of the Junior High School to a nicer and larger apartment on Oak Street beside the Methodist church. When Sue Ara Harris' sister had decided to move out of the Oak Street apartment, she had called Mother about the opportunity. Although Mother and Uncle Melvin only moved one and one-half blocks, it was a move to a better neighborhood. They had one-half of the upstairs in a four-apartment house. She had use of the front porch, where she had a swing, chairs, and flowers.

The last week in May 1947, Ray, I, Howard, John and Mother attended the Boy's Club convention in New York. We thought it would be an educational trip for the boys. Mother went along to be with the boys while Ray and I attended Boy's Club activities. Mother especially enjoyed the rolling hills of the Virginia valley. She remembered her mother, Martha Jane Carney Simpkins, writing cousins in Virginia. One cousin wrote that his farm was so large it took him one whole day to ride over the acreage on horseback. Those letters would help solve family relationships if we had them today.

In Washington we toured the Capitol, the Washington Monument, the Jefferson Memorial, and the White House. As we were standing in line at the White House, I read a large sign, which said, "No smoking, drinking, or eating inside the White House." I had John (7 years old) by the hand. My mind was trying to absorb all the features of the White House. I looked down at John. He had an "all-day" sucker in his mouth, licking away. No one mentioned to us that our child was disobeying the rules. By the time I discovered the sucker we were exiting the White House tour.

We stopped in Baltimore to see Polly and her family. Polly told Ray, in private, that she didn't see why we had brought my mother – that we should have brought Mr. White instead so he could visit her. I didn't know about that statement until we returned home. I would have told her my mother paid her own way, including food, hotel, and part of the gas. Mr. White would have expected Ray and me to pay all his way.

In New York we went to Radio City, made a tour of the new television studio and the radio station. The immense size of that operation astounded us. During a demonstration of the new television technology, the speaker asked John to come on the stage to see and hear himself on TV. We rode the subway to the zoo – both were firsts for the boys. We took a ferry ride around Manhattan Island, and took a general bus tour of the city and a boy's club. One day when I returned to our room at the Commodore Hotel, Mother was beside herself with fear. The boys had been making airplanes out of paper and sailing them out of the open window on the 12th

floor!. She was afraid they would fall out the window. She was right. There was danger in that as we explained to the boys.

We were away from home one week for this convention. Our trip home was quick, but by a different route, as much as practical. We passed over the mountains and spent the night at a bed and breakfast. It was cold outside. The room was cold and the blankets were thin. We asked for more blankets. All night I was cold from underneath. Not much sleep for us.

Howard and John had one more week of school, therefore, we had to be home by Monday. Both of the boys had been given special permission to take the trip. Make-up schoolwork had to be done the last week of school.

When school was out, our new house on Lynwood Blvd. was ready for us to move in. But Ray thought it might be better for us economically to sell this house and build another one. So one Sunday we had open house. There were only a few new houses on the market. We had many, many lookers and some bids. Some bids we seriously considered, but we liked this lot, the location, and we were eager to get settled.

Therefore we prepared to move. By moving so often we had not accumulated much "stuff." I did want to keep all the toys, books, and clothes the boys had outgrown. I had already given their baby clothes to Polly for Bill and Tom. The truck had pulled out of the driveway. Our car was packed and we were following the truck. I looked back and saw the box and the wooden toys Ray had made for the boys still on the porch. I pleaded with Ray to stop. I wanted to take those playthings. He said "no." He had already told the tenant family they could have those items for their children – never saying a word to the boys or me if we wanted them. He did not stop the car. The next time we went to the farm I asked Mr. White about them. He said the tenants got them the day we moved – a sad experience for me.

So ended our eleven years of moving from rented place to rented place and into our own home at 410 Lynwood Blvd. This new home has brought much happiness and joy into my life and my family's lives, for which I feel blessed!

Chapter 15 – Early Years at 410 Lynwood Blvd.

We moved into our new house on Lynwood Blvd. – different life style, friends and values. I had first seen Lynwood in 1936 when Med Ransom had interviewed Ray and me for the summer camp job. At that time Lynwood ended at Abbot Martin Road, which had not yet been paved. Beyond that point, to the left where we would build our house, I had seen a riding academy and barns, and a small riding ring located at the end of a dirt, one-lane track. To the right I had seen a rock house with a large yard. Much of the land in the vicinity was covered with scrub growth, tall Johnson grass canes and ancient trees. When we had come back to Lynwood Blvd. in 1945 to look at lots, we saw lots marked off and a two-lane paved road from Abbott Martin to Harding Place. On what would become our side of Lynwood we saw four new houses, and two others being built. And we saw four additional new houses on the other side of the road. Slowly the remaining lots began to sell and more new houses were built. Curtis Snell and her mother and father lived on the left. Dot Demonbreun, then a senior in high school, lived with her mother and father to the left of Curtis. There was a vacant lot to our right, which we considered buying, but we feared we could not pay for it. Ernest and Ann Moench lived to the right of the vacant lot. The Moons lived across the street in the rock house. He owned Moon Drug Store on Harding Road in Belle Meade. The Moskovitz family, who had formerly lived in Springfield, lived left of the Moons' house. The Rolfs, who owned a jewelry store in Nashville, lived next to them. And John J. Hooker lived next to the Rolfs. John Hooker would later run, unsuccessfully, for Tennessee Governor. He married Trish Fort. These were the only houses on Lynwood when we moved into our house.

The small rooms and lower ceilings were not suited to our furniture. Ray cut 3 inches off the legs of our bed, chest of drawers and walnut storage chest. He cut 2 inches off the legs of the boy's single beds and about 6 inches off their oak desk. The dining room table did not need modification, but he cut 4 inches off the legs of our Pembroke living room tables and 2 inches off of the legs of our wingback living room chair and sofa. My antique oak piano was completely out of keeping in the living room. I sold it for $10, but kept the piano bench, for which I had paid by picking strawberries in Portland when I was a teenager. We bought 8 cherry Empire chairs from Bradfords, which matched the dining room table that Ray had made. Ray refinished the Jackson press, which Mother had given me. This completed our down stairs furnishings. We bought room-size wool rugs for the living room. I had Castner Knotts make silk twill floral draperies, which I used for 35 years. I had turned the edges over and re-stitched the hems twice before I would consider them to be worn out.

We went to Boys' Club Camp for two weeks soon after moving into our new house. Again I planned the menus, bought the food supplies and acted as hostess and mother for the camp. This year we relocated to Group Camp Site 2, which had frame cabins with screen windows on all four sides. Our cabin was next to the dining hall. Howard and John shared this one room cabin with us. They were old enough now, 10 years and 7 seven years, to follow the morning activities. I ran errands in the car to Dickson and to the grocery store on the highway.

When we returned from camp, Ray and I were invited to a large luncheon at Belle Meade Country Club, which was given by Mr. Silliman Evans of the Nashville Tennessean. I had not had time to buy any clothes for the summer. I wore something I had and felt improperly dressed. I wore a hat and very few ladies wore hats – that was the beginning of women going hatless. I wore a crepe dress – most women had on summer cottons. After that I tried to be more conscious of dress trends.

The house had cost us $14,000. We had borrowed $2,000 from Ray's sister Margaret, and $2,000 from Mother (who had sold some telephone stock to help us). And we had signed a mortgage for $10,000 with Whitsitt Real Estate Company, where Ray had his Boys' Club office. We decided to rent out the upstairs to try to pay off some of our debts. Ray put an inexpensive floor covering over the hardwood floors to cut down on the noise of feet moving across the floor; made a kitchen unit out of the dormer window area in the left-side room; placed a screen between the kitchen unit and the rest of the room, and extended water from the bathroom through the wall to a sink in the kitchen unit. To give renters privacy when moving through the upstairs hall he hung louvered doors at the top of the steps. This made an attractive apartment.

Our first renters were a young couple from New York. They rented during 1947-1948 school year. She was

Gentile and he was Jewish. They had just married. He entered Vanderbilt Medical School. They were fun and made themselves part of our family. During our 1948 Boy's Club Convention they looked after the boys for us, a responsibility they offered to assume. But, for some reason, at the end of the first year at Vanderbilt, he decided to drop his schooling and go into his father's clothing manufacturing business in New York. On one of our trips to New York, we spent the night with them and had an enjoyable time. We exchanged Christmas cards and letters for many years (they also visited us in Nashville for a weekend). Much later he wrote us that he and his wife were divorcing. Their two girls were out of college, and she had found another man and left home. It was a sad letter.

During the 1948-1949 school we rented to a young Vanderbilt couple, the Neiderhouses. He was the son of the dairy farm people on Elm Hill Pike. The following year we rented to a Mrs. May Buntin, who lived in Robertson County and wanted an apartment in Nashville to use when she came into town for luncheons, dinners and other social engagements. I remember she was of the Buntin Berry family and knew my family in Springfield. She stayed one or two years, then moved permanently back to Nashville.

Our next project was to prepare for school. My school, Joy Grammar School, was in the northeast part of the county, in the Old Edgefield section, across the Cumberland River near First Street, which became Dickerson Pike outside of the city. Joy School was named from the Joy Floral family, who gave the land for the school and had a home and greenhouse next to the school. The school was eleven miles from our house on Lynwood Blvd. The school year for teachers started in the middle of August 1947. Our in-service training was held at Isaac Litton High School in the gym. I remember it was cool for August and I wore a suit, which was unusual for that time of year.

Students came to school one week before the Labor Day weekend. To get to Joy School I had to ride the bus. My schedule was a rough one. My alarm went off at 5 o'clock. I dressed, had breakfast, packed my lunch, and then Ray drove me to Harding Road and Lynwood Blvd. We waited in the car until the bus came by at 6 o'clock. On the way to town I would review my plans for the day. I got off the bus at Fifth and Church (across from Cain Sloan and next to the Presbyterian Church). I walked from Church Street to Union Street on Fifth Avenue. It was sometimes dark, rainy, and working class people, mostly blacks, were on the street at that time. I would wait on the corner of Union and Fifth, in front of the First American Bank, for the bus marked "Meridian Street." There were mostly blacks on the bus. I would get off at the end of the city street, for that was as far as the bus went. Then I walked another block to the school to start my class at 7 o'clock. Schools were segregated and my students were white. They were well behaved, courteous, and they loved me. I worked at Joy a half-year, until a position teaching home economics opened for me. When I left the school in January 1949 to go to Hillsboro High School, I received from the students many letters and cards of appreciation and love. I regret that I did not save them.

School attendance had increased in Davidson County because of people moving in and building new houses. Therefore, there were not enough schoolrooms. I taught one second grade class from 7 o'clock to 11:30. Another teacher taught another 2nd grade class in the same room from 12-4:30 o'clock. But I was not free to leave school until I had put in a full day. My free time was spent on records, planning, and preparing illustrative materials in the school library. I left school at 2 o'clock by the same way – by bus, transferring to town and riding the Belle Meade bus out of town and on its round through our neighborhood, directly to my driveway. Soon after I got home Howard and John came home from Woodmont school on their school bus.

Howard was in the fifth grade and John was in the second grade at Woodmont School on Estes Avenue. Their schedule depended on Ray. When he returned from seeing me on the bus he would awaken the boys, oversee their dressing (I had their clothes laid out for them), prepare their breakfast and drive them to school on his way to work downtown. The boys came home on the school bus.

John had to follow Howard's afternoon schedule, for he was supposed to go home at 11:30. Special permission was obtained from the school board for him to stay at school all day. He was bored – not enough activity – same studies twice each day. I believe his teacher had a difficult time keeping him in his seat. If she had given him some special creative project in art or science he would have been happy and contented. I firmly believe that second grade teacher was harmful to John's academic growth.

Having attended a variety of schools, most of them country schools, Howard was still behind in his grade level. His class stayed all day with full class activity. All of my time at home during the week time was spent helping Howard with his school work; seeing the boys were bathed for the next day; getting their school clothes ready; preparing supper for them and Ray, and getting my own clothes in order for the next day. Ray often times had Boy's Club meetings in the evenings. We all tried to be in bed by 9 o'clock – 8 o'clock for the boys.

I had a maid 3 days a week that year – Monday, Wednesday and Friday. She was one of Felix Hayne's granddaughters, who lived in Nashville. We paid her $1 per day plus bus fare. She cleaned house, washed, ironed, and prepared supper on the days she came.

Both John and Howard joined the Cub Scouts at Woodmont School. On a night program for parents at Woodmont a magician gave the program. This intrigued John immensely (7 years old) and continued his interest in doing magic tricks. I remember helping with simple projects for their Cub Scouts.

We needed to make a decision on our church affiliation. First we visited Calvary Methodist Church on Hillsboro Road. We knew no one there – and no one spoke to us. At Rotary Club the next week Dr. Hill (President of Peabody College) asked Ray if he had made a choice of churches. When Ray said no, Dr. Hill invited him to visit Westminster Presbyterian Church, because Ray had told him I was a Presbyterian. Ray knew several people there, who spoke to us and invited us to join. Everyone was so friendly – Dr. Currie, the pastor, was a Rotarian – so we decided immediately to join Westminster. It has been a good relationship. We made the right choice. We started going to all the activities: Sunday School, young peoples' groups on Sunday nights for the boys; Men's Club for Ray, Evening Circle for me, and the main church service for all of us. We sat in the balcony where parents with young children generally sat. Across the aisle sat Dr. Larson, Mrs. Larson and their daughter, Michael, who was in John's second grade class at Woodmont, and his secret love that year.

In the early fall, Dr. Larsen found another lump in my other breast. This required surgery. I was out of school (Joy) for one week.

My schoolwork was coming along fine. I heard my principal, Mr. Parks, tell a faculty member that I was on my way to being an excellent teacher, which was the rating I would receive later at Hillsboro High. During the fall, J. E. Moss ran for Superintendent of Davidson County Schools. Ray worked hard for his election. Mr. Moss won; the next morning the "Tennessean" newspaper carried an interview with Mr. Moss, in which he said his wife Dot would retire from her position teaching Home Economics at Hillsboro High. Over breakfast Ray read the article to me and said: "That's the job for you. I will call John Koen and J. E. Moss this morning." Mr. Koen said he would definitely offer my name to Mr. Moss as a replacement for Ann Moss. Mr. Moss told John Koen, "Have Martha come by to see me this afternoon." I went by his office, which was in the courthouse and on my way home from Joy School. He asked me one question: "Do you feel you can get along with John Koen?" I said "yes. I will try my best." Then Mr. Moss said: "The job is yours. Report to Hillsboro on the first day following the Christmas vacation." My getting a job teaching home economics so quickly surprised teachers who had been waiting for years to get such a plum of a job as Hillsboro High School, but I never explained the friendship angle. For years, Ray and I had exchanged dinners and played bridge with the Koens and Mosses. But I also benefited from my double major of English and Home Economics, both of which would pass state education requirements, and this helped John Koen and Jewell Moss justify what they had done for me.

The next morning I went to Joy School for my teaching day. Mr. Parks, the Principal, had been notified that I would be leaving at the end of the week before Christmas holidays. Mr. Parks and his wife were from Robertson County and knew my second cousin, Phillip Bell, who at that time was Superintendent of Robertson County Schools. When I went into Mr. Park's office to discuss my leaving Joy School, he asked "Are you sure you want to go to Hillsboro High? Mr. Koen is a most difficult man to get along with – he's very demanding and wants everything his own way." I answered, "Yes, I think I can get along with him. My husband and I have known him and his wife for a number of years." Mr. Parks seemed surprised that I was so positive about John Koen. Ray had told me to never take any abuse from John Koen and to always stand up for myself when I thought I was right – this I was determined to do – to stand up for my rights.

My first day at Hillsboro, January 1948, was a quiet uneventful day – two classes of Sophomore English, 2 classes of Junior English and one class in Home Economics. The class members had been coached well by Dot Moss to tell me which textbook to use, where the class roles, grade books and lesson plans for the week were kept, I walked into a completely foreign situation. Mr. Koen walked me to the classroom, introduced me, and left. I stood in front of the class holding a notebook, pen, pencil and Bible (at that time devotion was held first thing in the morning). I sat down at the desk and read the Twenty-third Psalm, expressed my appreciation for being at Hillsboro, and asked if anyone had instructions for me about the class. In each class someone had been appointed to help me. I noticed Mr. Koen passed by the door several times during the day. At the end of the day he expressed praise for my handling the classes – and warned that there were several in my classes who were considered troublemakers.

I felt at home at Hillsboro. It was the type of high school I attended, and I had known several faculty members before arriving. I already knew John Koen; Jim Lee Allen, the math teacher was a sister of my good friend, Blair Stephens; Mattie Pearl Regen, the history and business education teacher was in my Sunday School class at the Methodist Church we had attended before we had left Nashville to live outside of town; Elinor Stroh, the Latin teacher, whose aunt was a lady friend of Mr. White's following Mrs. White's death; Nina Williamson, the librarian was an aunt to Elinor Stroh and a sister to Lura Williams, Mr. White's deceased lady friend; Henry Nance, the basketball coach, who Ray and I had known at Middle Tennessee Teachers College; Ed Hessey, the football coach, who we had also known in college; Margaret Batey, the Spanish teacher, who was also in college with us, and one year behind me. We knew many people in common. As a result of previously having been friends with these people, I was readily included in the faculty family.

The spring was the time for the principal's teacher evaluations. Mr. Koen came to my classroom, during a class, and sat down to observe. This slightly upset me because I had not been notified he would be evaluating me that day, and I had not planned a "showy" lesson. It popped into my mind that several years before I had heard him speak of, when attending Vanderbilt, being a friend of a noted writer of Kentucky hill country people, culture and dialects. At the moment Mr. Koen walked into the room, it so happened that a student was reading a section from this noted writer's work. This was a lucky break for me. I immediately told the class of Mr. Koen's association with this writer, and asked Mr. Koen if he would share some of his remembrances with the class. This made a hit both with the students and with Mr. Koen! So my rating was high. Mr. Koen later told me he was surprised I had remembered the association.

I tried hard to have interesting home economics classes. We had refreshments for the large spring P.T.A. meeting. Mr. Koen brought some beautiful gladiolus flowers for the table arrangement and asked me to arrange them. I found a flat ceramic bowl with an attached stem needle control in the bottom. I arranged the gladiolus in an elongated arrangement, an oriental style. The arrangement and the refreshments made a good impression both on the P.T.A. members and Mr. Koen. The next time there was something important happening at Hillsboro, he called at 6 o'clock on a dark morning to ask me to buy fresh flowers for the stage that morning. I said "Mr. Koen, I have two sons who have to be dressed, breakfasted, and on the way to school. I have no time to buy flowers this morning, but will be glad to arrange them at school if someone else will buy the flowers." I think he was surprised at my answer. Never again did he ask me to run errands for him before the school day started. However, I arranged many "bunches" of flowers for him for special occasions.

In the room next to me was a male teacher whose morals and teaching techniques were questionable. It was said that he used a copy of his exams and reviewed each of his classes on the answers to the specific questions in his exams. A student told me what he was doing, and a teacher also told me before the day was over. That weekend the faculty and student council picnic was held at the summer camp house on Stones River that was owned by Mrs. Mayfield, the biology teacher. Mr. Koen asked me if I would go with him and his wife, Madeline, and stay until the end of the picnic. I told him I would. Most of us went swimming in the afternoon in the river; then, we had an outdoor picnic. At dark we went into the house – faculty in the living room and students on the screened porch – playing cards and singing and playing musical instruments. Gradually, faculty members began to leave; then student council members left. This questionable teacher stayed on the porch with the remaining students. Mr. Koen, Madeline, and I were the only faculty members left. Mr. Koen always sat so he could see this man – and asked Madeline and me to change seats so we would be nearer the porch. The man teacher left about 11 o'clock. Later the 2 students left. Then we left. On the drive home Mr. Koen wanted to know if we saw anything out of line or any immoral conduct on the part of the teacher. Both Madeline and I said we did not. Mr. Koen said he had to make a decision to present to the superintendent because of parental charges against the teacher. The teacher did not return to Hillsboro the next year. He was hired by another Middle Tennessee county and later in the year was charged with sexual misconduct.

At that time I did not have a car. Ray drove me to school in the mornings, and I rode the school bus home. This sounds strange now. Margaret Batey was also riding the school bus.

When the school year was over, I began preparing for Boys' Club Camp – clothing, food lists, menus, food orders from the different vendors, and first aid supplies. Again, I acted as hostess, mother, and dietitian. Our boys stayed in our cabin. They participated in all camp activity; improved their swimming, and enjoyed Mr. Barton's food – especially those delicious pancakes made with government surplus flour, synthetic eggs, real butter, and homemade syrup made from sugar and maple flavoring. Mrs. Miles was our camp nurse. I enjoyed our association that summer. Ray would oversee making ice cream, a treat the campers enjoyed.

One camper from North Nashville, nicknamed Rooster,

stands out in my mind. His name is Marion Cook, a local artist of note. He started to camp at seven years age – a slender, freckled face boy who would win the rooster crowing contest on stunt night held each camp session. He came each summer as a camper, junior counselor, and senior counselor until he was 16 years old. Over the years, Ray and I kept up with him and have two of his paintings – a barn, and the stone bridge across the old Louisville and Nashville highway. Many times he would tell us how he wanted Ray to be his father; how much he enjoyed camp activities, how camp opened a new vista to his life, and that it was the first time he had tasted bacon and had a full breakfast with plenty of milk to drink. In fact, camp was the first time in his life he had had enough to eat and three square meals a day. As long as Ray lived, Marion helped support Boy's Club with money.

When we returned home from camp, preparations for school had to begin. John and Howard went to the new school, "Julia Green," on Hobbs Road, less than a mile from our house. We were so close to school that we were not qualified for bus service, but we received special permission for them to ride the school bus, which came by our door. Howard was in the sixth grade and John was in the third grade. John's teacher was a young pretty lady who married during the year. She invited each student and parents to the wedding, which was a beautiful affair at the downtown Presbyterian Church. We arrived early enough to get an aisle seat near the front – John was so excited about this event because he cared deeply for his teacher. But she hurt his feelings several times that year that made me angry, and I regret not talking to her about them. One day the Civil War was being discussed in class. Having lived a year on the old battlefield site of the Battle of Murfreesboro, and having gone to the military park a number of times this discussion greatly interested John, who was eight years old. He raised his hand and said, "My grandfather lives in a house that was used as a hospital, and there are blood stains still on the floor." She passed over this information as not important and said, "Now, John, don't tell stories like that." He tried to assure her the bloodstains were real. But she was ignorant of the fact that blood could soak into the very cells of the wood and become part of the wood – never to be removed. I was so angry. I explained to John the staining process and explained he knew more than she did. Ray and I talked it over, and he advised it best to let the subject drop.

Another time John wanted to bake his teacher a cake because the new box cake mixes were out and he had helped me bake a cake. One afternoon when I got home from school he had mixed a cake and had it baking in the oven. I then showed him how to make a confectionery sugar icing. He was so proud of the big slice of cake that he took to his teacher the next day. When he told her he baked it himself, she said, "You know, John, you didn't do that. Your mother baked this cake." Again I was angry. But Ray said "No, don't create a problem."

Another time the class discussed Fort Nashborough and the beginning of the settlement of Nashville. John raised his hand and said, "My family has ancestors who were at Fort Nashborough." Again this teacher said, "Now, John, don't say things like that." She never questioned him about who they were, how he knew, or anything. The Leiper's, a prominent pioneer family at Fort Nashborough, were of our family line. My great, great, great, great grandfather was a Leiper whose granddaughter married James Bell and she and her brothers, sisters, nieces, nephews, and cousins were at Fort Nashborough. I had read to John and Howard from a book telling of this Leiper family in the settlement of Nashville. He remembered, and felt it was an important piece of information to share with his class. Again I was angry with that pretty young thoughtless girl who was trying to teach my son. It makes my blood boil now to think how John was treated.

Howard was in the sixth grade. Occasionally, his deaf ear presented difficulties. Each teacher was told of this problem and given the doctor's report – that he needed to be seated near the front of the room on the teacher's left side and be aware that he did not hear from his right side. Some teachers remembered, but others did not. Howard was diligent in keeping up his homework and always did his own work. The principal of Julia Green, Mrs. Mathis, sometimes taught arithmetic classes. She was a short, loud mouthed, strident, arrogant, person, who was in school at Middle Tennessee College with Ray and me. We did not think highly of her capabilities or her manner with children. In her math classes she would walk around the room – give out a problem quickly, snap her fingers, point at a student, call the name, and expect a quick answer. When Howard missed the answer, she would become angry with him. Ray had several sessions with her in regard to this as well as the treatment that John received. Ray and Mrs. Mathis did not always agree, but she had to give him respect and attention because each year that Howard and John were in Julia Green, Ray was on the Men's Club Board – as Secretary, as a member of several policy-making committees, and as Program Chairman. I was never able to go to the Julia Green P.T.A. meetings because I was always in Hillsboro teaching, so Ray had to handle the grammar school problems for the boys. At the close of Howard's eighth grade year, Mrs. Mathis, held the door open for us and said, "I believe Howard is not college material" – right in front of Howard. I remember how anger built up inside of me as I thought to myself, "you just wait and see, old sister." Howard says he said to himself "Oh yes, I will graduate from college." She was one teacher and principal who was unworthy of the position she held.

I had one grand surprise at the beginning of the school year (1948). Ray bought a car, a Ford, for me (of course, I paid my share of it). For the first time in my life (almost 34 years) I had my own transportation. Ray was using his Mercury and still supervising the Boy's Club activities in the evenings. So my own transportation meant I could pick up the boys at school and drive them to different activities. It also meant I could be home earlier to be with them and run errands. The spring before I got the car we had experienced some difficulty with Billy Morehead, an older boy who lived on Walnut Drive (a nearby road). Billy would come to our house before I would get home from school. One day I came home to find him jumping up and down on Howard's bed; another time I was told he had run through the house slamming doors and throwing things at Howard and John; another time I was home and I looked out the window and saw him bending

Howard's right arm back as far as he could (the arm he had broken twice and could not yet fully extend at the elbow). I went out in the yard and told him to go home. I called his mother and explained the condition of Howard's arm and the seriousness of another break, which her son appeared to be attempting to do. He never came back to our house. Later in life, he gave his family trouble and was known as a troublemaker.

There were several boys in the neighborhood who formed friendships with Howard and John. The boys would go to each other's home for refreshments, games and basketball. At our house we always had ice cream in the freezer and they liked to play basketball in the backyard. The basketball goal was on a locust tree and, of course, they wore the grass down to the brown earth. Chuck Smith, Spencer Iverett, Jake Libby, Tommy Hopkins and Sonny Miller formed the small group of friends for Howard and John.

Hillsboro High School started at 7:30 in the morning and Julia Green started at 8:30. I would get the boys out of bed, prepare breakfast and go to school. Ray would see them eat breakfast, dress, and get on the school bus. Our faculty meeting was one hour before school started. I was able to get home before Howard and John got off the school bus.

This year, 1950, I had a maid twice a week. She did not cook supper those two days. In looking back over those years, I should have had a maid each day of the week and used my energy to better my health with more rest. Every moment of my time was scheduled. But, at the time, I enjoyed the fast pace resulting from centering my life on family, home, school and church.

This was the year, 1854, we bought our first television. We placed it in the living room in front of the back window. John was captivated with TV. Before us, the family next door, Dr Kurzrock had the only TV in the neighborhood, he was allowed to go next door once a week to see "Suspense" a scary creaking door program.

We had telephone troubles. Because of a shortage of material and manpower following the war we were able to have only a party line. The other party was the Roth family across the road and down two houses from our house. They had a son older than Howard and John and a daughter younger than either of them. One night Ray's sister Polly Clark called to say that her husband Bill had died from his surgery operation. When I answered the phone, Mrs. Roth was dialing a number even though my phone was already connected with Polly in Baltimore, Maryland. With Polly crying and trying to tell me about Bill and Mrs. Roth's dialing in my ear I said to her "Mrs. Roth, we are on a long distant call." She said to no one in particular, "since those people have rented rooms I never can get the line," and slammed up the receiver. Ray came to the phone then. Polly started screaming and said, "Oh, he has died." It was a traumatic situation for us all. Ray called the telephone company to tell them of our difficulty with Mrs. Roth and found out they had had trouble before with her. The next day we had a private line. Following a church service in Baltimore, Polly came to Nashville with Bill's body by train. Ray and I met the train and made arrangements in Nashville for the burial. A graveside service was held at the White family plot in the Nolensville Cemetery where he is buried.

At this time we knew Mr. White was not well. He rode the bus to New Albany, Mississippi, so that Dr. Bob Shands, his son-in-law, could conduct tests at the Shands Hospital. After a few days in New Albany, Mr. White returned to Nashville on the bus. Ray met the bus and Mr. White stayed a few days with us. Then we drove him to the farm. At this time Mr. White had not received a report from Bob's tests. Mother came over for a visit on the day we drove Mr. White to the farm. The next day was Monday. Each of us went about our schedule at the Boys' Club and at our schools. When I came home in the afternoon, Mother was upset because Ed had called for Ray to come to the hospital in Murfreesboro, and she couldn't reach Ray by phone. In the morning Mr. White had sharp and intense pain in his abdominal area followed by vomiting and nausea. He had been taken to the hospital and diagnosed as having a ruptured colon, which had thrown feces in the abdominal area. The doctor operated. He said it was impossible to get all the feces from his abdomen and there wasn't a chance for him to live. Ed was calling Mr. White's children to come immediately. By phone we found Ray helping a group of Boys' Clubbers from the "Neighborhood Boys' Club" build a float to be in the fire department parade. He and I arrived at the Murfreesboro hospital at dusk. We went into Mr. White's room; spoke to him; held his hand, and were told by the nurse to leave. Soon Margaret and Mrs. Floyd, the head nurse of Shands Hospital, came to the Murfreesboro hospital from New Albany, Mississippi. The diagnosis at the Shands hospital had been advanced colon cancer, but the news had not reached Mr. White before the colon had ruptured. If it had arrived in time he could have undergone colon surgery and lived a bit longer. Mrs. Floyd took over private duty nursing for Mr. White. Polly flew in at about 10 o'clock. Ray and I met the plane. Margaret and Polly spoke briefly to Mr. White. For some reason I don't remember John A. there. He and Martha Lou were living with Aunt Bertha and Uncle Buford in Springfield, Tennessee.

Mr. White died in the early hours of the morning soon after midnight. He was buried in the White plot beside his wife in the Nolensville Cemetery. His funeral service was at Woodfin Funeral Home in Murfreesboro.

After the burial, the family met at the farm. John A. wanted to buy the farm from the other siblings, Ed, Ray, Margaret and Polly. They all met in the kitchen, sitting around the table. I was in the living room with Martha Lou, Mother, Aunt Bertha and Uncle Buford. Martha Lou was called into the meeting. I remained in the living room. Martha Lou and John A. did not want Ed to stay on the farm if they bought it. Ed decided to buy the old grocery store (which was vacant at the time) next to the Stone's River Military Park on the Old Nashville Highway. Agreement was reached around 12 o'clock that night. John A. would pay each brother and sister a little over $2,000 for his or her share and would buy from Ed the farm equipment, cattle and produce. That was not a good business deal for Ray and the girls, for the farm was worth more than $10,000. The siblings allowed sentiment to take over business judgment – as later years have proven. There was a verbal agreement with John A.

that, at his death, the farm and his estate (except furniture, monies, belonging to Martha Lou) would go to the grandsons of Mrs. White, whose inheritance had paid for the farm. Soon after that time John A. and Martha Lou took over the farm. Ed bought the grocery store, where there was also room to live, and he later married Jenny. I believe Ed was happy in his work and it suited his health limitations. Jenny kept a clean house and was a good cook, but she was not an educated or traveled person. Ed explained, "she didn't always understand or comprehend things."

Howard and John had joined the Cub Scouts at Julia Green School when they entered school. John excelled to the level of webalos. They then joined the Boys Scouts their scoutmaster was a former World War II soldier, Mr. Crossman, who believed in roughing and toughing up the boys. At the meetings he sent each boy down the paddle line. Some of the boys were older, larger and stronger than my boys. Ray heard of this paddle line. He was against any form of rough treatment to young boys. He took both John and Howard out of the boys scout program – I wonder if that was the appropriate thing to do for their social development.

The music teacher at Hillsboro, Mr. Thompson, started a beginner's band with the older students at Julia Green. Both Howard and John entered the program. Howard played the cornet and John played the drums then clarinet. I was anxious for them to have a basic appreciation and knowledge for music, but not elaborate training. After he became proficient Howard played evening taps and morning reveille at camp.

Westminster Church started a youth choir for young children under 10. John joined this group. I made him a white cotton choir robe – all materials were furnished by the church, cut out and ready to sew. He continued his interest in singing through twelfth grade. Later, in high school he would sing tenor in the main church choir and in the school chorus, and All State chorus. Julia Green School had an arrangement with the Nashville Symphony to play children's concerts following the school day and taking the children by school bus to attend a concert. Both Howard and John had tickets for that program which offered them greater appreciation of good music. Ray and I had season tickets for the night symphony held in the War Memorial Building. Our seats were in the balcony, front row, which we kept throughout the years until the new concert building was erected.

John had a used red Schwinn bicycle, it was an adult size but he enjoyed riding with the neighborhood boys. He begged and begged to ride his bike to school. Finally we gave him permission. On Hobbs Road he was coming downhill breaking with students on the right gavel side of the road where he was riding. Suddenly a girl walked on the pavement in front of his bike, he hit the breaks so hard he flew head first over the handlebars. He hit his head on the pavement. John was befriended by two elderly ladies who took John home and he came to there, probably unconscious for about 30 minutes. Needless to say John rode the bus to school after that. He loved to stand inside our front door and wait for the bus to stop in front of our house for him.

John went out for football at Julia Green. Ray and I had a

big disagreement over his football shoes. Auntie offered Bill Worsham's shoes, which were two sizes too large. I remember Ray said, "Just wear two pairs of socks." I pleaded with him to buy John a pair of football shoes. I made the mistake of not taking matters in my own hands to ensure that John had perfectly fitted shoes. He made the team, even when only wearing no jock strap. His team played one game at MBA. I went late (as soon as possible after Hillsboro closed). Walking up the driveway at MBA a man passed me; spoke; and called me "Mrs. White." I did not know the man but something inside me said, "John is hurt." When I got to the field, Mr. John Sloan, met me and said John was hurt and needed to go to the hospital to be checked – it seemed to be an ankle injury. Mr. Sloan followed me in his car to Vanderbilt and Dr. Tom Zerfoss' office. That injury ended John's football playing for the year, but Julia Green played in the Clinic Bowl after the season was over, John was well enough to play. They did not bring a jersey for him to the game and had to share #11 with Graham Woolwine, John's name was not on the announcer's list, so when John would be in the play, we heard "the tackle was made by Graham Woolwine. That ankle would bother him during high school basketball tryouts.

John also played Little-League baseball. I remember Mrs. Libby told me I would have been so proud of John sliding into home plate for the winning run if I could have seen him. John could not attend weekly practice since he was at camp, he had special consideration since he played hardball at camp. He played first base since he was left handed, he was first string for 2 years.

Chapter 16 – My Boys, Howard and John, and Boys' Club Camp

Boys' Club Camp was held for five weeks each summer at a group campsite in Montgomery Bell State Park. At camp Howard and John became competent at swimming, hiking, archery, riflery, diving, badminton, ping-pong, baseball and volleyball, and each received his Red Cross junior and senior life certificates two years before the allowed age. When each became of age, he took responsibility as leaders in these activities – serving as junior counselors at 12 and senior counselors at 14 (two years younger than normal because of their familiarity with camp methods).

Following camp we would take a vacation, often going camping in the mountains with Jimmy and Henrietta Durham and their boys. We always slept in a tent and cooked on a Coleman stove or a campfire. The Durham's were our college friends. Their two boys were the age of ours. All of us loved the mountains. We traveled and camped on all the back roads and campgrounds of the Smokies. Henrietta Durham believed in cleanliness. We had to wash all dishes in hot soapy water and pour boiling water over the washed dishes. Drinking water was boiled. Hands had to be thoroughly washed before eating or preparing food or handling food. She was from Chattanooga and said "warsh" for wash.

One day at Boy's Club camp, on or about 1949, I experienced a very heavy menstrual period, passing a large mass of blood. For some months I had experienced unusually heavy monthly periods, so I didn't think too much about it. I drove to Nashville, picked up eggs and chickens at Alloway's on Second Avenue. At C. B. Ragland, also on Second Avenue, Mr. Beck placed my order in the trunk of the car. Then I went to the State Department building on Charlotte Avenue to get movies to show that night at camp. By that time I was trembling, weak, and nauseated. I asked the clerk if there was someone who would take the heavy load to my car. That woman looked at me and said, "No, there isn't. I've seen teachers carry out many more than you have." I stumbled to the car – and drove straight to Dr. Tom's office. He was aggravated with me for not seeing him immediately. He concluded that I had suffered a miscarriage, and he told me to go to bed and lie flat of my back until the bleeding stopped. I told him I had to drive back to camp because of the eggs and meat in the car. He said have Ray drive me home that night. I drove to camp in a weak trembling condition. Upon returning to camp Ray asked me to be hostess to Louie Phillips, a member of the Boys' Club Board, and his wife, who were spending the afternoon at camp and planned to eat dinner with the boys. I tried to tell him how weak I was and that I had suffered a miscarriage, but he wouldn't listen. When the Phillips left camp I insisted he drive me home and call Dr. Tom. I remember how pale he became when he was talking to Dr. Tom, who told him I was in danger of hemorrhaging to death and that I had to have someone with me all of the time. He called Mother, who took days off from work and stayed with me for 4 days – would not let me off the bed or even sit up. After that Ray drove me to camp where I stayed in the clinic room with Mrs. Miles, the camp nurse, who brought me my food and would not let me walk until all signs of bleeding had stopped. For the rest of the summer I took it easy at home.

The next summer we lived in the cabin on the hill on the road leading into camp. A bathroom was added to the one-room cabin. It only supplied cold water, but it was wonderful to have a flushing commode, shower, and lavatory. That summer we had several visitors – friends and family, who stayed a few days or one day with us.

In Montgomery Bell State Park there were some plum trees and blackberry bushes. I made preserves and Jam on the camp cook stove to carry home for the winter months. One day I was cutting plums away from the seeds. Ray brought a 9-year old crying boy to stay with me. He wanted to go home – a very home sick little boy. He talked about his family, school, and why he wanted to go home. He said, "my grandmother wants me to go home; my mama wants me to come home," and, with tears running down his cheeks, he said "and God wants me to go home." He spent the morning with me and went to the afternoon swim with the other boys. The next day was Sunday, visitor day. That afternoon I went downhill to the waterfront. This homesick little boy was there with his parents, all of them grinning from ear to ear. When he saw me he came running to me and said with sparkling eyes, "I floated today – the first time I have ever floated." He put his arms around my waist and said, "I'm glad I didn't go home." That was a very happy experience for me.

One year Mrs. Miles could not come to camp because she was getting a divorce. Her husband was a Peabody

College professor. We hired a retired nurse for the camp. We were spending the camp session at Lake Woodhaven Campsite across the lake from where we had previously camped. She was afraid of each bug, each insect, and the out of doors. Our cabins were nicely built of rock – but she stuffed toilet paper in each crack and crevice she could find and rarely came out of her room except to the dining hall for meals. Someone came to me with a camper and said the boy had hurt his arm when jumping off his iron bunker bed. I saw he had broken his arm between the wrist and elbow in a green twig break. I sent him to the nurse and went about my duties. In about an hour I saw Ray and said, "Why aren't you at the hospital with the boy who has a broken arm?" He said, "What broken arm? The nurse said he just hurt his arm and she had bandaged it." When Ray saw the definitely broken arm he was so mad at this nurse that he told her to pack her bags, he was driving her to Nashville – that he and his wife would see to the nursing. I was a certified Red Cross Home Nurse and First Aid teacher and therefore qualified as a camp nurse.

I drove the young boy to Goodlark Hospital in Dickson to have his arm set and protected by a cast. This was my second trip to the hospital that day – earlier I had driven another young boy there with a sore throat. Then around 6 o'clock that evening I had to drive a third camper to the hospital with a sprained ankle. He had been on a hiking trip to the lookout tower and tripped over a rock – had to be brought back to camp in the car. As he and I were waiting in the emergency room, a nurse came by, recognized me, patted me on the shoulder and said, "you are having a rough time with your children, aren't you?"

In camp that summer at the Woodhaven group campsite we had a 15-year-old boy from Juvenile Court. One day he was on a hike with other campers. The leader of the hike brought in a fat copperhead snake. Someone said, "I believe she's pregnant." So while the hike leader held the snake to the ground the boy from Juvenile Court slit the snake's stomach open. She was pregnant! Baby snakes crawled out of her body and went in all directions. Someone said, "kill them, they are as poisonous as an adult copperhead." Everyone grabbed something to kill a snake – there must have been twenty baby snakes crawling about. No one was bitten and, I believe, all the snakes were killed. That was an ordeal I would not want to live over – a dangerous one!

That year was our only summer at Camp Woodhaven, for it was normally used for girls' group camping. We liked the rustic beauty of the old camp across the lake from Woodhaven, and held Boys' Club Camp at that site thereafter. The boys and Ray made a council circle with benches on the side of a wooded hill. Here we held camp devotions on Sunday with an invited speaker, who would give a talk on character building, morality, and living a good, clean life. This would not be allowed today in a youth group of varying religious denominations and beliefs. The boys would gather by units with their leader and march single file, without talking, down the wooded path to the circle and silently be seated for the program. With songs and prayers it was truly an inspirational time. We drove Church of Christ campers to White Bluff for church each Sunday.

Once Howard reached high school he played reveille on

his cornet to wake up the campers. Then campers would get up and dress, unit leaders would check cabins, and campers would gather around the flag pole in front of the dining hall for the pledge of allegiance and the raising of the flag. Each afternoon before supper, the ritual was repeated with the lowering of the flag. John learned enough cornet to carry on the tridition after Howard got a real summer job.

At the end of each camp session we had our "Camp Fire" ceremony where the leaders and instructors gave awards to deserving campers. The campfire, itself, was a work of art, built over several days time in a pyramid of logs about 5 or 6 feet high. The fire was lit by a counselor, who held a lighted torch as he was paddled across the lake in a canoe to the swimming dock and then raced to the pyramid on the hillside and lit the campfire. The campers, the other leaders, and visiting board members watched while sitting around the fire in a large circle. It was beautiful, a sight to behold! John added additional drama by being an archer receiving the flame and shooting a flaming arrow into the campfire to start it.

John began a fun activity that was enjoyed by the campers. After the noon and night meals he would start the campers singing camp songs, activity songs, and action songs. One of their favorites was the "hiker song," where, while singing and patting on the tables or their chest, the campers would act out a thunderstorm, walking through grass and rain and meeting a bear. Everyone had to repeat the sounds in reverse order to escape the bear, at 5xspeed. John was an excellent motivator and song leader during his camp leadership days. By this time

Howard had outgrown camp and was off working at a summer job at Redstone Arsenal in Alabama.

John carried this type of leadership into his church activities. He was youth fellowship chairman for Westminister, Middle Tennessee Synod, and UCYM (southeastern United Christian Youth Movement.) He also served as vice-president and president of Westminister youth group and chairman of UCYM. The last postion allowed him to attend Lake Geneva, Wisconsin National UCYM.

When Howard was in the eleventh grade and John was in the eighth grade, Hale Harris asked Ray if he would take a few Hillsboro High School basketball players to camp as leaders. Ray thought it might be a good idea – but one which he later regretted. The parents of one boy insisted that he should have a car at camp for emergencies. This gave the Hillsboro boys a chance to sneak out at night and during our rest hour. Although they were Howard's friends, they did not want him to know about the trips. Ray had to constantly, monitor them. One night, about 11:30 A.M., I was awakened and immediately felt that something was not right in camp because there was dead silence, which was unusual. I awakened Ray. He took his flashlight and made the rounds of the cabins. None of the Hillsboro boys were in camp and the car was gone. He waited at the gate for them to drive back and gave them a lecture on responsibility. He also had trouble with them telling the campers horrible stories about what would happen to them if they didn't behave; also teasing them on the fire tower climb about throwing them off the tower. This type of treatment of the campers was not the policy of the Boy's Club Camp. Needless to say, the next summer, when Hale Harris asked Ray to take Hillsboro boys to camp, Ray had a ready answer: he had his staff positions filled – so much for the "advantaged" boys working with the "disadvantaged" boys. Although Howard and John were "advantaged" boys, they never thought in those terms during camp.

For the 19 years that I was at Boy's Club Camp with Ray, I planned the meals; ordered the food and related supplies; bought all supplies needed daily and weekly; supervised the cooks; the serving of food, and cleaning up the dining room. For 14 years I was camp nurse. Each day following a meal, campers would line up outside the clinic door for treatments. Ray or a senior counselor would help me. I drove campers to Goodlark Hospital whenever treatment or medical attention was needed.

One interesting camper I cannot forget. This 9-year-old boy got off the bus in camp without any luggage – only the shorts, shirt, and shoes he was wearing. I got together some clothes, swim shorts, tennis shoes, and underwear for him. (I always had a large bag full of clothes – outgrown by my boys and their friends.) The first evening following supper Ray brought the boy to the clinic. He had impetigo of the worse sort. Of course, he could not swim or participate in any action sports. These places had to be dressed 3 times daily. The next day I drove him to Goodlark Hospital to see a doctor. He was given medication and a routine to follow. We kept him in camp for 4 days – treating him, taking him to the doctor each day (all paid for by Boy's Club). He was beginning to show good improvement but could not actively participate in camp life. Ray thought it best for him to go home for the betterment of the other campers. He called his mother. I drove him home. His mother was absolutely furious with me for bringing her son home. She said some mean bad things about Ray, the camp, and me for not keeping her son (I might say here: he was a charity case; she had not paid one cent for his camp). I gave her the bundle of good clothes; explained the routine of washing the sores and applying medication; gave her the medication. She grabbed the boy by the shoulders, shoved him through the door, and slammed the door in my face. I shall always remember the pained, hurt, humiliated look on that little boy's pale face – so much for giving your time and talent to someone who has no appreciation.

In the mid-fifties the State Park Commission built a building containing two bedrooms, a bath, a kitchen, and an office for the director of Camp Site II. This was directly across from the dining room. I enjoyed the privacy of a bedroom with a real bed and mattress, chest of drawers, and clothes closet. The other bedroom was used in conjunction with the clinic with two beds ready for a camper who was sick with an elevated temperature or other symptoms requiring bed rest. The kitchen was used as the clinic. It had a sink with running hot and cold water, a range, a refrigerator and cabinets. The bathroom had a shower, a lavatory, a commode and hot and cold water. The office was roomy with a large desk, couch, chairs and a single bed next to a closet for home sick boys or our visitors. By this time we were staying 5 weeks at camp, which took up most of our summer. This house added to my duties; however, because it always had to be kept clean and in order. We never knew when board members and their wives or children would show up in the afternoon for a dinner meal.

This added hostess duties. When wives came with husbands we would sit in the office, drink Coca Colas and talk. One of my favorite wives was Mrs. McGovern, wife of the President of Union Planters Bank. She was a domineering large woman who spoke her mind. She had no children. We got along well – and had many laughs together. I showed her a pocket watch Ray had bought me from the estate of the woman founder of Boy's Club. The next time she came to camp she brought me a gold pin for my pocket watch so I could pin my watch on my blouse. Her mother and father had given this pin to her as a teenager. I cherish the pin and her memory.

During the mid-fifties, the Boy's Club had been given 2 or 3 old war surplus cars. They were old manual shift models. I had a rough time driving those old cars (my car was all automatic and I loved it). On Highway 70 on my way to Nashville I had a flat tire! Good luck was with me, there was a filling station a few hundred yards up the highway and I got a ride with the man who pulled up behind me after my flat. One day I was driving up Second Avenue from Alloway's and couldn't shift the gears fast enough; stalled the motor; and the car behind me hit the back end of my car. No damage was done to either car so no papers were filed. One night at dusk I drove out to Cathey's grocery store on the highway. On the way back I had a flat tire in the park. When I got out to look at the tire a carload of teenage boys passed, hollered at me and made signs. A car with a man, woman, and 2 children pulled up about this time. I asked them to drive me to the campsite. As I was getting in their car the teenage boys drove by again. I was grateful for that family. I told them about the car passing me earlier. John met us as we drove into camp because he and Ray had gotten concerned about my being on the park roads after dark. When I saw him I threw myself into his arms and started crying – then the man and woman told him what happened. After that I never went by myself after dark. On another day I had driven to Nashville for supplies. As I returned to camp John (then a little boy) with a bunch of boys met the car in an excited manner. John's first question was, "Where is my snake." Scared the daylights out of me! He found his green snake dead – stretched out across the hood of the car. It seemed he had put the snake in the car for safe keeping not knowing I was going to Nashville in that car. I shudder to think what I would have done if that snake had crawled on me while I was driving.

My daily trip to Cathey's grocery store was always a treat. I took the mail out and collected the incoming mail; bought any small supplies needed; and chatted with Mr. and Mrs. Cathey about park news. She always had a cold bottle of coke in the corner of her drink box and sometimes a special dessert for me. Our summer friendship lasted through my 19 years at camp. Whenever I am going by their store I always stop. My last time was in 1992. We all three cried when I left. Mr. Cathey said, "he would never see me again" (he had had a heart attack). He also said Ray was one of the finest men he had ever known. One year Mrs. Cathey and I decided we would go cat fishing off the swimming dock at dusk – this was against park rules. She brought the poles and I supplied the dough balls. We sat on the dock and caught any number of catfish before the mosquitoes and gnats drove us away. It was fun; but the park superintendent found out about it – so no more cat fishing for us.

On my trips into Nashville I would stop by my house on Lynwood; pick up the mail; wash clothes; go to town for supplies; come home and dry the clothes if I had the time. One day when I got home I had no house keys. I was so aggravated because I had a large bag of clothes to wash. I pried off a pane of glass in the basement door; turned the lock and got the door opened. Then I found the door locked going upstairs. Anyway I washed clothes; relocked the basement door and pounded the glass pane into the frame with a rock. Such tribulations to wash a load of dirty blue jeans, socks, shorts, and T-shirts!

An enjoyable thing happened to me one summer. Mother and Elsie Elam visited us for a few days. Elsie was my age; had a beautiful trained soprano voice; had sung a leading part in "The Messiah" in Nashville, and she was a church friend of Mother's. We went to the little chapel (Cumberland Presbyterian) on the grounds of Montgomery Bell State Park. The pump organ was open; the songbooks were there; so, I decided to attempt to play the organ while Elsie sang. We were having such a good time with the old gospel songs. I looked at the sanctuary and there were several people seated in the pews listening to us. Elsie knew they were there and was singing her best. The people thought we were giving a program. They were so complementary!

Ray did not have anyone on the staff he thought suitable to direct the arts and crafts program, so I got the job. I kept it for 10 years. Two counselors helped. One had responsibility for lanyards. John helped with other crafts – enamel work, potholders, etc. Each camper had to have a great deal of help. My job was to organize, keep supplies on hand, and stay in the craft cabin when I did not go to Nashville or the hospital. Craft hours lasted 2 or 3 hours in the mornings. Some 10 feet from the front porch was an old rotten stump. Ray had told me there was a nest of copperheads in the tree stump – to stay away from it and keep the boys from it. One day I started to step up on the porch and saw a baby copperhead stretched out sunning on the step. Just in time I adjusted my stride so as to step over that snake. I had nightmares about that! They would not come out when people were around, so there wasn't any great danger if we watched our step.

The cooks were always very important to camp. As Ray said, "At any cost, keep the cooks happy." So I stayed out of their way as much as possible and let them have their way. They had a printed menu for each meal, snack, and camp-out for the entire one-week camp session, and had supplies to work with that printed menu. I have mentioned Mr. Barton, who was an excellent cook, organizer, and loved to see the campers enjoy his food. After him we went to a man cook and his wife. The man was a hard drinker all 24 hours of the day and his poor wife had to do most of the work. The next year we had 2 black women who had cooked in Nashville City Schools and had come with excellent recommendations. I knew something was wrong the first day. They seemed lost. I gave them the printed menu and they looked blank. I read the menu for the day. Then it popped in my mind. They couldn't read! They were accustomed to doing what someone told them to do and no more. They chose canned goods by the pictures on the labels, and, if the can had no pictures, we would be surprised by our food. So I had to give them more supervision, which was boring, Ray helped me out, so together we got through that camping year. The next cook was a huge black man who was a good cook and a good organizer – but he had to be handled with kid gloves – we were afraid of him really! One day I was in the kitchen, John, who was then 12 years old, walked in and said "Mama." Well, the cook threw a knife at him. On his shoulder John had a lizard, which the cook was afraid of, he had told John that. I almost fainted. John had entered the kitchen forgetting he was "with lizard". While we had this cook Polly Clark's son Tom spent the summer with us and went with us to camp. This cook fascinated Tom with his stories and he taught Tom how to play poker. Ray and I had to monitor Tom every minute all summer long to keep him away from the cook. Tommy felt he was special and did not have to follow camp routine or rules. He was a headache for Ray, John, Howard and me. I doubt if Polly appreciated all we have done for her two boys – she never invited Howard or John to visit her. This cook stayed with us for several years – drinking all night and in the kitchen all day. However, one morning he didn't show up for breakfast – too drunk – Ray came for me and together we got breakfast on the table for 110 people. Have you ever tried to stir oatmeal in a 10-gallon pot? It is as heavy as lead. So that was the last camping session for that cook.

Our next cooks were two black women, about 60 years old, from Davidson County School system. They were good cooks, organizers, and could read! They stayed with us as long as Ray and I were going to camp. Their fault was – aspirins! It seemed every other day I would buy them a bottle of aspirins. So they stayed high on aspirin day and night. Ray said "keep them happy." I continued buying aspirin. They kept a clean, orderly kitchen. Each had a small bedroom, shared a bath on the back of the kitchen and kept a radio playing. We never saw them outside the dining room. During the five weeks they never left camp. The boys didn't bother them and they didn't bother the boys. It was a good situation.

My supply orders were given one month before camp. The salesman would call me; give me pointers on good buys for the summer; send me a copy of the order of the previous year with changes in prices. I would make changes for the summer and mail it back to him. He would send Boy's Club a copy of the bill. I would call Alloway's for eggs, chicken, other fresh meats, current prices and delivery schedule. They would send me the order to fill and send the bill to Boy's Club. I would go to McKesson Wholesale Company on Second Avenue for medical supplies. Ray would make out this order after talking to several doctors for recommendations about the best medicines to use in camp. The Program Director would buy supplies for all group and waterfront activities.

Both Howard and John made excellent group leaders and activity leaders – each taking his job seriously and with maturity of thought and action. Both Ray and I were so proud of them – as I am today. Their strength of character, ability to see jobs finished, and caring thoughtfulness for other people – have all contributed to their success in life.

We got special permission from the state parks to build a natural rifle range on a hillside away from the camp. Am experienced NRA certified riflery instructor took charge for two years. He was the first person to get bitten by a copperhead at our camp. It was near the swimming area during afternoon general swim. He came back to camp and trained John to take over for the next year, John was the youngest riflery instructor ever to be certified by the National Riflery Association. he had charge of the rifle range, where campers shot 22 gauge rifles at targets for scores. He also taught swimming at the waterfront. As a camper both Howard and John had won several "Best Hiker" awards, so, as a counselor, they often led the hikes. Howard had a lot of endurance, and loved to explore caves with other Nashville cavers, but this was not allowed at camp.

Between John's senior year and freshman year in college, he was hired by the Tennessee State Game and Fish Commission as a Nature and Conservation Counselor to teach nature classes in different state parks throughout the summer. There was a two week training period for all the counselors, John was the youngest and most experienced about walking in the woods. He was at Boy's Club Camp for our five weeks. He drew presentation charts, created a small zoo, kept poisonous and nonpoisonous snakes in jars, and kept live snakes to show as examples in his programs for the State Parks. This bothered me – having a live poisonous snake in my cabin. Of course, it was tied up in a stout bag, but I kept thinking it might get out – it never did. One day John came running to the cabin with a copperhead snake in his hand. He had banged in the snake's head, but it was still dangerous – John yelled for me to get out of his way, and I did! John threw him in the sink and finished killing him. My job that afternoon was to go to the drug store in Dickson to get a gallon of formaldehyde for pickling the copperhead for John's nature class. I had been to the drug store before for medication so the pharmacist knew me. I told him the story of my son's new job, so he sold me the formaldehyde without any questions asked and charged it to Boy's Club. That snake in the gallon jar spent more than one winter in our garage. That year John was delegate to the national UCYM youth conference. At the end of the conference he was asked to fly back to Tennessee by the Department of Parks to teach a class at Natches Trace State Park. He said this impressed the other young people at the conference.

Ray was an excellent disciplinarian. He had no real trouble with the boys. They respected him; and he kept them busy with activity. One summer Ray brought to camp several boys who had been in serious trouble with Juvenile Court. Two of those boys were found guilty of taking a Boy's Club canoe, rowing across the lake to the girls' camp and stealing some money. This happened after dark. Within two hours Ray had found out who had done it, and informed the two boys he was shipping them out of camp. I had gone to bed and was asleep when Ray awakened me to dress and ride with him out to the highway with the two boys so they could catch the bus back to Nashville. The boys were in the backseat of the car. I noticed when I got in the car one of the boys had a leather belt with a heavy metal snap which he continued to pop. I knew I was not turning my back on those two boys, and I knew then why Ray wanted me to ride with them. I sat sideways so I faced both of them and started asking them questions – they went to North High School, they said, and I immediately began talking about faculty members I knew and subjects they were in, etc. – and kept them talking all the way to the bus stop. The boy was still popping his leather belt when he got out of the car. We never mentioned why they were leaving, why he had his leather belt out – anything that would cause them to react negatively. We saw them off on the bus at midnight. They were 14 years old – old enough to take care of themselves. You had better believe that night the two doors to our cabin were locked. That was the summer when I told Ray, if I stay in camp, the doors are going to be locked.

Howard's last year at camp was 1956 because after entering Vanderbilt University he no longer came to camp to work during the summer. After John graduated from Hillsboro High School in 1959 he went to Southwestern College in Memphis, now Rhodes College. His last year at camp was 1960. So, with Howard in Cincinnati and John overseas, Ray and I were alone in camp. All joy went out of camp living without my two sons. Camp was drudgery. I told Ray I was not going back to camp unless he paid me. He paid me all right –

$50 for 5 weeks of hard work. This went on for several years. By then Ray's heart was giving him serious trouble – sapping his energy and drive. He had to leave more and more of running the camp to his program director and to me. The worst year of camp, came in 1958 when a small camper drowned at the public swimming area (a different place from our camp swimming area). We had gone over for a hike, swim and picnic – everyone in camp had gone. The waterfront instructor saw the boy jump off the dock but was too late in realizing he had not come up. By the time they pulled him out of the water he was dead. He was a poor boy from a large family. Ray went into a trance – he couldn't cope with it. He turned to me and said, "You will have to take over." The program director, the staff, and I got everyone and everything back to camp. The program director had to manage everything. Ray went into the bedroom and didn't come out for 2 or 3 days except for decision-making sessions with the program director. Directors from the camp across the lake came to offer their sympathies and he would not see them. I sat outside the cabin with them and talked with them. The family did not sue Boys' Club. I believe this was the real beginning of Ray's heart failure.

During the spring of 1964 I told Ray, definitely, I was not going to camp. I was going to have a summer to enjoy and rest from teaching school. Ray didn't believe me until the food broker called for my supply order, and I told him I was not going to camp that summer. I thought the person responsible for the meals should order the supplies. Then Ray got busy hiring people for camp. He sent Mr. Mac from the Boy's Club staff to head the camp. Mac's wife went with him to help. Ray decided that, if I were not going, he would not go. We visited camp several times during the session. One time they had five kinds of peas and beans, but no meat. The food was terrible and the camp was not efficiently run. The next year, 1965, Boys' Club had campers for only 2 weeks. After that, there was no more Boys' Club camp. All activity was centered at the new Boys' Club building on Thompson Lane in Nashville. A few years later Boys' Club lost lawsuits and had to admit girls. It became the Boys' and Girls' Club.

Those 19 summers (1945 to 1964) were a great experience for me – I was lonely for lack of lady friends, and missed going to luncheons, playing bridge, and shopping – doing all the lady things I wanted to do in the summer. The close companionship with Ray, Howard and John made up for those ladylike activities that I now enjoy. Therefore, I would not for the world take away from my life and memories those years of summertime family togetherness and loving companionship.

Chapter 17 – More About Howard and John on Lynwood Blvd.

Now I leave thoughts of Boy's Club Camp and come back to our home at 410 Lynwood Blvd. I begin with Howard entering Hillsboro High School, where I am teaching, and with John entering the sixth grade at Julia Green.

Howard and John enjoyed playing pickup basketball at school and at home. But they and the neighborhood boys also liked to play in the rock quarry behind our lot. Also, the creek running behind our house out of the rock quarry, meandered through Woodmont Golf Club; a splendid place for snake catching and golf ball searching. The kids allowance money was extended by selling golf balls from the creek back to the golfers. One day I saw a metal minnow bucket on our back terrace; I lifted the top; the bucket was tightly packed with withering snakes of all descriptions – the result of a snake-hunting hike along our nearby creek banks.

Ray and I had some discussion about sending Howard, and later John, to Montgomery Bell Academy, but both times we decided on leaving them in public school. Hillsboro was an excellent school in those days. Howard, and later John, preferred Hillsboro, where there were more activities. The Hillsboro High School building burned when Howard was a freshman. The fire was caused by faulty wiring between the old building and a new addition that was being built. Howard spent 1-1/2 years of High School in makeshift quarters on the Belmont College campus. He entered the new high school building his junior year, when John was in the eighth grade at Julia Green.

High school fraternities and sororities were big social powers at Hillsboro. And with it were formal dances held almost every weekend. Most Julia Green students attended ballroom dances in the 7th and 8th grades. Howard and his best friend, Chuck Smith, visited dancing classes for once, but did not continue. Mrs. Libby called me about John taking ballroom dancing at Fort Nightly Dance School, to which many other students were going. So I called Mrs. Fort to enroll John to attend with her school class. John really liked it. The boys wore jackets, dress shirts, and ties – all of which both my boys had been accustomed to wearing to church. We shared rides in taking the boys to Fort Nightly on West End Avenue. This was a manners class as well as ballroom dancing – they learned how to behave at concerts and plays; how to go down a receiving line; about making introductions; how boys should treat girls; about holding coats and car door, and when to remove gloves, etc. – all those little niceties of life which are so lacking in today's society. John enjoyed this activity a great deal, and attended in his seventh and eighth grade years. The Fort Nightly graduation party was at the Centennial Club downtown. He and Cela Edwards won a prize for their costumes of two stoplights, which John had designed, built and painted. Aflashlight shined through the green plastic when moving, yellow when about to stop and red when stopped, the boxes covered them except for the feet. During the dance they took them off to dance.

I believe it was John's eighth grade when square dance became popular among his friends. Each student gave a roller skating party or square dance during the year. John and Tommy Fike had their square dance at the Peabody Demonstration School gym. Joe Gibson called the dance. Their pictures were in the paper.

Howard excelled in math and science at Hillsboro and was admitted into the National Honor Society. His math teacher, Jim Lee Allen, said I would be so proud of him when he stood at the blackboard and explained math problems. His hearing loss still gave him some difficulty with new or substitute teachers but he always made the best of his hearing problem. One incident I remember clearly. A substitute teacher called for order in her classroom. Howard continued to talk to Ted Lee. She became angry and said, "Just because your mother teaches here doesn't mean you don't have to obey orders." She continued to harangue him. Howard said he was sorry, but that he had not heard her. That made her madder. When class was over Ted Lee went to her and told her about Howard's hearing disability. Ted came to my room and told me what had happened. Soon this substitute teacher came to me with all kinds of apologies. She was never sent to Hillsboro again to teach – the word got around about what she had done. Howard played trumpet, then French horn in the band. Ed Hessey, the football coach, once told me he considered Howard White the most honorable young man to have graduated from Hillsboro High.

Howard's best friend, Chuck Smith, was also his cave

exploring buddy. They joined the local caving group, the Nashville Grotto of the National Speleological Society, which met at the Geology building at Vanderbilt, and together they explored scores of caves in Middle Tennessee along the Cumberland Plateau. It is hard to believe the mud and dirt that came home with Howard's caving clothes. On two or three occasions Howard and Chuck attended national conventions of the National Speleological Society. At the time Tom Barr, a speleobiologist was doing state-funded research on the caves of Tennessee. Howard, Chuck, a few other Hillsboro boys and some Vanderbilt students helped with Barr's study, but Howard and Chuck spent more time with Roy Davis and Tank Gorin at Higginbotham cave near McMinnville (now Cumberland Caverns). I spent much time worrying about Howard's safety – even today, I react with horror thinking about his crawling in complete darkness over slimy dirt and breathing fowl air. Ray said, "Let the boy be a boy – don't hold him back." One night we were expecting Howard home from a two-day caving trip around 9 or 10PM. It came time for bed, and he had not come home. We waited for 2 or 3 hours, and I was about to lose my mind – no word from Howard. It was easy to be afraid: a student at Hillsboro High School had been killed in Higginbotham cave a few years earlier. Ray called lots of people: State troopers, local police, hospitals, McMinnville police – a policeman went out to Higginbotham cave and reported back that, from all sources he could find, the group of cavers was still in the cave and no accidents had happened. We were happy and overjoyed to see Howard home the next day. Howard continued his interest in caving until he married. He made beautiful photographs of cave passages and cave formations, winning a prize at the national convention for one of his photos. He wanted to celebrate his sixteenth birthday in the Volcano Room at Higginbotham cave, then renamed Cumberland Caverns, where he had helped widen the entrance, string lights through some of the passageways and helped find and document new areas of the cave. Ray, Howard, John, and I went to the cave with a chocolate birthday cake and a picnic meal. It was a beautiful cave with nice lighting. Howard wanted us to see the Monument Pillar formation in a passage, which had not been prepared for the general public. At first the passageway was wide and easy (this was the long Big Room); then we climbed and worked our way across a large room littered with breakdown. The passage became smaller and we had to turn sideways to get through. Then, it stopped. Howard crawled through a round hole above his head and held his arms down to pull me up – into a small barrel shaped hole with a hole above it to be pulled through. This was frightening. I couldn't breathe. I started to cry. Howard swiftly went through the hole above his head, pulled me through into a gorgeous, beautiful display of color and columns. John and Ray followed. We took pictures. I found the return trip easier. I appreciate the caring attitude of my family to see me safely through that ordeal. When Howard worked in Huntsville, Alabama, during summers after his second and third year of college, he also explored many Alabama caves.

Howard and John wanted to hike the Appalachian Trail with the Durham boys. Their big trip was from the main road about halfway up from Gatlinburg to the old Mt. LeConte, south to the Appalachian Trail, westward along the trail through Newfound Gap and on to Fontana Dam. The 41-mile hike traversed the main ridge of the Smoky Mountains. Ray and I hiked with them along a brief section of the Appalachian Trail toward the end of the first day. Ray built a fire, set up our pup tent, and spread our sleeping gear. I prepared to fry hamburgers (we thought they would be eating dried food for several days thereafter fresh meat would be an excellent send off). As I was turning the hamburgers, I heard a grunt and a noise. There was a grown black bear standing on his hind legs about 20 feet away from me. Ray said, "Don't move. Stay perfectly still," which I did and he did. Evidently the bear thought neither the hamburger meat nor we would make a choice dinner. He suddenly dropped to all fours and lumbered off. Ray and I spent a miserable three days waiting for the boys to appear at the Fontana Dam trailhead. They were tired, dirty, hungry and thirsty – the first thing they wanted was food and drink. They had one story to tell that frightened me. They had set up camp at a shelter and built their campfire when three grown men came to the shelter for the night. They were carrying packs of all can goods, our boys had looked every where for dryed foods. They were rough talking and evidently had been drinking. One fellow pulled out a glass unlabed flask from his hip pocket and with outstretched hand said "Younuz wouna ave uh dryink?" There were only four beds in the shelter so Howard, John and the Durham boys moved out of the shelter hiked another mile and slept on the ground – which was also dangerous. They remembered unusual terms the men used, including "Yee","twixt and tween" and other Elizabethan phrases and mountain expressions, which our boys had never heard. Both Howard and John hiked other stretches of the trail, but that hike seemed the most dangerous.

Ray bought an aluminum 16-foot fishing boat from Bob Crownover. It had a 10-horsepower Mercury motor just powerful enough to pull the boys up on 6' long 6"wide water skis. We towed the boat to Center Hill Lake where both boys learned to water ski. The most fun was in the early fall or late spring on a Saturday or Sunday. We would put the boat in at Cleese's Ferry and spend time going up the Cumberland River to Ashland City, stopping to have a picnic meal. Going to Center Hill Lake was a longer run and usually involved camping overnight. By this time we had a 100lb. heavy tent with a floor, zippered window and door flap with sleeping bags for more comfortable sleeping. The tent had a oily tent smell. This boating was most enjoyable the summer after Howard graduated from Hillsboro.

At the end of this summer Howard entered Vanderbilt University to study Chemical Engineering. Except for one year he commuted from home while at Vanderbilt, utilizing a bed and desk he and Ray set up in the basement. This gave John sole use of the upstairs bedroom. That year Ray borrowed for a few years a donated pool table, it had stood in 3 feet of water for many years. There was not a place for it at the Woodbine Boys' Club on Nolensville Pike. Since it was in need of repair Ray, Howard and John replaced four legs, the damaged wood areas and covered it with new professional felt. The pool table was set up in the basement recreation room. They would put a ping-pong board on top of the pool table to play that game as well. Howard, John and their friends enjoyed the pool table, convertible ping-pong surface and the space in the basement for many gatherings and parties.

During the first summer following his Freshman year at Vanderbilt Howard went to the Vanderbilt survey camp at Monteagle. During the second and third summers he worked in Huntsville, Alabama, for Thiokol Chemical Company, where they made rocket motors.

Howard enjoyed playing French horn in the University band. He played with the band at all the home football and basketball games. During his sophomore year, he met Judith Hunt Willis in the Vanderbilt band, where they both played French horns. They began dating during the Christmas holidays. Judy was far more skilled than Howard at playing the French horn. She had a gift for music, had worked hard at practicing and had been in the Youth Orchestra. Howard had just enjoyed playing. In late May they were engaged to be married. They had a wonderful wedding on August 24, 1959 at Emanuel Baptist Church on Belle Meade Blvd. Judy's parents were Dr. Larry Willis, Supervisor of Nashville Elementary Schools, and Edna. Judy's older sister, Suzanne, was married and an accomplished violinist. After the honeymoon in Florida, Howard and Judy lived in a small apartment near campus, to which we were never invited, there Howard finished his senior year. Judy played French horn in the Nashville Symphony and attended Peabody College during that time. She had switched from Vanderbilt to Peabody to get into a stronger music program. When Howard graduated Magna Cum Laude in May 1960 he and Judy moved to Cincinnati, Ohio, where he took a job with Procter and Gamble.

John played the clarinet and e flat alto clarinet in the Hillsboro band and was drum major of the marching band his senior year. John and some band members formed a dance band and practiced in our home. They played at several small parties, including Bob Clement's 16th birthday party at the Governor's mansion, and at Assembly at Hillsboro. John also played in the Vanderbilt Marching Band, including some road trips to away football games. During his senior year the band director, William O. Sims developed Bell's syndrome in his face muscles and did not teach band. John prganised the band officers and went to Mr. Koen to request that the officers be given responsibility for the marching band. This meant planning music, show formations, partice with everyone after school and get chaperons for the bus trips. John was vice-president, Mary Bea Peek was secretary and carried most of the responsibility and planning. The football team won an invitation to the Freedom Bowl in Murfreesboro and the band played at halftime, each performance was dedicated to Mr. Sims, each week we went to his house and reviewed the plans we had made.

During the eighth grade John's interest in magic began to take shape in the form of giving shows. His first major stage show was at a Julia Green assembly. He was good with his hands in more ways than one; had a great deal of poise for an eighth grader; and spoke well on his feet before a group of people. He did several birthday shows for which he was paid; during his freshman year at Hillsboro he gave a magic show to the entire student body from the stage every year he was at Hillsboro. It was well received. He started a magic club at school, which about 30 students joined. John was president of the Hillsboro Magic Club for four years. He gave a show in the Maxwell Ball Room before a group from the East Nashville Civitan Club House. Ray and I attended. John looked so handsome in his tux and handled the whole program with a great deal of poise. He performed at many Boys' Club activities, camp and dinners. He was asked to do tricks on the Saturday afternoon local TV dance parties, WSIX, WSM and WLAC. Hje became a regular member of the WLAC show with pantomime talents, John did magic. His good friends were members of the Society of Magicians SAM), including David Cobb and Jimmy Sanders. He was too young to join, but was invited to many meetings. This interest in magic has continued in his adult years. For several years he was active in the Atlanta Magic Club, held office including President received awards and certificates for his skill and talent. Presently John is a member of national organizations SAM, IBM andHollywood's Magic Castle. He has designed magic related crystal lapel pins.

John and Howard began stamp collections during grammar school. John took a lifetime interest in this hobby, but Howard had put his collection aside, he took both collections to a meeting of the Civil Air Patrol meeting at the downtown YMCA and gave them to "someone" to appraise. He never saw them again, John found that his was gone 5 years later!

While John was at Hillsboro, he was very active in outside activities. In addition to the band and the magic club, he sang in the All State choir, was a vocal soloist in the senior class play, was Master Lighting Technition of stage lighting, curtains, microphones and props; played 1st string HI-Y basketball and played in the state turniment in Memphis. Furthermore he was a participant in the talent shows including East High for four years. He was elected to the Burro Circle for the time, talent, and energy he had given to the Hillsboro activities. He also played on St Luke's Boy's Club basketball team during the winter. He was moderator of the youth service at church his senior year. He participated in all these activities in addition to the academic work at school.

The fall after graduating from Hillsboro John entered Southwestern College at Memphis, now Rhodes College. During the spring of his 1961 junior year he became interested in the Peace Corps, which became a popular way for young people to give their service and time for our country. John Kennedy had given a speech at a University proposing a Peace Corps. He was attending Peabody College for one quarter, was youth director at St. Lukes Boys' Club, coaching the same basketball team he had played with, working at Petway Reavis clothing store in Green Hills Mall and later at the New Orleans Restaurant on 8th and Church Street. He took the first Peace Corps exam in January of 1962. By April he had become assistant manager at Green Hills and mai'te d at the restaurant, including doing magic at tables. He was accepted in April for Ceylon I project and went to the University of Pennsylvania for training, but became very sick when there was a 40 degree change of weather from 90's to 50's with no night cover, a result of the battery of shots and general fatigue. Officials notified Ray and me that John had infectious mononucleosius and would come home the next day/ We were at camp and what was required was total rest for several weeks. Every week he would go with me for a blood test when I came home from camp. In August he was given "cured". He then called the Peace Corps doctor to tell him the news, he was asked "Where would you like to go?" I'm sure one of the few Peace Corp Volunteers that was able to select where and when they went to training! After his complete recovery John chose the Philippines VIII training which was in Hilo, Hawaii at the University of Hawaii.

Chapter 18 – Teaching Prior to Desegregation

My first 17 years of teaching gave me much pleasure and joy with white girls from strong educational backgrounds, full of eagerness to learn how to become excellent homemakers, caring and giving mothers, wives and community leaders. Of those years I will relate a few stories. During my first year at Hillsboro I taught four English classes and one Home Economics class. Finding that I enjoyed the classroom activity of my Home Economics more than the sedentary nature of the English classes, I worked through the P. T. A. to encourage more students to choose Home Economics as an elective. My second year consisted of three Home Economics classes and two Junior English classes. The third year consisted of five Home Economics classes and no English classes. Within ten years the school needed a second Home Economics teacher and enough units of work had been added to permit a student to take four years of Home Economics. Each of the four years consisted of different units of work, including: food preparation and serving, textiles, sewing, child care, interior design, entertaining, Red Cross first aid and home nursing, and Red Cross pregnancy and birthing. When a second Home Economics teacher came to Hillsboro, she picked up some of the Home Economics classes. I remained head of Home Economics Department for 27 years.

In addition to four classes of Home Economics, home room and sociology, I was historian for the PTA; served refreshments for PTA meetings and in-service meetings; served luncheons for Board of Education and PTA board meetings; held two fashion shows and open houses featuring items made in sewing and food labs each year; was sponsor for the Junior class for several years; was chairman of the home economics department at Hillsboro, and was sponsor of the Future Homemakers Club. My FHA activities included: class activities toward the degree requirements in the FHA national organization; club meetings at Hillsboro each week; district meetings each month, and Tennessee State FHA conventions each year – all of the above requiring transporting students at my expense. I felt this activity added to the interest and advancement of my home economics department.

I was selected by Peabody College, Belmont College and David Lipscomb College to be the Davidson County Metro high school student practice teacher. This added greatly to my other responsibilities because I had to have conferences with the student teacher's professors and grade the student. The college girls were top students, well organized and respectful – a joy to have in my classes. Only one gave me trouble. She could not organize her material to make a point to the class. Dr. van Amwirt and I didn't know what to do about her grade. If given less than an A, she would have a most difficult time getting a teaching position. My work with student teachers discontinued after desegregation.

My students gave fashion shows. We generally presented

our fashion shows in our Home Economics lab during Open House or in the afternoons on the auditorium stage for P. T. A. meetings. I especially remember one, given before parents, the P. T. A. and the Men's Club. It was narrated by Bob Clement, who was my homeroom class president. We wrote our script, which had a story line and added background music. Bob and the girls made an excellent presentation.

I entered my better sewing students in the Middle Tennessee "Wool Contest," which was held by The Singer Sewing Machine Company. Each year my students would win honors or place in the contest. One of my former students, who won each time she entered, has received her PhD degree at the University of Tennessee and operates her own consultant business, giving seminars and lectures throughout the United States on diet and medication.

Interested students also entered the Regional Kroger "Bake-Off" contest. One year a student won first place in our region. She and I received a trip to Cincinnati for the National "Bake-Off," but she did not place in the National. In recognition of her accomplishment, the "Bake-Off" presented an electric turkey baker to me and our school, which I left at the school upon retirement. I wonder where it is now!

I entered my Home Economics program in the "Sterling Silver" contest and won. The prize was a place setting of sterling silver to be given each year to the student who received the highest grade average over four years of Home Economics. Over the years, the girls who received this expensive gift have thanked me over and over.

Every year Harvey's Department Store held a "Table Decoration with a Theme" contest. My girls generally placed and one time we won a sterling silver Revere bowl.

A student moved into the Green Hills area from California with her parents. The parents opened a restaurant featuring steaks. I had difficulty understanding her and she had trouble understanding my southern speech. One day I called the role requesting each person to answer a question on the assignment I had given out the previous day, expressing it as "For tomorrow you may read pages 10 through 20." The girl from California had figured the assignment optional and had not read it. The girl seated next to her explained, "When Mrs. White says, "you may" she means "you had better read the assignment or suffer the consequences." The California girl had a strange look on her face as a result of being called down by a fellow student who was taking up for the teacher. The California girl and I became good friends. She laughed at herself for not realizing how much my students loved and respected me.

Mr. Koen had a way of putting boys in my Sociology class who had been asked to leave the area's private schools. I remember one day during the school year a boy who had been in a private school entered my class whose parents I knew from Westminster Presbyterian Church. And I knew that this boy had recently been in Juvenile Court and, at his parents' request, had been counseled by Ray about those difficulties. I paid no special attention when he turned in his enrollment card. When he asked where he should sit I said, "over there," for I had prepared by adding a chair on the front row just before he had arrived. Deciding not to introduce him to the class, I handed him a textbook and a class paper to fill out. I paid him no special attention. He was quiet and courteous that day in class. At the end of the day Mr. Koen came by my room and said, "What did you do to Charlie? You were the only teacher who did not send him to the office." My tactics worked. Charlie sat in my class day after day; I paid the basic attention to him. During that semester he had a role in a school program in which he drove his little red Austin Healy roadster across the stage. When he arrived in our class I commented, "Charlie, I really like your Austin Healy." He looked at me and said, "How did you know it was an Austin Healy?" Off handedly, I replied, "My son Howard and his wife Judy, have one like that and it is red, too." After that encounter Charlie was a changed boy – friendly, cooperative and interested in his class work. However, he did not graduate, choosing instead to join the Army. He came by to see me the following year in his Army uniform. Charlie was one boy I believe I helped "find himself."

I remember another boy who transferred to Hillsboro from a private school. One day at the lunch table an older teacher was upset because this new boy had caused a fight in her English class – chairs were thrown and, all in all, it was a real fight. When I asked her about the boy I realized he was the son of the President of the Nashville Boys' Club Board and had, when considerably younger, visited us at camp with his father. I passed by his lunch table where he was eating alone and said, "Dan, I don't think your mother and father would like to hear about what happened in English class." He was surprised to see me. The next day at the lunch table his English teacher said she had never seen such a change in a boy – he had been courteous, cooperative, kind and a real gentleman in her class that morning. I never told her I had known the boy since grammar school and that Ray had counseled him recently in Juvenile Court.

Ray counseled many boys when requested to do so by their families. He would always tell me when a Hillsboro boy was involved, but I was obliged not to tell Mr. Koen or any of the teachers. Therefore, I knew a lot about students others did not know.

One day at the Nashville Rotary Club luncheon Ray heard a physician say some ugly things about a Hillsboro math teacher who had "given" his son an "A" rather than the "A+" the physician thought his son deserved. The physician added was going to do something about it, too. The next day at school this math teacher came into the ladies lounge full of excitement because the boy's mother had just called and invited her to Sunday dinner at Belle Meade Country Club. So that was how the physician and his wife arranged to obligate the math teacher to "give" a better grade to their son. Looking at the math teacher that day in the ladies lounge I said to myself, "Oh, if you only knew the terrible things the boy's father said about you."

One Christmas season my senior home economics girls were preparing and serving a Christmas luncheon to their mothers. The icing failed in class period. She asked if she could stay the next class period to try again. I said, "yes." She failed again. I felt so sorry for her because she so wanted to make that icing. She said she knew she could make it if she tried one more time. I said, "yes," again. This time, she made beautiful icing, iced the white cake balls and rolled them in freshly grated coconut. Never have I seen a student as happy over her project – and the girls were complimentary and happy for her. When the mothers came to the luncheon the girl's mother asked about her daughter's icing. When she saw the beautiful cake balls, tears rolled down the mother's cheeks and she expressed over and over her happiness that her daughter had completed the project so well.

During 1957, give or take a year, I underwent a double mastectomy to alleviate a recurring problem with cystic mastitis. I had undergone six earlier lumpectomy operations; so complete breast removal had become the recommendation of all four of the doctors I had consulted. The surgery proved to be very difficult. I was given several pints of blood during and after the surgery. In fact, some months later I learned that a request for blood donors was broadcast over the intercom system at Hillsboro that day. I remember waking up from my sedation and seeing Howard sitting by my bedside, only to go to sleep again. I had much drainage from the two incisions in my back as well as the incisions in the front. It was six weeks before I could write with a pencil or pen. I don't remember how long I stayed out of school, but it was a long time. I do remember the kindness, consideration and helpful attitude of my students during that time. My entire chest, both back and front was numb for a year. Gradually a tingling feeling began, then extreme sensitivity to touch. Finally, after two years a normal feeling returned.

My classes gave me Christmas presents – usually silver, perfume or flowers. Sometimes they would remember my birthday, and they always gave me a red rose corsage for the FHA banquet honoring girls who had earned degrees in the national home economics club for high school students.

My professional organizations included association with teachers on the local, state and national levels: Nashville area Home Economics Association for which I served as president and on several committees; Middle Tennessee Home Economics Association, for which I served as vice president and on several committees; Tennessee Home Economics Association, for which I served as Middle Tennessee vice-president and state career chairman. I was asked if I would run for state president and be on a national committee. I declined because Ray was planning to have heart surgery.

I was invited into the Phi Sigma Alpha group, an international sorority for outstanding older professional women. I served as president and on several committees.

In 1965 my mother died after a long hospital stay of three months, with nurses around the clock. Each day after finishing my work at Hillsboro I drove to Springfield to check on mother and make sure she had a nurse for the night. In her room I graded exam papers, averaged grades, made report cards and other reports. I would leave the hospital around 7:00PM, drive home through the black section of town and arrive in time to take a shower and prepare for the next day at school. The principal told me anytime I had to leave school early he would see to my classes. Only one time did the hospital call at school and request that I come to Springfield because Mother's condition had become critical. Ray went with me that day. Sometimes I would spend the night in Mother's apartment and leave Springfield after checking on Mother at the hospital in the morning, leaving to arrive at Hillsboro by 7:00 am. I am glad I had the strength to look after Mother and finish the school year. Each night the minister of Mother's Presbyterian church would come by the hospital room and read the Bible and have a 15-minute devotion and prayer for mother. He was a most caring Christian minister. I was with Mother when she died, holding her hand, and her last words were, "I love you" – a wonderful mother! And Mother was loved by so many people in Springfield. It seemed that everyone knew "Miss Myrtle" – if not through church or social organizations, then through her career as a telephone company employee. Flowers were everywhere during the funeral service. I reflected on the years. So many had passed since that Springfield girl had left town to attend college in Murfreesboro. With Mother's passing my ties to Springfield lost their immediacy. I went back to visit cousins on occasion, but it was thereafter always so different.

I should tell about my work toward a Master's degree at U.T. In 1967 I decided to obtain this degree by adding additional hours already accumulated at the U. T. Extension in Nashville. I finished the summer in Knoxville with 30 hours toward my Masters degree in Related Arts, having attained a grade point average of 3.43 out of a possible 4.0. I needed two classes that met only in the fall and winter at U.T. Knoxville. However, during that time Ray became increasingly ill from heart disease and I decided it was not possible to leave him and school for two days each week to take the two remaining courses. Therefore, I never received a Masters degree in Related Arts.

Chapter 19 – A Six-weeks tour of Europe

In 1966 Ray and I went to Europe. It was a trip we had long wanted to take, but family responsibilities had previously always kept us at home. For transportation we bought a Volkswagen "Beetle" to be delivered to us in Germany, it was to be John's graduation gift for obtaining his Masters degree at Emory University. The president of the Nashville Boys' Club board paid our fares to London and later to Frankfurt, where we received the car at the airport. We were guests of the parents of the Boys' Club president in Newcastle, England, for six days. They drove us around the eastern side of England each day, served us good English food and had guests in to meet us. They gave us wonderful tips on how to travel in Europe and on getting back to England from the Continent.

We saw the eastern side of England including Cambridge University; we punted on the Cam River and had high tea at Cambridge; we saw John Constable's birthplace and the site of some of his noteworthy oil paintings; we saw a section of an original Roman road; we saw the place where King John had signed the Magna Carta; we saw Sandhurst, the country home of Queen Elizabeth and Prince Phillip, where our hostess said she had once had tea; we saw Falstone seaside resort where our hosts had a cottage on the boardwalk, and we ate lunch in a pub near Newcastle. Our hosts' daughter, a student at Cambridge, was visiting home at the time we were there. I was aghast at the short, short skirt she was wearing, because they had not yet been fashionable in The States.

We rode the train from Newcastle to the airport and boarded a flight for Frankfurt, Germany. The car salesman was helpful getting Ray accustomed to the little Volkswagen Beetle and the German road signs. I was the navigator for the five weeks, using my AAA International road maps and town information. My four years of Latin and three years of French helped me translate information on menus and signs.

We headed south to Austria, the mountains and Switzerland. We had a AAA booklet of homes, hostels and small inns recommended for spending the night. They were clean, restful and hospitable. Breakfast, tea and dinner were served – home baked, cooked, and the best food they had to offer. One of our favorite midday activities was to stop at a bakery in a small town and buy pastries and cheeses, then stop at a place to buy wine, and take it all to a high place in the mountains and enjoy a picnic lunch with a wonderful view. One day we rode the train up the mountain and through the ice tunnels to the lookout station for a delectable lunch overlooking a glacier. The sun was shinning on the brilliant glacier ice.

Our next memorable stop was Salzburg, Austria. A tour in a horse-drawn open carriage included Mozart's birthplace, the open concert hall where they were practicing for a night concert, the lovely stone fountains and two historic churches. On the second day we rode the tram to the castle overlooking the city and had lunch on the terrace restaurant. The ice cream desert was delicious.

Heading west, we drove through the Black Forest region, where I bought a coo-coo clock that had been made there. We crossed over into rural France; then up the Loire Valley, stopping at each castle listed in our AAA booklet.

Our stay in Paris was for three days. We picked up our mail at the American Express station across from the beautiful Opera House; toured the Louvre Museum; shopped at Lafayette Department Store, where I bought shoes and a pocket book, and toured Notre Dame and Versailles.

Leaving Paris, we drove into Belgium. Spending one day in Brussels, we saw the square, the famed boy statue, toured the Battenburg lace shops; bought a large banquet tablecloth with 12 napkins.

We drove on to The Netherlands, with its windmills, and saw the waterways of Amsterdam. We stayed at a nice downtown hotel on the canal – a clean room with a hall bath. Our dinner was especially delightful because we were seated at a table facing the canal, so we could see the lights and the nightlife on the canal boats. The next day we toured the city in a canal boat and walked the shopping streets. The valet, having noticed the USA license on our Volkswagon Beetle, commented, "It's always a pleasure to have the embassy people stay with us." So, we then realized, that was the reason we had been given a prime dinner table and special attention each time we walked through the hotel lobby. We left Amsterdam for Belgium & ferried across the Channel.

As the ferry took the "Beetle", Ray and me across the

English Channel the first view was of the magnificent white cliffs of Dover. We drove off the ferry, through Dover and on to Canterbury Cathedral, surrounded by the sixteenth century overhanging second story houses. We went into the middle of England to Sulgrave, the home and farm of the Washington family, from which John Washington, son of Sir John Washington, came to Jamestown, Virginia, and there married Mary Flood, daughter of the ancient Jamestown planter, John Flood – both of them my ancestors. Sulgrave is a country manor house with original Washington family furnishings. One large window has a coat of arms similar to the United States flag. The village is quaint. The Washington Church, also built by the Washington family, has large Washington floor brasses. These people represent the eleventh, twelfth and thirteenth generations of my Washington linage. Ray and I walked the streets of nearby Oxford University, where Sir John Washington (my eleventh generation ancestor) had attended. We toured Windsor Castle and the surrounding town. Windsor began as a wooden fort built by William the Conqueror, and it continues as a royal home. It is now a beautiful castle with staterooms opened to the public. From the middle of England we crossed to York in eastern England, where we toured the cathedral and walked the fortifications surrounding the town.

We then crossed the river over a Roman arched-stone bridge into Scotland; crossed the highlands into Edinburgh; stayed in a doctor's home and ate dinner in their living room at a beautifully set table containing excellent food. The doctor and his wife seemed to enjoy talking to us about The States. We toured Queen's Park,

Holyrood Castle; Edinburg Castle; saw where John Knox lived, and attended the Sunday morning service at the Presbyterian Church where John Knox had preached. After the service, the minister stood at the church door telling everyone goodbye. A couple came up to us and said, "You are from the south." We replied, "Yes, from Nashville, Tennessee." They said they had formerly lived in Nashville and had attended Westminster Church there, where they had been in the Good Sam Sunday school Class. There we were in Edinburgh, Scotland, being greeted by people who had attended our church, even our Sunday school class. We had the same Nashville connections!!

Another connection I had to Edinburgh was my great, great, great grandfather, William McMillian, who had studied the ministry at Edinburgh and had come to Virginia as a Presbyterian minister and mission worker. I had joined the DAR on his service record in the Revolutionary War.

Our next interesting stop was Fort Williams on a fiord below the highlands and at the beginning of the lowlands. Then we entered the territory of the Bell clan, where we saw the damaged keep still standing with the Bell coat of Arms and the date 1511 engraved above the doorway. Next we went to the Presbyterian Church and graveyard where many, many Bells are buried, dating back to the 1400's. The tombstones were in excellent repair and could be easily read. It appears these Bells were ministers of the church and some probably started the congregation. The Bell clan property boundary went to Hadian's wall. We walked on the wall and could easily understand how the Bells were lowlanders, bordering Scotland, switching between Scottish and English loyalty according to the outcome of sequential political wars.

We continued on to western England where we bypassed Glasgow. We enjoyed lunch above the bypass while looking down at the traffic. Our next stop was Washington Hall, the first home of the Wessington family, who had come from France with William the Conqueror. It is a country manor house on top of a low hill, with the town, river and church below. The sexton was extremely polite and informative when he found out I was a descendant of John Washington who had come to Jamestown in 1654 and married Mary Flood. The sexton showed us where the first Washington was buried and wrote me several times after we returned to The States. Of course, he was interested in our contributing money to the upkeep of Washington Hall and the church.

We visited the Featherstone manor house, which was being used as a day camp for children. We were shown the stone courtyard, dating from the 1100's. The Featherstone's also came over with King William. My fourth grandfather was William Featherstone.

Stonehenge was a wonderful place to visit, and I wonder about its history. At nearby Bath we saw the marvelous water system and baths built by the Romans. The town is also noted for its row houses.

We next saw the site of the Battle of Hastings, where the English army was defeated by William the Conqueror. I noted a plaque on which the name of Sanford was listed as being an English hero in that battle. This was of interest to me because my great grandfather was named Robert Sanford.

By way of the Crystal Palace we drove to Southampton to place our "Beetle" on board a freighter bound for Norfolk, Virginia. From there we rode the bus to the London airport. We flew from there to Dublin, Ireland, arriving late at night. We found a place to stay in Dublin – the smallest room I have ever seen. The suitcase had to be put under the bed and we shared a hall bath with other guests. Everything was spotlessly clean. The first day we took a city bus tour, had dinner at the best hotel in town and then attended a musical. The next day we took a bus tour north across the border into Northern Ireland to a beach and had lunch at a hotel. At the border of Northern Ireland we were searched for guns, knives, etc. It was frightening to be in that situation. The third day we rented a car and drove "the circle" through the western part of Ireland. We toured Knappogue Castle in County Clare, which included dinner with about 100 other guests. The master of ceremonies invited Ray and me to be Lord and Lady of the Manor. We felt honored; sat at the head table with the master of ceremonies; were often toasted, bowed to and saluted in recognition of our special roles, and drank hot mead, which was delicious.

We returned to the airport at Dublin and flew back to London, where we stayed at the Doncaster Hotel, one of the better hotels in the city. We took an all-day bus tour of London. We attended an evening songfest at Westminster Abbey. A full choir marched in to begin the service and presented beautiful music with organ accompaniment. The next day we toured the city on our own seeing the Tower of London and the crown jewels; the British Museum, where we viewed Egyptian relics and oil paintings; Westminster Abbey; Harrod's Department Store; Green Park, and the riverside government houses, including the house where the Prime Minister lived.

The next day we visited the Boys' Clubs of Britain. As we walked into the club, we were greeted by Grand Old Opry music. They probably expected two hillbillies. We visited the Boys' Club executive offices in a beautiful townhouse in one of the circles. A beautiful wooden facing surrounded the fireplace. I recognized it as being by Robert Adams. The Boys' Club official was surprised that I knew about Adams and his magnificent work. The next day we went by bus to the airport and flew from London to Nashville by way of New York City and Atlanta. We had been traveling for six weeks. Never had iced water tasted so heavenly!

Chapter 20 – My Two Grown Sons

Howard and Judy moved to Cincinnati, Ohio, after he graduated from Vanderbilt, and there he went to work for Procter and Gamble. On February 21, 1962 they had a boy, Howard Ray White III, whom we all called Howie. He was my first grandson. Then, two years later Howard went to work for Celanese Corporation at a fibers plant near Pearisburg, Virginia. There they had another boy, Keith, born on February 19, 1964. Howard became active in politics and for a time was chairman of the Giles County Republican Party. In 1972 Howard was transferred to Charlotte, North Carolina, where he and Judy remain today.

Howie was full of life and fun to be around during his childhood and teenage years. Ray and I were very proud of him. But a great tragedy befell our family in 1978, when Howie was killed instantly while driving home from school. He was 16 years old.

On September 4, 1981, Howard and Judy were blessed with another child, David Howard White, who has grown to be a handsome young man. Now 21 years old, David is starting his own business.

Keith married Kelley Morris. They had met in high school and had been sweethearts throughout college at North Carolina State University. Keith received a BS degree in Electrical Engineering. Kelley received a BS degree in Premed Studies and continued on to The University of North Carolina Medical School, receiving a MD degree in Internal Medicine. They have two children, Alexandria and Stephen. These are my two great grandchildren, both of whom are now in grammar school. Keith, Kelley and the family live in Richmond, Virginia. Keith, a Principal Engineer with Infineon, is expert in the testing of semiconductor memory chips. Kelley practices medicine with a group of physicians in Richmond.

When Howard and Judy moved to Charlotte Judy played French horn professionally in the Charlotte Symphony. After several years of playing she resigned to spend more time with the boys. But Judy remains active in her music. She plays French horn in the Charlotte Civic Symphony – a very good volunteer orchestra – and in a professional horn quartet, and she teaches ten-to-fifteen young horn players.

Howard retired in 2000 at the age of 62 from the consultant firm. Retirement gives Howard and Judy more time to enjoy their lovely lake house on Lake Tillery, which is just over an hour's drive east of Charlotte.

Retirement also gives Howard more time to write his histories. Having thoroughly studied for ten years the political causes of the American Civil War, he is currently publishing, in four volumes, that history, which is titled, *"Bloodstains, An Epic History of the Politics that Produced the American Civil War."* I have read the first two volumes. The educational experience is remarkable.

As mentioned earlier, John took time off from college to

work in the Peace Corps. He went to the University of Hawaii, in Hilo, to complete his training and to prepare for work in the Philippines. For two years he served in Sarrat, Ilocos Norte, a remote village in the northern part of the island of Luzon, where he taught English and Science to the Elementary teachers at Sarrat Central School. During his training in Hilo and during his two years of service he learned the language of northern Luzon "Ilocano", it surprises me that he can still speak the language after 40 years.

Following his Peace Corps work John traveled to Hong Kong and Japan by boat, spent two weeks in Japan returned to Hong Kong for a week and proceeded to Saigon the week following the Tonkin event. He spent five months during 1964 in Siagon, Vietnam, teaching English at the Vietnam American Association School, Hoi Viet Me and the Chinese High School, Khai Trie. He had a draft deferment for being a teacher in the country where they wanted to send him as a soldier! He then traveled for two months through Cambodia (ankor Wat),Thailand, Burma, India (Calcutta, New Delhi and Agra), West Pakistan, Iran, Iraq (Baghdad and Babylon), Syria, Lebanon, Egypt, Greece, Italy, The Netherlands, and finally returned to the United States through New York City. This world travel helped establish John as a "Citizen of the World."

John then returned to his college work, where he adhered to the American Chemical Society curriculum and finished his B. A. degree in Chemistry with a minor in math at Rhodes College in Memphis, Tennessee, in 1967. Part of the degree program required German as a foreign language, he spent in 1966 2 months in Germany at the Goethe Institute in Iserlohn. Utilizing a fellowship, he then earned a Master of Arts in Teaching Science at Emory University in 1968. John then began teaching science, chemistry and physics in the Atlanta School System at Dykes and North Fulton High Schools.

John taught at North Fulton for 20 years. Four times the faculty nominated him "Teacher of the Year." He became Head of the Science Department and for five years the "Star Student" elected John as his "Star Teacher." One year, John's student, John Sparks, won the top Science award in the State of Georgia. They were honored together, receiving the A. T. & T. award and a trip to the Bell Labs in Menlo Park, New Jersey. During his teaching years John continued his interest in stamp collecting, including being elected President of the Atlanta Stamp Club and the magic club. He also became interested in antiques and art and became proficient in appraising the value of both collectibles. John retired from teaching in 1988, due to the closing of North Fulton High School, the highest academic school in the city.

While still maintaining his home in Atlanta, John moved to Fairfax, Virginia, and established his own antique store, which he ran for two years. Then he relocated his store to Centreville, Virginia, and operated it there for five more years. At that point he began working trade shows for Oriental Traders Corporation, which designs, manufactures and distributes crystal fashion jewelry that uses Austrian made Swarovski crystals. He is now Sales Director and designs some of the product line. When John is not at trade shows, he is with me in Nashville.

Chapter 21 – Dealing with Desegregation

Let me say that I endured school desegregation at Hillsboro High School, a Davidson County school prior to the city-county merger. Those were trying times for all the teachers, and it is impossible to relate those years in detail. But I will pass on a few stories that stand out in my mind long after retirement. The major national lawsuit by which the Federal Supreme Court ordered schools to desegregate was the famous Brown versus Board of Education decision handed down in 1954. A lawsuit against Nashville City Schools, Kelley versus Board of Education, was decided in 1955 with a directive that Nashville City Schools desegregate. Nashville City Schools began holding desegregated classes in 1957, starting with the first grade and moving up one grade each year in step with those students. The City and County Schools merged in the fall of 1963, at which point the City Schools were desegregated through the seventh grade. I will not give any more history or dates, but just relate a few stories as I remember them.

It was a bright sunshiny afternoon when Dr. Prentiss Pugh and I walked down Capital Blvd. following a luncheon at the Andrew Jackson Hotel held by Nashville businessmen in support of Ray's second bid to be elected Juvenile Court Judge. The newspaper boy on the corner of Church Street and Capital Blvd. was shouting the news: "City Schools desegregated." Dr. Pugh and I both said, "and that means trouble." The First Baptist (Negro) Church was not far from where we were standing, and a mile or so down Church Street was Fisk University, the Negro college founded during Reconstruction. Both were hotbeds of racial activism. Now these activists had obtained what they wanted – black and white children in school together.

When school started at Hillsboro the following year, the faculty was told we would possibly be the target of protest demonstrations by desegregation activists who were pushing to desegregate the county schools. At our 6:30 am faculty meeting held before school started on the first day of school we were instructed on how to react to racial unrest. During class we were to keep our doors open but with the lockset to engage if the door were closed. If a racial disturbance were detected outside the school building, a male faculty member would rush down the hall and slam each door shut so it would be locked from the outside, but not from the inside. Teachers were to keep the students busy in their classroom until the bell rang, even if moving to the next class were delayed several hours. We quickly got our chance to drill on this procedure. Halfway through the first period on that first day I heard sirens and loud noises from outside the building. I was on the back side, second floor and could not see what was going on in front. Immediately, my door was slammed shut by a male teacher. My students drew long breaths, opened their books and notebooks, and were completely quiet and studious for three hours. No one talked. We could hear the noise from outside – and the question in each of our minds was, "will the racial rioters get into the building?" A girl came to my desk at the end of three hours asking if I would see her out of the building because she had a job at the ice cream store in Green Hills Mall across the street from the school, and needed to be there at noon. Then I opened my door, walked to the second story balcony and was astounded by what I saw! Two bus loads of black men and women screaming and hollering; many patrol cars with lights flashing and sirens going; many, many television people, radio people and photographers recording the event, and, in conference, a group of men from the central office of education, some Metro school officials and our school principal and his staff. I followed my student to the end of the hall; saw her down the stairs, and out of the north end of the building. From that point she could run across to the mall without getting very close to the agitators. Within the hour the noise stopped, the class bell rang, and students went to class normally scheduled for that time segment. There was no talk among the students of why they were kept in one room for over three hours – no student mentioned it to me or to another student when they were leaving my room. They all seemed to understand and felt a need to be cooperative. I want to compliment my students on their understanding and courteous behavior toward me and each other during this stressful time.

Many interesting events took place in my home economics class after Hillsboro was later desegregated. My classes contained black and white students, both boys and girls.

In a sewing class there was one black student who had announced to me and to the class that his ambition was to eventually become a tailor. He learned sewing machine operation, sewing terminology, and pattern selection and fitting. For his major sewing project he selected a standard slacks pattern and a suitable dark purple fabric. He was happy with his selection and studious in his approach to sewing – sometimes humming or singing to himself in a low monotone as he worked. The girls seemed to respect him for his studious approach to his work. The boy finished his slacks, but then dropped out of school. I often wonder if he did become a tailor.

There was a black student in my cooking preparation class. He was also serious about his work and planned to be a chef. His unit prepared and served a luncheon to themselves. He brought to my desk a plate of the food and a glass of iced tea. As he put the serving on my desk he looked at me, smiled and said, "We're gonna fatten you up, Mrs. White." I wonder if he became a chef.

In my beginning sewing class there was a huge (250-300 pound) black student. She enjoyed running the sewing machine at full speed with her fat vibrating in time with the machine. She missed her final exam; but showed up the next day after exams were over seeking a private exam. I talked to the principal about the matter, and he said, "Give her any kind of exam and pass her because we want her out of this school." That I did! I wonder what kind of trouble she was in.

One day I was wanted in the counselor's office in regard to a grade a stident had received, Dr. Kelley Smith's daughter for her work in one of my sewing classes. I asked the principal to accompany me to the conference because "I didn't want to be the only white person in the conference." He immediately agreed. Together we walked into the conference room. There sat the black counselor, the student and her sister, who looked very impressive in her uniform. I allowed the counselor to bring up the issue of grades and listened to the reasons the student and her sister thought the grade should be and "A" instead of the "D" that she had received. I simply opened the folder containing the student's tests and samples of her daily work. I passed around the six-weeks test paper, on which she had signed her name without answering any of the questions. The test was completely blank. The principal then asked the student if she had signed her name to that paper, and she replied, "yes." Then, he handed me the paper and said, "The grade stands as Mrs. White has recorded. There is no need for further discussion. Come, Mrs. White, we will now leave." We walked out of the room. The girl continued in my class without giving any trouble. On her last exam paper of the year she wrote me a note of appreciation for not throwing her out of my class and for standing up for my principles. However, I lost sleep over the incident, for not knowing what might be done in retaliation.

In the middle of the semester a student reported to my sociology class. I inquired why the counselor had sent me this student. She said the boy's father, a black councilman, had requested my class for his son, and that the boy had been dropped out of several schools. The councilman knew Ray and his work with delinquent youths and was hopeful I could help his son. But the boy merely sat there in class through the second half of the semester with his head in his hands on the table, apparently in a doped stupor – never with paper, pen, book, or any knowledge of what we were doing in class. I was afraid of this student and never aggravated him. The students left him alone.

In my interior design unit we were studying and drawing house plans. I suggested to one black girl that she could add shrubbery to her drawing. She replied, "What is that?" Another girl told her, "Mrs. White means bushes." So language and words did not always mean the same to us.

At lunchtime one day I decided to go through the cafeteria line rather than remain in my room and eat the sandwich I had brought. A big black male was standing at the beginning of the serving line begging everyone for money. I told him that I had no money to give away. I then told the faculty members at the teachers' lunch table that the boy was begging money. A black female teacher jumped up from the table and went over to the boy and asked him to leave the school. As he was going out of the cafeteria he asked several boys for money. When one rather short student refused to give him money, this big black beggar grabbed him by the neck and began banging him against the brick wall. The men faculty immediately went to the victim's aid. The big black beggar knocked a white math teacher down onto the floor and began kicking him in the groin. For about four minutes there was a general fight until the police arrived. They had come so quickly because they had been in the area patrolling the streets around the school. The big black beggar was not a student – just someone off the street trying to get money. The math teacher who had been kicked in the groin had to have medical attention and had to stay out of school several days.

I want to describe two other incidents that I did not personally see. I was in the office when a coach rushed in and said a robber had held him up. It was routine for this coach to take the school's money for the day across the street to the bank. He went the same route each day. On this day, when he opened the north side door a black student had pulled a gun on him and demanded the money. The coach knew the boy so he called him by name and said, "Now you really don't want to shoot me, do you?" The boy turned and ran away, and the coach came to the office to report the incident to the principal. That coach was one shaken up man, who afterward changed his routine for taking the school money across the street to the bank.

Another coach gave out report cards at the end of a six-weeks period. When this black student looked at his report card, he rushed the coach and knocked him flat on the floor. He ran out of the room and the school building and never came back to school. The coach turned in his resignation at the end of the semester.

One day in a girl's gym class a white girl and a black girl got into an argument. Punches were thrown; hair was pulled; chairs were thrown – a big general fight was engaged.

On another occasion a fight took place in the hall outside my room over a black student, his black girlfriend and his white girlfriend. I held my students in my classroom until it was over.

For ten years the percentage of black students in my classes steadily rose, and I often thought of retiring. But the determining factor came one morning around 7:00AM. I had arrived earlier than usual to prepare for lab work. No one was in the upstairs hallway when I arrived except two black male students who were in my first period class. They were known as troublemakers. I had to make a choice between turning around and going back downstairs or facing these boys while unlocking the door to the classroom. I chose the latter. With a "good morning" to each of them I began to put the key in the lock. Immediately, I felt an arm go around my shoulder and neck. I thought I was going to be mugged and robbed right there, but one said, "Mrs. White, you are my girlfriend, aren't you?" I turned the lock, opened the door while his arm was still around me and said, "No, I am not your girlfriend; I am my husband's girlfriend." I walked into the classroom and they walked in after me and took their seats. I still thought I would be mugged and robbed; but I sat at my desk and took something to read. At that point I said to myself, "Why am I exposing myself to danger and turmoil? I have a husband; he makes a good salary; my two boys are grown and no longer need my earnings for schooling. I am retiring!" That afternoon I told my principal I would not be returning the next year. I did not want a general announcement made regarding my decision to retire. The principal gave me the appropriate papers to fill out and they went in the afternoon school mail to the Metro education office.

Those ten years of desegregation were years of education for me. I tried to be fair, courteous and understanding of my black students. I did succeed with some, but for some

I failed because those were racial in their own thoughts.

I retired from teaching at Hillsboro High School in 1975. My principal, Mr. Hagan, ranked me aas an excellent teacher through the last years of my career. At the Metro teachers retirement dinner my principal had the following statement read when I was handed my retirement pin.

"Mrs. Martha White has devoted her teaching career to becoming a master teacher. She has discovered that basic truth about commitment that many seldom discover, that through genuine commitment we get back much more than we give and it is through this means we find our true potential."

Chapter 22 – The Close

Ray took great pride in the new Nashville Boys' Club facility that was built beside Thompson Lane under his leadership. It is a beautiful facility with a fine indoor pool, gymnasium, activity rooms and outdoor ball fields. But his health was declining. He had heart surgery in 1969, having his diseased mitral valve replaced by a metal ball check valve device. As long as he lived the metal ball made a noise when his heart beat. He was determined to live with this metal ball check valve and continued to work at the Boys' Club.

Ray escaped the ordeal of changing the Nashville Boys' Club to the Nashville Boys' and Girls' Club, for that took place shortly after he retired in 1977. Ray's health was seriously declining by the time he retired. Howie was killed about a year after his retirement and the grief over the loss of his first grandson worsened Ray's decline.

Ray died in his sleep on May 3, 1979. The previous day he had worked on the garage, which he planned to turn into a woodworking shop. He was happy in his work and looking forward to working with wood again. However, he died as his surgeon had told him he would – suddenly and in a way that nothing could be done to save him. I went into hysterics when I found him dead in bed. I called 911; the neighbors came in when they saw the ambulance arrive and heard me screaming. Auntie was visiting us at the time. She tried to calm me by saying I would lose my mind if I didn't stop screaming. Even to this day I cannot carry a tune by singing, read the Bible or say a prayer without crying. The woman across the street put her arms around me and said, "God loves you and will take care of you." Only then did I stop screaming.

That morning the light went out of my life never to return.

And, my friends, this concludes my story about a Springfield girl named Martha Frances Bell.

Acknowledgements

Oral history and memoirs by:

Myrtle Simpkins Bell

Joseph Gideon Simpkins

Grace Franklin Bell Worsham

Susan Davis Bell

Mary Elizabeth Bell

Howard Ray White

Howard Ray White, Jr.

John Walter White

County Records of Tennessee:

Cheatam County, TN: marriages, wills, census tabulations and deaths, 1850-1910

Davidson County, TN: court records, deeds, wills, deaths, census tabulations, marriages, 1789-1923

Dickson County, TN: marriages, deeds, deaths, census tabulations, 1820-1900

Robertson County, TN: court records, deeds, wills, deaths, marriages, census tabulations, 1792-1965

Sumner County, TN: census tabulations, wills, deaths, deeds, marriages, 1792-1850

Goodspeed's History of 1886 for Robertson, Sumner, Cheatham, Dickson and Montgomery Counties.

Carolina Cradle by Robert W. Ramey, 1964

Clans and Tartans of Scotland by Robert Bain

History of Sumner County, Tennessee, by Jay Guy Crisco, 1909

Virginia Frontier by F. B. Kegley, 1938

Cavaliers and Pioneers (1623-1666) Vol. I by Nell Marion Nugent, 1974

Captain John Smith's History of Virginia edited by David Felman Haderke, 1970

NOTES:

NOTES:

NOTES:

LIMITED EDITION   /1000